Conversations with Writers

Vance Bourjaily

James Dickey

William Price Fox

John Gardner

Brendan Gill

Edward Gorey

Robert Hayden

Mary Welsh Hemingway

Ring Lardner, Jr.

Wallace Markfield

Donald Ogden Stewart

Thomas Tryon

Robert Penn Warren

A Bruccoli Clark Book

Gale Research Company
Book Tower · Detroit, Michigan 48226

Editorial Director: Matthew J. Bruccoli

Managing Editor: C. E. Frazer Clark, Jr.

Project Editor: Richard Layman

Editors
Margaret M. Duggan
Glenda G. Fedricci
Cara L. White

Transcriptions: Rhonda W. Rabon

Interviewers
John Baker
Matthew J. Bruccoli
C. E. Frazer Clark, Jr.
Robert Dahlin
Richard Layman

Library of Congress Cataloging in Publication Data

Main entry under title:

Conversations with writers.

(Conversations with ; v. 1)
"A Bruccoli Clark book."
1. Authors, American--20th century--Interviews.
2. Authorship. I. Bourjaily, Vance Nye. II. Baker,
John, 1931- III. Series.
PS129.C57   810'.9'005   77-9142
ISBN 0-8103-0943-2

CONTENTS

INTRODUCTION

Conversations With Writers has been planned with three chief goals in mind: first, to provide a forum for the leading American writers by preserving their comments on their work and careers; second, to provide readers with insights into the profession of authorship in our time; third, to present an accurate image of the authors as individuals—to reveal their aspirations, their feelings about literature, and their responses to the world they live in.

The interviewers for this series are selected for their knowledge of the material and for their interviewing experience. They have been asked to submit cassette tapes of their interviews along with short biographical sketches of their subjects and short descriptions of the settings of the interviews. The tapes have been transcribed and edited at the *CONVERSATIONS* editorial office. Transcriptions were then sent to the interviewers and their subjects for approval before final editing.

Recordings of these interviews are being preserved and will become part of a permanent archive of oral history.

CONVERSATIONS WITH WRITERS

Jill Krementz

Vance Bourjaily was born in Cleveland in 1922. He graduated from Bowdoin College in 1947. His principal books are The End of My Life *(1947),* The Hounds of Earth *(1955),* The Violated *(1958),* Confessions of a Spent Youth *(1960),* The Unnatural Enemy *(1963),* The Man Who Knew Kennedy *(1967),* Brill Among the Ruins *(1970), and* Now Playing at Canterbury *(1976). He was editor of* Discovery, *1953-1955. Since 1957 Bourjaily has taught at the Writers Workshop at the University of Iowa.*

2

Vance Bourjaily

Vance Bourjaily was interviewed at the home of William Price Fox in Columbia, South Carolina, by Matthew J. Bruccoli on 10 March 1977. Bourjaily had come to Columbia to give a reading at the University of South Carolina. The interview was conducted on the morning before the Foxes took Mr. Bourjaily to the Capitol Cafe, a colorful hangout for state legislators and less reputable types, for breakfast. Before he left Columbia, Mr. Bourjaily rode an elephant in a circus parade with Fox and James Dickey.

Conversations: How did you get into the business of being a professional writer?

Bourjaily: I really had no alternative. My mother had three sons; she and my father were both newspaper people and very, very much aware of the difference between journalistic writing and literary writing—rather in awe of it. My mother had three little kids to take care of, and when she could no longer work on daily papers, she began writing newspaper serials. As she developed her own skills as a writer, she became a writer of what was called women's fiction in the twenties and the thirties. But she was constantly aware, probably unfairly to herself, that there were writers whom the world held in a greater degree of respect than they did fluent women who wrote women's novels for *Pictorial Review* and *Cosmopolitan* and so on. So she was absolutely determined that one of her sons be a writer. I was the middle of the three, and I guess she probably worked us all over, but I was the one with whom it took.

Conversations: Was there literally a training program at home? Were you given assignments?

Bourjaily: No, not really. We were read aloud to; my mother read very well aloud. All through my childhood she read aloud to us every night from Dickens, and eventually Conrad, who is a great favorite of hers. She read us poetry; she read Emily

Dickinson; she simply talked and thought literature a lot. She had a pretty good collection of Emily Dickinson first editions; she used to lecture on Emily Dickinson. The very first things I remember writing were poems in an effort to gain her approval, which was not hard to do if one could write a childish poem. I think I had at the age of seven or eight some inclination to become an actor. That's the only other thing I can ever remember wanting to be. Well, the actor's personality and the writer's personality are so close anyway that I think wanting to be an actor and wanting to be a writer are virtually the same thing. But in any case, by the time I was eight or nine it was perfectly evident to me that I was going to be a writer.

Conversations: What was your first appearance in print?

Bourjaily: Well, in school papers and school literary magazines.

Conversations: High school?

Bourjaily: I think probably before that. We had a summer place in southwestern Virginia, in Craig County, in the mountains. This would go back to before I was ten. There was always a collection of my mother's and father's friends down there, including her younger brother, Bob, who, again a journalist, worked for the *New York Daily Graphic* at the time. In any case it was the custom to put out this sort of camp newspaper. It was an extended family camp, and there was a little newspaper that circulated once a week. It was typed up and a few carbons were made. Probably the first things that I ever published were submissions to that weekly journal. And I also went to the kinds of schools—sort of ambitious, little, progressive day schools which . . . .

Conversations: This was in Cleveland.

Bourjaily: No, no. We left Cleveland when I was one year old.

Conversations: Where did you grow up?

Bourjaily: Up and down the East Coast. My father and mother were divorced when I was . . . well, they were separated when I was about eleven. After this there were always two establishments—one in Virginia, because the summer place then became developed as kind of a year-round place where my mother and stepfather lived. My father, meanwhile, was pursuing a fairly big-time newspaper career; he was manager of United Features Syndicate, which syndicated Mrs. Roosevelt's column and Heywood Broun's column and so on. He lived in a town house in New York, and by the time I got to prep school age I was regularly going for vacations either to the town house in New York or down to this very rural part of Virginia.

Conversations: Where did you prep?

Bourjaily: At a school called Solebury, in New Hope, Pennsylvania, from which I was ejected at the end of my sophomore year.

Conversations: Why?

Bourjaily: It was not really because I was caught smoking so often—it was because I was so stupid as to let myself be caught. I think they really found me intractable as much as anything else. I wasn't a flamboyant violator of school rules, but I had a hard time persuading myself that they applied to me.

Conversations: You are now rolling your own cigarette. Have you been doing that for most of your smoking career?

Bourjaily: Well, I have for the last eight or ten years, I guess. After I left prep school, I went to public high school in Winchester, Virginia, near which my mother and stepfather had settled. The first job I ever had was picking apples in Harry Byrd's orchards near Winchester. Most of the people who were picking the apples were very tough late-Depression migrant laborers who had their own code of manners and behavior. One of the things that they very much held against one another was being too fine to roll your own cigarettes. A person who smoked ready-made cigarettes was considered affected. And I was not only a stranger among them, but I was a very slight kid and not particularly tough physically, so I thought it would be just as well not to call attention to myself by showing up with ready-made cigarettes. I actually rolled Golden Grain then. Golden Grain has disappeared—all you can get now is Bull Durham.

Conversations: After you graduated from high school you did not go to college; you went to work in an advertising agency. What dictated that decision?

5

Vance Bourjaily

Bourjaily: Well, the first thing I did after graduating from high school and having been admitted to college—as a matter of fact, again recalling it was late Depression, it wasn't much of a trick, but I got admitted to Harvard. I got admitted to Harvard without examination, which was just as well. I probably could not have passed college boards given the caliber of the high school I had gone to and the amount of attention that I paid to classwork in it. But the policy then was if you graduated from high school below the Mason-Dixon Line and were in the upper tenth of your high school class, you could get in anywhere—I mean you could get in anywhere in the North, because they were trying to spread out the geographic base in the entering classes.

I had graduated very young; I was sixteen when I had graduated from high school, and I decided that the thing for me to do before I went off to college was to write a book. I had spent the summer in New York; I bought a car and drove down to Winchester, where my mother and stepfather lived, and visited them a bit. Then I went on down to the southwestern corner of Virginia where this old summer property was and spent the fall there with an old mountaineer we called "Uncle George" in a very ancient kind of farmhouse and wrote a book. And it was a terrible book. I wasn't even trying to write fiction. It was a philosophical work of . . . I guess I can only say it was a work of sheer, self-indulgent self-expression.

Conversations: Did you submit it any place?

Bourjaily: Yeah. I sent it to my mother's agent, who was Diarmuid Russell of Russell and Volkening, a magnificent man. Diarmuid was kind of tickled with it, and he sent it over to Max Perkins of Scribners. Then he and Perkins, who were quite close apparently, had lunch and talked about it. Perkins said, "Look, it's fairly evident that this boy is going to be a writer, but he couldn't do himself anything but damage by having some publisher do this book as a stunt." Perkins thought possibly it could be done as kind of a stunt book: you know, sixteen-year-old boy tells the world how to be. But he thought it would be a very bad way to begin a writing career, and he was obviously right.

Conversations: How long did it take you to write this first book?

Bourjaily: About three months, I think. It seems to me I went down to Craig County in August and returned with this—it's about a 100-page manuscript—at about the end of October. The manuscript still exists. I think there's one copy in the Bowdoin Library. I can't say that I'm eager for anybody to go up and read it. I reread it myself once about fifteen or twenty years ago, and it's pretty embarrassing.

Conversations: You gave up on it after Perkins gave you this piece of advice?

Bourjaily: I had so much good literary advice when I was a kid from my mother and Diarmuid Russell and people like Perkins, whom I did not meet at the time but whose advice was available to me through Diarmuid. I was easily prevented from making that kind of mistake. But what happened with that manuscript was that my father then . . . let's see if I can get this straight. I had gone from Virginia up to New York to visit my father and took this manuscript up with me. My father, who had been an enormously prosperous man all through the middle thirties, had left United Features Syndicate. He was terribly successful there, with what was then a considerable fortune—he had about half a million dollars when he sold his United Press stock. But he had always had a newspaperman's dream of owning his own journal, and what he had done was to invest this money in a couple of ill-starred magazine ventures. The first thing he did was to buy from *The New York Times* a weekly photographic supplement they had called *Pictorial Review*. The idea of a picture magazine was very much in the air. *Life* was about to be started—its prospectuses were out, dummy issues were out. Dad had this kind of newspaperman's feeling that if you're going to do a picture magazine the thing to do is to be out first with it—you know, to beat the other guy. So he put together a staff, a wonderful staff of mostly European refugee picture-magazine editors—Germans, and Austrians, and so on. John Huston was doing movie reviews; Huston was a twenty-two or twenty-three year old. My father began publishing *Pictorial Review* about a year before *Life* actually appeared and lost piles and piles of money on it. It was quite a good magazine.

He lost most of the money on *Pictorial Review* and what he did after that, when it was clear that was going to fail, was to buy

Vance Bourjaily

the subscription lists and rights of the old *Life*, which was a humor magazine, and try publishing it. Then he bought *Judge* and tried combining that with *Life*, and he just kept going through the money until it was all gone. So by the time I was out of high school in 1939, he was around New York looking for a job. He answered a classified ad that the Erwin, Wasey advertising firm put in the *Times* for a copywriter. He figured he could probably do that. He went over to see them and they decided that he was far overqualified for the kind of job they had in mind. And so, being an indefatigable salesman by nature, my father said, "Well, I'll tell you what I'll do. I'll bring you this book that my sixteen-year-old kid has just written. Take a look at that and see if you don't want to hire him as a copywriter." The copy chief at Erwin, Wasey was one of those guys who had that twenties romantic feeling about advertising—that some of the great writers were writing advertising copy, and it was one of the art forms. So he was very much disposed to take on a kid writer. I went to work for Erwin, Wasey at a time when it was a glamorous business to go into.

Conversations: You were about seventeen years old?

Bourjaily: Yeah. I was seventeen, and the other new employees around there were the former spring graduating classes of Yale, Harvard, and Princeton. They were all working down in the stock room waiting to get promoted to jobs like copywriter. So my position was enviable and, I should think, rather envied. Some of these guys were very high-caliber potential advertising men. I suspect they resented me. I certainly wouldn't blame them if they did. I wrote ads for Kreml hair tonic, Barbasol shaving cream, Calvert whiskey. They were a little chary about my doing whiskey ads, as a matter of fact.

Conversations: Because of your age?

Bourjaily: Yeah. Did that for the rest of the fall, the winter, and most of the spring. Then decided that I had indeed better go on to college. By then my father did have a job; he had become editor of the *Bangor Daily News* up in Maine. It was because of that as much as anything, I guess, that I went to Bowdoin, though I guess I was still eligible to go to Harvard, but Bowdoin offered me a scholarship and Harvard did not. Harvard wisely did not—

8

no way in which I qualified for aid on the basis of my academic potential. You probably recall that colleges were really scraping around looking for people to fill up their classrooms. Bowdoin did give me a tuition scholarship, I think. That's where I went.

Conversations: Where you started writing a novel which became eventually The End of My Life.

Bourjaily: No, not for a time. By the time that I got to Bowdoin I had decided to try to channel whatever talent I had into play writing. Although I wrote some short stories at Bowdoin, the ambitious stuff I did was in play form.

Conversations: Were they produced on campus?

Bourjaily: Yes. Mostly one-act plays. And I continued to write poetry. So it went for a couple of years and a summer, by which time we were at war. I got impatient and left college to join the American Field Service in summer 1942. I remember talking to Bill Shawn at *The New Yorker* about the possibility of writing something for them, but which I never succeeded in doing. But it was all. . . you know, when I think about it all, there's none of the accidental quality about my having become a writer that I think is characteristic of most writers' careers. I was programmed for it from the time I was a kid and all through high school, through college. When I went off to the war I took a typewriter with me, a little portable.

Conversations: After your tour with the ambulance service you were inducted into the Army.

Bourjaily: Right. I did two years with the Field Service. I had jaundice very severely and went home to recuperate, was drafted, went into the Army, and had a rather inactive military career. It had been fairly active in the Field Service. In the U.S. Army I was assigned to an infantry regiment, 398th Division—I believe it is the only U.S. infantry division which was never committed to combat. Our assignment was the defense of the Hawaiian Islands, where I nearly expired from boredom. I hated Hawaii, and I just hated the general inactivity of it all, which went through 1944 until the occupation of Japan. I wrote quite a bit in Hawaii.

9

Vance Bourjaily

Conversations: Was any of it published?

Bourjaily: Well, there was a story which I think I must have written in Italy when I was still in the Field Service, which appeared in a publication called *The Southern Literary Messenger*. That would have been my first other than school publication. By the time I left Hawaii I had written a volume of poetry and a fairly ambitious three-act play. I duly sent that stuff back to Diarmuid Russell, who couldn't do anything much with the poetry but sent the play over to Maxwell Perkins. My next publication actually was a poem from the play which appeared in *Poetry Magazine* about 1946.

Conversations: After the war was over you returned to Bowdoin?

Bourjaily: Maybe it was 1945. Yeah, but before I was out of the Army, Perkins had read this play, and I became—like most of my subgeneration of writers—a beneficiary of probably the greatest inadvertent program of cultural patronage in the history of this country, a marvelous, marvelous device called the Wartime Excess Profits Tax. The Wartime Excess Profits Tax provided that anybody in business must average their profits—I believe for the ten prewar years. They could keep that much of their earnings at normal corporation tax levels. Anything in excess of that was taxable at ninety percent. Now publishing had done extremely well during the war. For one thing there was considerable inflation, which meant that the actual numbers that could be called profits were very high. But in addition there had been a considerable boom in sales. They made scads of money because of gas rationing and so on cutting people's travel down. This forced people to stay home, so they bought books and read them. There was also a four-year hiatus in the emergence of new writers. From a publisher's standpoint it was necessary to find some new writers and get the postwar era going. Since they had this available money which only cost them ten cents on the dollar, they were simply signing up anybody who could spell his name twice the same way.

Conversations: So Scribners gave you an advance?

Bourjaily: So Perkins, having read my play, said to Diarmuid Russell, "Do you suppose this young man would want to write a novel?" And Russell said he would find out. So I got a cable—I was by then on occupation duty in Japan—saying Scribners had offered I believe it was $500 advance if I would agree to write a novel. Naturally I cabled back and said, "Sure."

Conversations: You had still not actually met Perkins at this point?

Bourjaily: I had not. And didn't meet him for another year. But the thing that kind of fascinates me about. . . well, up until Perkins's offer, if you had asked me what sort of writer I was going to be, I would have said a playwright. I wanted to write a lot of poetry, too. But suddenly I was turned into a novelist by Maxwell Perkins, the Wartime Excess Profits Tax, and Diarmuid Russell. It was all so inadvertent in a way, just a matter of how circumstances went.

Conversations: So you started the novel immediately?

Bourjaily: I had written a story—I guess I had written it in Italy; it was waiting for me when I did get home from the Army—which is essentially the next-to-last chapter of *The End of My Life*. It is the chapter in which Skinner makes an appointment to take an American nurse whom he's met out to see the front lines. He picks her up in his ambulance the next day and they drive out to the artillery positions. This is a short story that I wrote, really out of guilt. I guess I wrote it the day after I had done a similar thing—it's kind of expiation, I suppose, for writers to indulge in. While in Naples I had met a very attractive blonde nurse who had just arrived in Italy, and she felt eager to see what she thought of as the front lines. I guess she thought she was going to see trench warfare lines as in World War I. I said, "There's nothing to that. I'll pick you up as soon as you get off tomorrow afternoon and drive you out there. We go out there all the time." So I had taken this nurse out to the British artillery positions. They were shooting twenty-five-pounders, actually. They were so tickled to see her up there; they let her pull the lanyard and fire a cannon. Then we turned around and went back to where my friends and I were billeted.

11

Vance Bourjaily

There had been a big party, and eventually I had driven her back to Naples very late at night and returned to the billet, had some more drinks, gone to sleep in a slit trench, and woke up the next morning just feeling terribly guilty about the whole thing. I had this very active masochistic fantasy of how easily I could have driven over a mine or gotten us into a counter-battery shelling situation. I just felt terrible and irresponsible and awful, so I did what writers do. I got up and I put all of my guilt into a story about somebody else doing the same thing and the whole thing going wrong and the nurse being. . . of course what happens in the book. So I had this story when I got discharged and by then had signed, or Diarmuid in my behalf had signed, a contract for me to write a novel for Scribners. I started from that story.

Conversations: What year was this?

Bourjaily: 1946. Let's see, I was discharged I think in January 1946. Within about two weeks of discharge, I would say, I was back in southwestern Virginia. My mother had by then separated from her second husband and returned from Winchester down to this kind of family territory in Craig County where she was established. I did a couple of things. The G.I. Bill of Rights had a business loan provision in it to enable the returning veteran to buy himself a small business. You got the money from a bank, but the government guaranteed it or guaranteed half of it or something. So I used that to buy the weekly newspaper in Craig County for my mother. Again, she had the old newspaperwoman's dream of having her own paper. Then I applied in addition to the Veterans' Administration for support as a self-employed writer. If you couldn't find a job, you got in what was called the 52-20 Club, which was twenty dollars a week for fifty-two weeks. But there was a similar thing for the self-employed, if you wanted it. If you were self-employed they would make up whatever the deficiency was between your earnings from self-employment and $100 a month. So there I was, really on government patronage, writing my first novel. I don't recall really what happened to the $500 advance from Scribners. I probably spent most of that buying a few civilian clothes and seeing some old friends in New York and partying.

In any case, I found a cabin down in Craig County into which I moved with my one chapter and started on the novel. The way I started on it, as I recall, I worked backwards from this episode trying to figure out. . . . I didn't think of myself as Skinner; I had no sense of identification with Skinner. Skinner really was—if he's based on anybody—a character who reappears in *Confessions of a Spent Youth* and is called Eddie MacCalibre. I was interested not so much by then in the actual act of irresponsibility as in what produced that kind of irresponsibility in so many of the people I knew, including myself to some extent, but most remarkably so in the Eddie MacCalibre-Skinner character. I started just writing about him and his friends to discover what they were like and what their educations were like and what sort of relationships they had with their girls and that kind of thing. And since I knew where the novel ended—it ended with Johnny's death—it was really a matter of figuring out how to get Skinner to the point of committing that act. I spent— February, March, April, May, June, July—probably spent about five months finishing the first draft.

Conversations: Which you then took to Perkins?

Bourjaily: No, no, I was unwilling to have anybody read it. When I got to the end of the first draft I wasn't terribly satisfied with it. I was beginning to get itchy for brighter lights, so I took the manuscript with me and went up to New York for awhile. I got a room at a rooming house, worked some at revising the novel, and mostly went through various sordid adventures, many of which are reported in *Confessions of a Spent Youth*. I was there most of the summer. I was there until a friend showed up who thought I was in dreadful shape from too much alcohol and too little exercise and persuaded me to go up to Maine with him in August, which I did. When I left Maine, and I don't recall that I did any work up there at all, I kind of recovered my health. It was a funny time for me in that I had no . . . . All my friends were people I had known in the Field Service; some of them were somewhat literary; some of them had written books and poetry. Bill Weaver, for example, a very close friend of mine, got the National Book Award for translation a year or two ago. But though I was in New York, I had no sense of being part of any kind of literary thing that was going on in New York. There was, I guess, a postwar literary scene there which consisted of Merle

Vance Bourjaily

Miller and Sam Baum, people around them. But I didn't know those guys at all. I knew my Field Service friends.

Conversations: Did you have your first meeting with Perkins during this New York period?

Bourjaily: I didn't meet Perkins until after the book was done. When I left Maine I was determined to finish revising the book so that I could show it to Perkins. Instead of going back to New York, which turned out to be a somewhat unhealthy place for me, I went down to Washington where my father had been working for the Bureau of Economic Warfare, I believe it's called. He had a house in the northwest part of Washington. I sort of fixed myself up an apartment in the basement and settled down to revise my book and court my wife, which I spent the fall doing—with success on both scores, I guess. Then the book got done I think around the first of November. I'm surprised at how fast I wrote it now. And finally it was read by Max Perkins.

Conversations: This is November 1947 now?

Bourjaily: No, we're still in '46. I can't actually recall the month and time of year when I finally did meet Perkins. But he read the book, and it may have been the end of the summer when he read the book. I probably had finished revising it once, after which I went in for my meeting with Perkins. I really only saw Perkins about two or three times. He took me to lunch after he had read the manuscript. I recall going into his office for our first meeting and being surprised that he had his hat on. I was feeling pretty defensive about my book. I knew what he wasn't going to like. I had by intention and with a feeling of enormous artistry left it unresolved after . . . I trailed off when Skinner gets back and Johnny's dead. I stopped right there, and I thought it was like a great unfinished chord of music. That was the way to do that. Perkins's technique with me was obviously very practiced and very good. He shook hands, started talking about Thomas Wolfe and we rode down the elevator. Having finished about Wolfe, he talked a little about Hemingway. I don't recall that he talked about Fitzgerald. I guess he did. Yeah, he must have, because by then I was terribly interested in Fitzgerald, so I'm sure we did talk about him. In any case, lunch consisted mostly of me waiting for him to say something about my novel, and Perkins instead telling fascinating anecdotes about Thomas Wolfe, Ernest Hemingway, Scott Fitzgerald, and other names which were to me utterly dazzling. I was so apprehensive and nerved up to answer what I assumed was going to be an attack on my manuscript, I couldn't really tell you what any of the dazzling stories were at this point. But it was enough to hold my attention.

When lunch was over he just sort of interrupted himself in mid-anecdote and made three structural suggestions about which he was absolutely right. I think the man was very good on structure; I think that probably was his strength as an editor, at least to judge by my own case. He said, "Now look, you've got to write a last chapter of that book and tell me how it all comes out." He said, "That girl is too interesting to be introduced as late in the book as you introduce her." Cindy had not been introduced till a big, long flashback in the middle. He said, "I think you ought to get her into the book first thing. And then keep her in the reader's mind some way through the long first section where they're on the train going up to Lebanon. Then I think you'll have it." And my will to fight back disappeared, because I just knew he was right, and the work that he was suggesting to me was all quite easy to do. There was a matter of writing an additional chapter at the beginning and an additional chapter at the end and one little sort of prior flashback in which Skinner thinks about Cindy as a sort of interruption to the long train trip. So those are the things I was doing in Washington in addition to—I can hardly believe it now, but running the whole damn manuscript through my typewriter again and sort of getting it homogenized. Then I turned the completed manuscript over probably in December, got married the day after Christmas in December 1946, and returned to Bowdoin for what was going to be two semesters, the winter semester and the following summer school. *The End of My Life* appeared in August of 1947, just before I graduated.

Conversations: After Perkins died. He died in June.

Bourjaily: Yes, that's right.

Conversations: So in a sense you may be Perkins's last author.

Vance Bourjaily

Bourjaily: He was working with James Jones.

Conversations: But From Here to Eternity *didn't come out until '51.*

Bourjaily: Right, and my feeling at the time, and I think it's probably so . . . although he did a little work with me, it was nothing like the amount of work that he did with Jones. I don't guess I knew it at the time; I knew it by 1951, when *From Here to Eternity* came out. But I was pretty much under Jones's shadow at Scribners without knowing it. I think Scribners was more interested in Jones than they were in me—much more disposed to assume that he was going to be their big post-war writer. They did not do anything much with *The End of My Life* when it came out as far as supporting it.

Conversations: *How was it received? Did you get some encouraging reviews?*

Bourjaily: No review at all in *The New York Times,* either Sunday or daily. The reviews were quite good or very bad. I remember one or two that were almost horrified by what they took to be the depravity in the book: really very mild drug scenes and drinking scenes and expressions of disillusion in religion and the establishment and so on. A few reviewers were clearly quite offended by those things. A few others were disposed to say, "Oh, boy, here come the postwar writers." I think the book might have been better received if it had come out a year or two later, though that's all speculation. Most of the books by new writers just out of the Second World War which did do well, those of us whose first novels were inevitably war novels, appeared in '48 and '49. Books like *The Gallery* and *The Naked and the Dead, From Here to Eternity,* and so on.

Conversations: *At this point you knew that you were a novelist from now on?*

Bourjaily: Yeah, I started right in on the next novel.

Conversations: *I have here a reference work called* Contemporary Novelists. *It includes a section on you, which begins with a summary judgment on your career: "Vance*

Bourjaily occupies a curious place in modern fiction." Do you know this?

Bourjaily: No, I don't.

Conversations: "A serious writer who deals thoughtfully with important themes, he has for the most part been ignored by the critics; a novelist who delineates in interesting ways the vagaries of American life during the past three decades, he has never been a genuine popular success. Bourjaily is, nevertheless, that rarest of phenomena in American fiction, the novelist who develops and improves his craft in successive books. Without attracting attention as an innovator, he has experimented in interesting ways with different methods of handling and presenting his materials, and he has consistently refined a style that is personal without idiosyncratic." How do you feel about that?

Bourjaily: Well, I would hope it's a fair summary. It sounds accurate to me. It's certainly accurate as far as the extent of popular success is concerned. I don't suppose it would be appropriate for me to comment on the critical conclusion. I recall being told, and I guess discussed, in somebody's scholarly article, that I was a writer's writer. If that is true, it's an uncomfortable thing to be. I think I am probably about as well read and thoroughly studied by my contemporaries as anyone. I hear occasionally from a younger writer that one or another of my books—generally it's *Confessions of a Spent Youth*—was very important to him when he finally came across it, and saw that you could do certain things. Fred Exley told me that, for example, and Fred Busch. So I think I can probably credit myself with having had some minor influence on the way literature is going the last three decades.

Conversations: Do you feel cheated in terms of big popular success?

Bourjaily: Cheated is not precisely the word. Each time there has been a book I've been, if not optimistic, at least hopeful that I would make some money and get more general recognition, and I suppose that one of the things that keeps one writing is the assumption that if it doesn't happen this time it's bound to next time. But meanwhile, I suppose, one constructs a life of what satisfactions are available.

Conversations: Do you get considerable satisfaction out of teaching?

Bourjaily: Yes and no.

Conversations: Yesterday when Bill Fox introduced you to speak at a University of South Carolina colloquium, he said that he regarded you as one of the most effective teachers of creative writing that he had come across. Since he is also in the trade, he knows what he is talking about.

Bourjaily: There are two kinds of effective teachers of creative writing, and I fall very much into one of the two categories. The first is the—and these guys are terribly effective—this does not describe me—very dogmatic teacher who really feels that he knows how to make it work as a program for how fiction should be written. Verlin Cassill is an extraordinarily effective writing teacher in that category. Verlin has very interesting theories of what writing consists of and how to do it and he teaches that way; for a certain kind of student that is an absolutely necessary kind of teacher. Another dogmatist—and I don't use the word at all perjoratively—is a guy like Bob Coover, who is just a tremendously effective teacher of how to write, both in and out of the classroom. I suspect that people like Cassill and Coover are more in the Ezra Pound tradition and the Gertrude Stein tradition—those who having become established want to help the apprentice. They've got programs, and the apprentice can understand in terms of these theories where he's fulfilling the master's requirements and where he or she is failing to.

I can't teach that way because I'm not that sure of myself and because I never do the same thing twice anyway. Whatever my personal faults as a writer, and I'm sure they are vast, I don't repeat myself. Having solved one set of technical and mechanical problems I don't want to do them again. I want to do something else. I think the other kind of effective teacher of writing is effective chiefly because of the changes in publishing. This other kind of teacher does pretty much what the Max Perkinses did. This kind of teacher accepts that there is a tremendous variety of good and serious writing possible and that, in Hemingway's phrase, one way that you will know a really fine piece of work is that it won't resemble any other really fine piece of work. And if you feel that way about it, you obviously can't be a dogmatist.

What you can do is to read a student's work and see if it works on its own terms, and then hope that in the course of talking it over you will not so much find the weaknesses and suggest the remedies as reaffirm what the student already knows. The student gives you this piece of work sort of thinking that this part of it is not too good but hoping it's better than that. All you do is really say, "No, I'm sorry. You're right about it. It is weak here, and you probably had better find a way to fix it." And then you may talk some about the remedies, but you try to pull it out of him or out of her, rather than making particular suggestions.

Conversations: This is done in face-to-face conferences, then?

Bourjaily: Yeah, what I try to do in the classroom is to do some of that in a more public way. In the conference situation I think my kind of teacher of writing is acting as editors once acted, or as Perkins once acted, and as they don't any longer. Editors are not given time these days to work with developing people. What an editor wants is the manuscript ready to go. They just don't edit much anymore. Some of them do; some of them try. Well, actually Dick Marek takes that kind of time with a manuscript, and I was surprised because it's a long time since I knew anyone who would. He was my editor at Dial on *Now Playing at Canterbury* and has just moved over to Dutton, I think it is, to do his own line of books. But in any case, I don't think even a guy like Marek could take the time now to look at a manuscript and say, "Yeah, there's some talent here. It's a couple of years away from a publishable book, but I'm so impressed with what this young writer might be able to do that I'm going to patiently read through several versions of this and several drafts of whatever the next thing he or she wants to do and see if I can't help this writer find some of the short cuts; learn some of the stuff that he or she would inevitably learn anyway by trial and error. But maybe by kicking it back and forth a little the learning will be speeded up."

19

Vance Bourjaily

Conversations: Who are the writers you feel you have helped to launch while you were working as a teacher?

Bourjaily: I really wouldn't want to say. If there are any I'd rather they say so. The teacher or the editor doesn't really do the work, you know. I think if credit is to be given it should be given the other way. What happens in the classroom is something a bit different and a bit artificial. As I was saying yesterday—Bill asked me to talk about what we do at Iowa. Because we operate under university patronage, we must be structured as if we were actually giving graduate courses, but it's really a concession so that a description can be given in a catalogue and it will conform apparently to other activities that are going on in graduate school. Essentially I think the course structure is—artificial is the wrong word—somewhat unnatural. What we should be doing ideally is sitting in cafes in Paris sort of gradually meeting the young writers who habituate the same cafe and reading their stuff because we want to. But okay, we're paid to do this by the university and what happens at a place like Iowa is a much less dazzling approximation of that sort of Left Bank situation. But because it attracts a lot of talented kids and they find themselves together in an ambiance, albeit institutionalized, I think very much the same kind of learning takes place that might have taken place around the coffee houses in London in Doctor Johnson's time or around the Deux Magots in Paris in the twenties.

   Meanwhile there is another change in addition to... as I say, my feeling is that we fill the vacuum left by the departure of editors from the role of helping develop talent. What happens in the classroom is—again in a very mild way for the student writer—the equivalent of first publication and criticism, and this is, let us say, in the absence of very locally important little magazines where they might first publish. Instead they first publish on ditto sheets and are read as a matter of obligation by their peers who are in the same class. And that's publication. The work is then analyzed and discussed in a two-hour meeting. Having had publication, you now have criticism. The sessions are obviously directed by somebody like myself, and again I think we get into the two different kinds of writing teacher. If he's a dogmatist, it's held up to certain standards of what should and should not be and discussed that way. I can't be a dogmatist. When I conduct one of those sessions. . . for one thing I try to let the students do most of the talking. But I can't be anywhere near as positive as, say, Bob Coover can about what I think is good or bad. So what I try to do is to take a real mechanics approach to it. When we find a problem in a piece I try to talk about it and its solution in a way that will result, partly for the author's benefit, in a class discussion of this problem and how it might be solved with particular regard to the story. But what seems to be more important is to try to derive a generalization about technique that will be a benefit to everybody there, including myself.

There are a couple of rewards from teaching. You ask me whether I liked it. The answer would be if I didn't have to do it, I wouldn't do it. It's how I support my family, but once that initial reluctance to do anything but write and indulge in one's natural hedonism has been overcome, and you make the commitment to teach, you may as well do the best job of it you possibly can. I feel a considerable obligation to give those kids their tuition's worth. They pay a lot of money to come sit in the classroom with me a couple of times a week. The rewards of it are of two kinds. One is that I constantly learn from them. I could itemize particular things I've learned this year that. . . . In the country they don't make any distinction between teaching and learning; they use the same verb, "to learn," for both functions. They say, "He learned me." And "learn" is a better word than "teach." When I learn somebody something, I learn it myself too. The other nice thing about teaching is it obviously keeps you in significant contact with a lot of energy and vitality and enthusiasm that is part of the condition of being young. And that's neat. I like it.

Conversations: What are you working on now?

Bourjaily: Just starting a new book.

Conversations: Another novel?

Bourjaily: Yeah. Starting another novel, and I have in draft now the Hemingway-Fitzgerald book. The Hemingway-Fitzgerald book is in need of just a nice three- or four-month period of concentrated revision. It's pretty much in hand, and I like what I

Vance Bourjaily

have, but it's thin in some places. Particularly thin in . . . when I first wrote a draft I found myself very diffident about trying to make new critical judgments. I thought so many guys who were such good specialists and such bright people have been through this stuff and found everything there is to find. Unless I first master all the criticism, which I will not have time to do in this lifetime, I don't have any business offering my own interpretations, because the likelihood is that I will simply be duplicating in a somewhat critically irresponsible way an observation that somebody else has made after years of work and research on it. I think that kind of diffidence about making judgments and offering insights on the works has created a thin part of the manuscript now. Since then I've taught through Hemingway and Fitzgerald a couple of times and read at least a fair amount of the criticism, and I think I trust myself to produce a few judgments—one of which I flatter myself is going to be of somewhat astonishing originality. It's a new reading of *A Farewell to Arms*, which tickles the hell out of me. As far as I know nobody has read *A Farewell to Arms* that way yet.

So I wish to get this new novel in hand and revise the Hemingway-Fitzgerald book, and that's probably the next two years. The new novel is going to be, I hope, quite a lot shorter than stuff I've been doing—for two or three very good reasons. One is—I shouldn't say I try not to repeat myself—I get very bored in writing fiction if I am repeating myself, and so I try to do things that I haven't done before. One thing that I have not successfully done before is to write a really short novel—a novel which will be accomplished within 150 to 200 manuscript pages, say, the *Gatsby*-length novel. I love that length. I love it as a reader. I've just never been able to contain myself within it. Now I want to learn how to write it.

So that's the intention of the book that I'm now messing with, and I think I'm going to do a couple of them, as a matter of fact, on very different areas of subject matter. I just am determined to get that form in hand because it has certain characteristics that longer novels don't have. It's more—we're talking about something that is a little more than novella length. But just as the novella more resembles a short story than it does a long novel, so I think this 60,000-word novel is essentially a

22

marvelously intricate, fully developed short story in form. That is to say it observes certain unities of tone; it avoids certain kinds of digression; it lays down the line it's going to take immediately and follows it without deviation in the way the short story does. Whereas when you write the four- five- six-hundred-page novel you've got room for everything. But there's a kind of discipline in that 60,000-word form that I just love and that I know I haven't done yet at that length, and I want to try doing it.

James Dickey, poet and novelist, was born in Atlanta, Georgia, on 2 February 1923. After flying in World War II he took his B.A. and M.A. at Vanderbilt University. He taught at Rice University, the University of Florida, Reed College, San Fernando Valley State College, and has been poet-in-residence at the University of South Carolina since 1969. His books of poetry include Into the Stone *(1960),* Drowning with Others *(1962),* Helmets *(1964),* Buckdancer's Choice *(1965),* The Eye-Beaters, Blood, Victory, Madness, Buckhead and Mercy *(1970), and* The Zodiac *(1976). He received the National Book Award for Poetry in 1966. Dickey's 1970 novel,* Deliverance, *was a best seller.*

James Dickey

James Dickey was interviewed at his home on Lake Katharine in Columbia, South Carolina, by Matthew J. Bruccoli on 4 March 1977. Every surface in the room was covered with stacks of books, so interviewer and interviewee sat on the floor. The phone rang repeatedly during the interview—which seems to be the normal condition at the Dickey household. Deborah, Dickey's recent bride, came in several times to relay messages from his Hollywood agent.

Conversations: Your career as a poet has been unusual in that most poets go through an elaborate stage of writing for college magazines, but you did not appear in print for the first time until you were beyond college and had started another career in business, is that right?

Dickey: Well, that's not quite right. I did publish in college magazines. I think the first time that I ever published was in the Vanderbilt literary magazine, when I was an undergraduate. And I had a poem accepted by one of the national quarterlies, the *Sewanee Review*, when I was either a senior or a graduate student—I just went to graduate school one year. It was printed in 1951, when I had gone back into the Air Force; I was about twenty-eight—twenty-seven then, or twenty-eight.

I didn't publish in a lot of very small places, although I was glad to appear in little magazines, like the *Wormwood Review*, and that sort of thing. It takes an author a good long time to get to the point where he's not fascinated with seeing his work and his name in print, you know. That seems wonderful at first, and I think that feeling never really completely wears off.

Conversations: Under what circumstances did you commence as a professional poet?

Dickey: I don't really know what that amounts to. Somebody like

James Dickey

Robert Graves would refer to himself as being a professional poet, but I myself don't feel that. Professionalism in poetry is not something that I think is especially laudatory. In my own case I hope for the rest of my life to preserve my amateur status.

Conversations: Let me rephrase my question. How old were you and what was your occupation when you began writing poetry seriously?

Dickey: Well, I was a student at Vanderbilt, a belated undergraduate, having had my education interrupted by the war, and having had my interest change during the war years from athletics to the more literary pursuits and the idea that the mind was at least equally worth consideration with the body. During the service years I just kind of gravitated over toward reading and writing and things that I had never really paid much attention to before.

When I got out of the service I didn't want to go back to Clemson to play football, which I had been doing when I went into the service initially. I wanted to go to another kind of school that would further the sort of new interests that I had kind of acquired during the service years. And so I went to Vanderbilt, and I was very gratified to have very good teachers like Donald Davidson and Monroe Spears encourage me in what I was trying to do.

It was already relatively late in the game. I started all over again. I didn't get any credit at Clemson. All I did was go through football season at Clemson before the war, just at the first part of the war. When I came back I started all over again on the G.I. Bill at Vanderbilt. I was twenty-three, and I graduated when I was twenty-six, twenty-five or twenty-six, and went a year to graduate school.

By that time my course was pretty much fixed. I was beginning to publish and I'd published in school magazines; I had a couple of national publications pending; and I had had some very good people encourage me to keep on with it. But still I was already past the age when John Keats died.

As soon as I got out of graduate school and got my first teaching job at Rice Institute, as it was then called, in Houston, Texas, I was immediately recalled into the service, so that was another setback. I tried my best to keep on with writing during the time of the Korean War, and I managed some little magazine publications, none of which have survived. I suppose I have them around somewhere, but I never collected them. Then when I got out I went back to teaching freshman English and composition and report writing for technical students and that sort of thing.

Conversations: Back at Rice?

Dickey: Back at Rice, yeah. But they gave me to understand that because I was a veteran I could have a year or two of grace, but that I couldn't be retained on the staff unless I had a Ph.D. degree which I had no. . . . I had already lost so much time as a writer that I couldn't go back into scholarship and so on at that age. I was thirty-odd years old.

Conversations: At this time you had made up your mind that you were going to be a writer?

Dickey: I had had sufficient encouragement to maybe take a kind of a wild hope that I might eventually be a writer, if I could just get the time to write and get some more publications and maybe get a book out, or something of that sort.

Conversations: How did you square taking time off to be an advertising executive?

Dickey: Well, that was later. I was given a Rockefeller Grant by the *Sewanee Review* and I went to live in Europe for a year or so. I wrote an awful lot of stuff there, and that did not survive either. I'd like to go back and read that stuff if I can find it in those old long-buried, dog-eared magazines in which they appeared.

Conversations: What year was the Rockefeller Grant?

Dickey: 1954. Then I came back and I was as much at sea as before. Andrew Lytle, who was one of the people who had given me the grant from the *Sewanee Review*, asked me to come and be his assistant at the University of Florida. We went down there and lived—I had a child by that time—and we went there, but I was living on really just a pittance of money. I had no money at all. I couldn't even get my child's teeth looked after or anything like that.

James Dickey

Conversations: What did this job pay?

Dickey: $3600. So then I immediately got into some very bad trouble down there having to do with an association called the Pen Women of America who asked me to read to them. I read some things of mine which they construed to be obscene. Then I saw I was going to get sacked. So in the dead of night I left and went to Jacksonville and caught the plane and went to New York to throw my hand in the business world. I thought if my chosen profession, teaching, was going to fall out to be that sort of situation, I'd rather go for the buck and make some damn dough in the market place. I had the confidence of Lucifer in myself by that time and I was beginning to appear all over the place; in the *Hudson Review, Partisan, Sewanee, Yale Review, Kenyon,* and so on. I was ready to roll.

I figured that the kind of thing that an advertising writer would be able to write, I could do that with the little finger of the left hand, and they were getting paid good dough for it. I happened to have been right. So I went to New York and I broke in with McCann-Erickson on the Coca-Cola account. I did the Eddie Fisher Show, which was short-lived. I think it had the lowest Nielson rating that's ever been on television. I did that and I worked on various accounts, mainly Coca-Cola.

Conversations: Can you remember any of your Coca-Cola writing?

Dickey: No, but I remember what was easiest for me to do. You've heard of Jungle Jim in the old days of the cartoons—I was known around the McCann-Erickson office as Jingle Jim. I wrote several jingles a day. It didn't bother me at all because I was really not seriously committed to it. It was just a way to earn a living for my family.

Conversations: How good was the money?

Dickey: I asked them immediately, I said give me twice what I've earned as a teacher and I'll come in with you. $7200 was $600 a month. That was it, and I had never had such a princely salary before. I was impressed with American commerce, because if they would pay an unknown guy $600 a month. . . . Well that's really not much now, but it sure was a lot to me then.

They proposed to move me down to Atlanta because the Coca-Cola account phased out the Fisher show, and the budget for radio-television advertising for Coca-Cola was to be diverted into local bottler advertising—that is, the budget was to be divided among 3600 bottling plants instead of having a network show. I was sent down to Atlanta to start up an operation in which we could furnish local bottlers with personalized local ads for their particular operations in the area where they were. This was the time when we changed into the other sizes—king size ten, king twelve, and the big, big family size, and all that sort of thing.

I went to Atlanta. We bought a home there, and we lived there five, five and a half, six years working in business and so on. What you do in the advertising business, after you get a certain cachet, you jump agencies. You say, well, all right, I had this job at this agency. You go to another agency and take your portfolio and that sort of thing and say I did these ads and these, and these, and these; and these commercials and so on; and you say I would be willing to leave my present job and come on with you.

So I went as copy chief to another agency, a smaller agency than McCann-Erickson, which was at that time the biggest in the world. This was a locally based agency. It had accounts like Armour Fertilizer and Lay's Potato Chips, before it was Frito-Lay, and so on. I worked on those as copy chief. It was a much better salary—almost double what I had gotten before from McCann-Erickson—so things were looking pretty good financially. We were not wasteful as a family. Maxine was a wonderful, wonderful wife and she managed mighty well. We seemed to be more or less set on our course.

Then I was chosen Atlanta's Advertising Young Man of the Year. On the basis of that I left that job and went with another agency as vice-president and creative director, on the Delta Air Lines account. Well, by that time my first book had come out with Scribners, and it looked like there was going to have to be a parting; the fork in the road had been reached. I was either going to have to stay with advertising and give it all my time, including my so-called leisure time, or not see get done what I knew should be done in the business end of things. I was either going to have to do that or pitch my hat in the ring as a full-time literary man.

James Dickey

So after a splendid conversation with my wife, she said, "Jim, you're killing yourself. You're trying to sell your soul to the devil all day and buy it back at night"—in my study trying to write my own stuff. So I quit. I sold my stock in the company, and we pulled what money we had out of the bank. We were given a Guggenheim Fellowship on the strength of my first book.

Conversations: That first book published by Scribners, how did that come about? Did you submit the book to them?

Dickey: No, they asked me on the strength of the magazine publications.

Conversations: This was John Hall Wheelock?

Dickey: John Hall Wheelock, who was one of Thomas Wolfe's editors, one of Fitzgerald's editors. . . .

Conversations: Who was editing the Scribners Poets of Today *series.*

Dickey: And the stories that that remarkable old man can spin about those. . . . Boy, Scribners really had a lock on American literature in those days, with Max Perkins and Wheelock and the other great editors that they had then. He can certainly spin some remarkable stories about them. They were so difficult to manage in different ways.

Conversations: What year was this?

Dickey: Oh, let's see; it was '60.

Conversations: You were how old?

Dickey: Thirty-seven.

Conversations: At the age of thirty-seven you walked away.

Dickey: Yeah, yeah.

Conversations: From a pretty good career.

Dickey: Yeah.

Conversations: To shoot crap on being a poet.

Dickey: This is right; this is right. And there could not have been a more unpromising kind of venture on earth than that of an American poet. I remember when we had Archibald MacLeish down here, he said to me, "Jim, the total—my net as well as my gross—for ten years of writing poetry when I started out was seventy-five dollars." There could have been no more unpromising possible enterprise or means of earning a livelihood than that of being an American poet. It's different now. They're still having a relatively rocky road but it ain't like it was when I used to give readings sometimes for maybe ten or fifteen dollars, where there would be five people in the audiences—three of them relatives.

Conversations: After the Guggenheim what did you do? Where did you go on the Guggenheim?

Dickey: We went back to Europe and some of the same places. Let's see, after the Guggenheim, what did I do? Oh, yeah, my second book had come out, *Drowning with Others*. And it was up for the National Book Award, and the Pulitzer Prize. It didn't get either one.

Conversations: That was Wesleyan University Press.

Dickey: Yeah, Wesleyan. I had gone with them, and I never regretted it, either. That's a very, very good house. Unlike a large publisher—just to throw a name into the huddle somebody like Macmillan—they don't publish poetry as a sop to the poet so that he will write a novel or a travel book or a cook book or something like that. They took him seriously as a poet, Wesleyan people did. I had a wonderful editor there, Richard Wilbur. They had very, very good people to work with, who all were vitally interested in poets and all poets themselves. They had very good designers. It was just a very good project, Wesleyan.

    Drowning with Others had come out and I had some job offers around to be writer-in-residence. The best one—it still wasn't very much money, but it was more than we had been offered at other places—was at Reed College in Portland, Oregon. So we went up there and lived in the Pacific Northwest for two and a half years, and that again I never regretted because it was such a wonderfully stimulating kind of far-out, offbeat type of experimental college—kind of like Black Mountain, something like that. Or Black Mountain is like it.

James Dickey

I don't think anything could be as far-out as Reed. But very good, very good people there, and it was a hotbed of folk music, which is another thing that I liked a lot about it. If we weren't talking about poetry or all those important subjects like love, art, death, time, poetry, imagination, and history, any subject. . . . We would talk about it hour after hour, and the rest of the time we would play music. We'd just sit around and play. It was a wonderful atmosphere for my children. I had another child by this time. They would sit around and listen to the conversation and the music and it was just marvelous. Reed College, I'll never forget it. It was just a marvelous intellectual stimulus for everybody that was connected with it.

But then my term—it was kind of a rotating chair—then my term was up there, and a college in California which is now California State, which was then known as San Fernando Valley State, offered me another residency. So I was just going from one residency to the other.

We moved down to California, and we were there for two, two and a half years, and I taught at Northridge. I also liked that in quite a different way. The Reed people were so intellectual—the rope-soled sandals and guitars and anarchist pamphlets and all kinds of causes and that sort of thing. The people at Reed College when I was there in '60—I don't know—'60, gosh, I don't remember, '60—in the early sixties—they were hippies before hippies had ever been heard of. They were naturally hippies. They didn't have to do anything about trying to become hippies or be hippies; they were hippies. I loved them. I longed sometimes—with all that hyperintellectualization and interest in the arts and in history and music and that sort of thing—I longed sometimes to see a dumb, adenoidal coed or hulking football player. There was nothing of that in Reed. When I came the only team they had engaged in intercollegiate athletics was a darts team—a good one, too.

When I went down to California to teach down there, there was nothing but the adenoidal coeds and hulking football players. I longed to see the long black stockings on the girls again and the guy with the guitar over his shoulder and a copy of *The Critique of Pure Reason*—it's in paperback—in the back pocket of his blue jeans. I liked them both. It was a lot of fun. It was a great contrast, and Maxine, my wife, was a wonderful woman. She could swing with any type of group. She enjoyed the Reed people and their superintellectualism and commitment to the life of the mind and the imagination, and she liked the kind of hearty outgoing sort of beefy, sweaty Southern California College atmosphere, too. She could take it either way. So in the end could I.

Conversations: Did you write Buckdancer *in California?*

Dickey: I wrote part of it in Reed and finished it in California.

Conversations: It came out while you were in California?

Dickey: Yeah, it came out when I was in California and then. . . .

Conversations: That one made you?

Dickey: Well, I don't know, it won the National Book Award. I went and made the acceptance speech and immediately the Library of Congress contacted me and wanted me to come give a reading there. I went and gave a reading. Then they communicated with me by mail to be the next incumbent in the chair of the poetry consultant at the Library of Congress, which I suppose is as close as we have in this country to being Poet Laureate. Although it, too, is kind of a rotating thing. It was supposed to be a one-year appointment—it was not due to my particular effectiveness at all—but during the time I was there it was changed to a two-year appointment. So I was there for two years.

Then that was up and I had to figure out what to do. I figured I'd go back out to California and take my family because everybody liked it out there so much. I liked it less than my children and my wife did, but I liked it enough to consider maybe going back out to Berkeley. But during that time the people at the University of South Carolina got in touch with me, and I thought, "Well, I'd kind of like to go back and live in the South. I love it; I miss it; I'm a Southerner myself, and I'd kind of. . . . Well, I'll go down and talk to them." I came down and talked to them. I liked the place and the climate and the kind of soft air and flowers and birds and things around. It was not too far from the remnants of my family in Atlanta, and it seemed like a good idea at the time, and I've never regretted it. I enjoy South Carolina, and I've kind of put down roots here. I have some property and a couple of homes here and very good friends.

Conversations: At the point when you accepted the offer from South Carolina had you already finished Deliverance *or were you still working on it?*

Dickey: No, I finished it here in South Carolina.

Conversations: Why did you decide to write a novel?

Dickey: Well, a couple of reasons. I think that first of all poets—every poet that I've ever known—have a secret and sometimes quite overt desire to write in another medium. They don't want to just write poetry.

Poetry for every true poet that's worth his salt—and I don't want to make this a cliche but it is anyway—the poetry for him is the center of the creative wheel, no matter whatever else he might write. Whether it's plays, or novels, or short stories, or screenplays, or even advertising copy, the poetry is the center. Everything else is a spin-off from that. If the poet is any good that center has got to hold firm, the center of poetry. But you want to try and see what you can do in something else, too, you know.

Now I've never had any wish to write plays at all. I'm afraid of the difficulty of the conventions of stagecraft, because I don't know it. I've never worked in the theatre, and I don't know very many people that have, although some; but I've never worked in that medium, and I hear lots of stories about how difficult it is to learn and how many years it takes you to learn how to get a character on stage and off at the right time and all that sort of thing. I'm always going to be scared of it, but novels—that's quite a different thing.

I love stories and I thought, you know, if I could ever think of anything with a plot to it that I would give it a try. I didn't really give it any serious concern. It's just one of those things that a writer will think: you know, if I ever got around to it I'd kind of like to write a novel, too, just to see what would come of it.

Conversations: How long did it take you to write Deliverance?

Dickey: Off and on under ten or twelve years, I guess. That's misleading because it implies that I was doing nothing but that, and I was not. That was relatively far down on the priority list. I wrote six or seven other books during the same period that I was working on that, and whenever I just felt like it or wanted to write a scene in *Deliverance* I would do it or block it out in some way, or maybe work on some of the sentences, you know, just little things like that.

I was interested in the story and then the further into it I got, the more interested I became, but it would never have been written if I had not leaked to the literary magazines. The contributors' items, for example, of one magazine—I forget which one it was, I think it was the *Partisan Review*—said James Dickey's written this book of poems and this other book of poems and so on; he is now working on a novel. Bam! The publishers began to call in. The novel—the magic word—that's where the dough is at.

Conversations: I thought the novel was dead.

Dickey: Yeah. Oh, no, no, no. You keep seeing articles to that effect, but it isn't dead, and it never will be dead as long as people have the age-old fascination that goes all the way back to the cavemen, of being told a story and wanting to know what happens next. The novel is going to live as long as that propensity survives in the minds of men, women, and children.

Conversations: Do you think Deliverance *is a poet's novel?*

Dickey: Oh, well, I like to think that it is, in a way, but it's not deliberately poetic at all. It was originally three or four times longer before I realized that I had a very bad defect in the way I was approaching the book. Poets tend to write too much description. They fall in love with their own descriptions.

I remember a John Aldridge article about John Updike. He was reviewing a book called *Of the Farm*, which is pretty good, I think, as far as Updike's work is concerned. I think it's one of the better ones. He says the trouble is that every time something starts happening to interest the reader in the people in the novel there's yet another endlessly long description of a tree or a mailbox or something, so that the narrative thrust and the interest are dissipated and so on. I saw that that was exactly what I

35

was doing, that the main thing that I had going for *Deliverance* was the narrative thrust and the wanting to know what happens.

Conversations: Did you cut it yourself or did the publisher cut it?

Dickey: Oh, yeah, I cut it. Yeah, I had a very good editor but we agreed that's what we needed to do: that whatever description or whatever might be construed as being essentially poetic in *Deliverance* was in just small touches, just in one word here or one there; but the floor of it, the narrative, must be kept going, you know.

Conversations: Were you surprised by its popular acceptance?

Dickey: I certainly was, yeah. I didn't even know if it would be published or not. Or whether it was publishable. I really didn't know. I didn't have any record as a prose fiction writer. I had never even published a short story. I had not the slightest idea that it would become some kind of an international best seller published in thirty languages, or something like that, and be made into a movie. It's completely amazing to me. I still am somewhat startled by it.

Conversations: Now Deliverance *led to your moonlighting as a screenwriter.*

Dickey: Well, yeah, when you have a novel that you worked on a long time and there is the eventuality of making a film of it, you naturally want to do it like you think it ought to be done. I hadn't any background in screenwriting at all, except a couple of documentaries I had done when I lived out in California for which I did the voice-over commentary. I had never done a feature film at all, and when Warner's contracted with me to do my own film, they sent me some sample film scripts of other writers. One of them was *A Clockwork Orange* by Stanley Kubrick. I read through them, and I swear—God, I don't mean to put Kubrick down; I admire him very much—but I thought, Lord, Lord, if these guys get paid good money for this kind of shoddy, slipshod, hit-or-miss type of writing it's going to be easy to do it.

Conversations: And it was.

Dickey: Yeah, it was, very. I had to learn to work with the director, and the actors, and the people with the camera, and the sound people and all of that, but that's really not very hard to do.

Conversations: And since then you've done what—half-a-dozen more screenplays?

Dickey: Oh, no, not that many, no. I've done one major thing for NBC, The Call of the Wild. Then I have a new one that's coming out called To Gene Bullard which Warner Brothers is doing, and I have some other possible projects, but whether I'll do them or not I don't know.

Conversations: What drives you now to do screenplays? Is it the money?

Dickey: No, no.

Conversations: Or do you get a kick out of it?

Dickey: No, no, well it's mainly this. I have come under. . . some of the people that I admire the most have been in the way of convincing me, or all but convincing me, that film is the great art medium of our time. It's not the novel or the poem, although poetry is always going to be my big thing. Always. I can't deviate from that and will not because I like it. That's my thing, my schtick.

But people who are fascinated with film, say people like James Agee, who's a very great screenwriter as well as a great writer, at least to me, can go a long ways toward convincing you that the film is the great art medium of our time and is roughly the equivalent to the Elizabethan drama of Shakespeare's time. Now that's saying a lot, but if we've got a great medium, a very great visual medium such as the play, the stage, it's going to have to be movies. It seems to me it's better to make good ones, memorable ones, than just waste it on a lot of schlock and junk.

Conversations: Are you also excited by the size of the audience?

Dickey: Well, yes I am. I think that any writer of any sort, whether he's a poet or a screenwriter or whatever—one of the motivating drives that he has is reaching people and moving them. With a mass medium like films or like television you've got that opportunity par excellence. You can reach millions of people. And God knows, maybe one person would see your film and want to tell you that if it hadn't been for that you would never have reached him in the sense of the artist reaching a member of his audience.

Conversations: I'd like to switch to your writing plans now. You have perhaps your biggest most ambitious project going—the two connected novels.

Dickey: Yes, the trouble with my particular situation is that I have so many I think I'm overextended and overdiversified: too many various kinds of projects. I want to make films and I want to write more poems and these two long novels and so on, which will require an incredible amount of research. I'm a very slow worker, anyway. Let's see, I'm fifty-four now. If I can last until maybe seventy my work will be done, and I will be able to lay my burden down. But right now I've got to take it up.

Conversations: And if you shuffle off tomorrow will you feel that some of your best work will not have been written?

Dickey: Yes, I would feel that. For years I felt that I had the potential to do good work but I didn't know enough in order to do it. Every plane trip I took or everything that I did every day that I lived I felt that if I could only last, I could do the work that I felt that I was capable of doing. But I always felt like I would be cut off before I could ever do it. I'm at the stage now where I believe that if I were to drop dead from a heart attack or the airplane that I was on blew up and I was snuffed out I would still be willing to rest on what I've done now. That's a very good feeling when you wake up at a middle-aged 4:30 in the morning and think: "Well, I wouldn't want to have to rest on it, but I would. I would rest on it if the circumstances where that was necessary were to happen."

Conversations: Let's focus on these connected novels which are called Crux *and* Alnilam.

Dickey: Yeah, *Alnilam* is the first one and the other one is called *Crux.*

Conversations: These derive from your experiences in the South Pacific.

Dickey: Well, they derive from the general experience that many members of my generation underwent in the air war of 1941-1946. The novels concern an elaborate plot hatched by a remarkable and perhaps insane boy who's an aviation cadet in the first novel and who has a complete kind of mystique. He's a kind of crypto-Fascist of mystical leanings.

His father, who has not known the boy—having been divorced from the boy's mother since the child was an infant—is a man who has gone blind from diabetes. The boy is killed or he disappears under very mysterious circumstances on a training base. The father, who has been blind only a few months, is summoned as the next-of-kin, which is already very strange to the father who's a man of around fifty, because he has never known the boy. The boy's mother has raised the child and so on.

The father is notified that he's designated as the next-of-kin. He goes as a blind man with his dog to this air base, where this boy has been killed. But the body has never been found. The novel *Alnilam* is a very slow disclosure of the boy's character— Joel Cahill's character—as it's revealed in the conversations of the father with his fellow cadets and flyers and so on. You might almost call them, well you could call them, you should call them his disciples who have been with him in hatching this elaborate takeover plot that's going to spread through all of the service— all of the services—and kind of transform the American system and that of all Western man through this mystical philosophy and so on that the boy has hatched in these enigmatic Heraclitian epigrams and so on.

The boy has been a spellbinder. He's the stuff of which political demagogues are made. He's kind of like a political Rimbaud, in that you can't explain him. He's just got almost supernatural and superhuman gifts to influence and move people to do what he wants them to do. The plot in *Alnilam*— Alnilam being the central star in the belt of the northern constellation Orion—is unfolded in just little bits and pieces of conversation and so on.

The father realizes to his consternation and horror that his appearance on the scene is going to trigger an enormous revolt because the son has said in his usual cryptic manner to his cohorts: "When my father comes then we spring the plot. We start." Now his coming will be the sign of the springing of the *Alnilam* plot—which starts out in mass destruction of the aircraft on the base, under the guise of making it appear like an accident and so on. Well, I needn't go on and on, but anyway the first volume is the blind father learning what his son was all about, and also learning some things about himself through learning about his son that he didn't know about, that he hasn't been able to explain to himself. All right, now the next part of it. . . .

You never do know whether the boy has actually been killed or not. He's supposed to have gone down in a fire, a brush fire, and so on. The plane has been found with blood all over everything and so on. He's not been found; but he's missing and presumed dead. But there is the hint at the end of the novel that he has staged the whole thing, that he has wrecked the airplane and disappeared into the flames of this forest fire and so on. But also that he will come back as though resurrected and appear to his disciples and that sort of thing. Now, in the second of the two novels. . . .

Conversations: Called Crux.

Dickey: *Crux,* which is the Southern Cross, a southern constellation. Orion is the northern winter constellation and Alnilam is in the belt of Orion. But Crux is a southern constellation and this takes place in the South Pacific.

Conversations: The disciples are now in the South Pacific.

Dickey: Yeah, and they are all in relatively influential positions and so on. But they believe in the plot more than ever. They think that they are going to be men of tremendous influence and power, not only in the service but after the war and so on. The plot is working. They're getting more and more recruits. They've got all kinds of elaborate codes and things the way they communicate with each other. This will appeal, I think, to almost anybody's interest in secret societies and takeover plots and that sort of thing and so on.

They are doing some remarkable things and they're all brave men; they're decorated men and so on. But some people feel that the game's afoot in some way—that this organization within the regular military organization is a terribly sinister thing, if they could pin it down and find out what it is. This is going to be a real Hitlerian plot, a takeover, and so on, and that there's got to be some way to keep its sinister machinations from taking things over as it seems to be doing. Well, most of the second novel is about that, but it takes place in a most intense combat.

There is a general in it. The chief guy, the chief plotter, is a major named Malcolm Shears, who back in the cadet phase when Joel Cahill disappeared was his number-one man. Cahill was kind of a Machiavellian-poetic-dreamer type visionary boy. As I said, kind of a combination of Christ and von Clausewitz and Machiavelli and Rimbaud and that sort of thing—Heraclitus.

But Shears is an organizer, and he's a practical man. More or less, the second novel, *Crux*, is his situation and so on as he takes over first the squadron and then larger units of the Air Force and so on. They fall under his sway, his spell, and so on. He's opposed by a fellow who is kind of a gentle liberal, who's a colonel, who's just right over Shears. The general who's head of the Fifth Fighter command is just as much in Shears's spell as any of his disciples is. But the guy that's right over him, the colonel, feels him as a terrible and sinister force who must be gotten rid of; he might even kill him or arrange to have him killed in some way and so on. He just feels that Shears is a terribly malevolent, sinister, menacing type of person, and the people that he controls are the same as he.

The climax of the novel is when several of the members of the squadron, including two or three of the old *Alnilam* group, are shot down and tortured and castrated and beheaded and blinded and that sort of thing by the Japanese. Shears sees that this is his opportunity to make a big gesture, to take the damn squadron's planes and go down there on a retaliatory raid and blast the Japanese. A lot of publicity, a lot of avenging your buddy, a lot of sympathy for what he's done and so on.

The general gives him carte blanche to do it, but the squadron commander—I think we call him Conway or Connell or something like that—goes along on the raid. They're getting ready to go in at low level and start strafing these Japanese positions and so on at the place where this torture and mutilation of some of these guys has occurred. The colonel, the liberal, feels that if he can make a wrong formation turn or something and run into Shears and kill him that he will be willing to sacrifice his own life; he does do it.

The last part of the book is told by one of the old Alnilam plotters, a very confused young guy named Harbellous, a Greek Orthodox kid, who is terribly confused about all these happenings. Everybody else that was an original Alnilam plotter is killed and he's the only survivor. The end of it is when he's on occupation duty in Japan and he gives up that whole idea. It's too abstract; it's too inhuman. He's the last survivor of it and he can maybe in some way carry it on, but he decides that he won't.

Conversations: How much of volume two, the Crux *volume, draws upon your experience as a combat pilot?*

Dickey: Well, it's just scenes and, well, incidents and physical details and that sort of thing; but I never participated in anything like that. Wish I had.

Conversations: Some of the people you flew with were captured by the Japanese and tortured.

Dickey: Yes, they were. That is true enough, yeah. In the most horrible ways you can imagine. One of them was castrated; one of them had his testicles squoze until the guy died—in some kind of thing like a meat press or something like that. It got pretty grim over there. I'm glad I don't have to go through that again.

Conversations: How many missions did you fly?

Dickey: Oh, 100 at least. I don't really remember. I don't have my Form Five anymore.

Conversations: I notice you're wearing five wrist watches. Does that have something to do with your research for the novels?

Dickey: In a way. One of the characters in the first novel is a character known only as The Navigator, whom I hope sincerely that I can make the most sinister figure since Captain Ahab. I've been doing a good deal of research on navigation. One of the things that you have to know in navigation is the time at various places, in Greenwich and various places and so on. I just got them. I mean it's kind of an interesting thing in itself. Why I might even eventually buy a sailboat, and sail around and see some of the watery part of the world. I like that sort of thing, anyway. I never really did want to be a pilot. I wanted to be a navigator. So this is my belated chance to learn something about it.

Conversations: You have just published what is your longest poem, your major poem, The Zodiac, *which has received a good deal of attention. Do you feel that the poem has been fully recognized?*

Dickey: Well, yes. I couldn't ask for any more recognition. It's unusual for a poem to get that much attention—say like in *Newsweek* and the national magazines. That's really very gratifying indeed. I think that the sales have been really very, very heartening. I'm kind of at a loss to account for it, but I'm not questioning it. I don't argue with them.

Conversations: In The Zodiac *you attempted a new form for your poetry, which you described as the "rewrite"—not imitating, not translating, but working from the poem of a Dutch poet. Why did this form appeal to you?*

Dickey: I really don't know except that I had read the poem years ago in a very inept translation and it struck me that it was such a wonderful idea and was so congruent with my own thinking about poetry, the stars and the universe and that sort of thing, that it would be a wonderful thing if somebody just took this dead poet's poem over and did it right. I didn't see anybody else do it so I figured I would have to. I was tremendously excited about doing it, and I would do it again. And it seems to me that maybe this will bring in kind of a new genre. I'm quite reconciled to seeing some of my own poetry rewritten by other people. But that's all right, I'd like to see what they'd do.

Conversations: Apart from the two novels, do you have another major poetic project marinating?

Dickey: No, no, no. Really I don't. I have a new book of shorter poems coming out and then maybe a larger retrospective volume with all the stuff that I will have done by the time that I finish this new volume of short pieces. Maybe this will be around 1980 or something like that. The rest of it, I suspect, will be miscellaneous poems. I don't have any big. . . . I have one idea that might turn into some long, major—well, I shouldn't use that term on my work—but a long, ambitious poem, I could say. I'm doing some medical research on that—not personal research, thank God.

I've always been fascinated with the mind-body problem and how one affects the other, especially how the body affects the mind—the changes in the mind that occur when various things happen to the body. I've wanted for a long time to write a poem about the effects, the shifting effects in the personality and the mind of a man who for medical reasons has been surgically castrated. How would one feel? How would that affect one's view of existence from the larger effects of existence and the smaller details and that sort of thing. I have as my working title "The World Without Balls."

Conversations: You see this as a long poem?

Dickey: I think so, yeah, because it's the kind of subject that admits of a very great deal of speculative proliferation, I would think. I don't plan to get castrated to research it but there are a lot of things. . . . This is, for example, a main operation for the relief of prostatic cancer. I know several people who have undergone it and I've talked to them and corresponded with them and so on. I don't know what it is—my preoccupation with disease and mutilation—but such as it is, as a writer I feel that I should go ahead and use it.

Conversations: What acknowledgments do you have to make; what people—living or dead—shaped your career, helped you to be a better poet?

Dickey: Oh, many, many. I don't believe that any writer could ever truthfully assess in his own mind what were the big influences on him as far as other writers are concerned. I have a very pronounced mystical strain in that I like unexplained things to be said to me, so when Heraclitus says the sun is new every day, that speaks to me. I have that part—I suppose that you would call it a romantic mysticism—that appeals to me powerfully, not because of what it is but because of what I am. That kind of thing appeals to me.

I am also very much impressed and even awed by the extreme classicists or neoclassicists like Alexander Pope, who can say a reasonable thing with great aplomb and tact and bring it off with great finesse—say like a couplet: *"True Wit is Nature to Advantage drest, / What oft was Thought, but ne'er so well Exprest."* Things of that sort. Really, I love the epigrammatic couplet very, very much.

Conversations: But you don't write them.

Dickey: But I don't write them because the masters of the epigrammatic couplet are in another part of the ball park from me. I admire them. I think it's true that you tend to overestimate mastery in a genre that you yourself don't do, or don't want to do, or feel that you can't do. I love the guys that are neoclassical epigrammatists and so on. I would not wish to emulate them. But I love them doing it.

My genre is quite different from that. I work in an extremely cloudy emotional climate, kind of nebulous, but I hope with some depth to it: the sense of mystery and the sense of the darkness surrounding everything that we do. I've never been afraid of the dark at all. I like it. Although I consider myself pretty much of a day person, and I like the sun and those things, I think that my own work is informed by a sense of a darkness surrounding a small kind of event or an action out of which it has evolved and is seen or experienced and then will disappear back into the dark, just after a moment.

Conversations: If you had a chance to chisel your tombstone, what would you put on it?

Dickey: All right, let's see. Well, I would like to be buried by the Chatooga River at the most savage part of the section four—Bull Sluice, or Sock-em Dog, Woodall Shoals, somewhere in there. I would have put on it: JAMES DICKEY 1923-19-- AMERICAN POET AND NOVELIST HERE SEEKS HIS DELIVERANCE.

William Price Fox was born in Columbia, South Carolina, in 1926. He declined to follow the family occupation of bootlegging and graduated from the University of South Carolina after serving in the Air Force. His first book, Southern Fried, *a collection of short stories, appeared in 1962. His other books are* Doctor Golf *(1963),* Moonshine Light, Moonshine Bright *(1967),* Southern Fried Plus Six *(1968), and a novel,* Ruby Red *(1968). He has worked for several studios as a screenwriter and publishes widely in magazines. Fox has taught in the Writers Workshop at the University of Iowa and is currently writer-in-residence at the University of South Carolina. He has recently completed a musical based on* Southern Fried.

William Price Fox

William Price Fox was interviewed by Matthew J. Bruccoli in the Department of English at the University of South Carolina on 28 February 1977. They used the interviewer's office because Fox was avoiding his own to escape the telephone. Fox enjoys talking and telling stories, and he frequently interrupted himself with laughter.

Conversations: You didn't go through the college literary magazine apprenticeship that so many writers go through. What do you regard as your apprenticeship as a writer?

Fox: I don't think I had any. What I did was just go right into it in New York.

Conversations: How old were you at that time?

Fox: Thirty-one or thirty-two.

Conversations: And what were you doing?

Fox: I was in sales in New York.

Conversations: Selling what?

Fox: I hustled packaging: cellophane paper, laminations, squeeze bottles, everything.

Conversations: Then you decided you really wanted to write?

Fox: I've always done a lot of talking, you know, and I entertained with that stuff. I'm pretty good at conventions and that kind of crap. A friend of mine named Bill Manville worked for the *Village Voice*—that was back when Mailer and Jean Shepherd and Shel Silverstein. . . .

Conversations: What year was this?

Fox: This is '61. And we'd sit around the White Horse drinking, and he had a hangover. He said, "Can you do an article for me for

William Price Fox

the *Voice*?" And I said, "Sure." He said, "I can't do my article for tomorrow." I said, "Hell, I'll do it for you." He said, "Try it and see what happens." So I did a thing called "Moncks Corner," or it may have been "Tourist." I'm not sure which; it was one or the other. It later appeared in *Southern Fried*. Then he ran it, and it ran on the first page, which was incredible.

Conversations: That was your first appearance, then?

Fox: Yeah, it was in the *Voice*. This was back in '61 when the *Voice* was quite small; there were only ten or twenty pages of it, you know. No one took it seriously. But it was read pretty well by the editors in New York and, you know, in the newspapers and the magazines and all. And so they ran two pieces in the *Voice*, "Moncks Corner" and "Tourist"—I'm not sure in which order— and then I got a call from Knox Burger. Knox Burger was the editor then of Gold Medal, a division of Fawcett. Knox is the one that discovered Kurt Vonnegut and John D. McDonald, and discovered me, I guess. He asked me if I could do more of those stories and I said yeah.

So I was then in the middle of a bad marriage and was going to the New School for Research in the Village and studying under Caroline Gordon. She is a very good teacher. She asked us about this time to write a short story for the class. It was a short story class, not in its writing but its reading. We were reading Joyce and Hemingway and Fitzgerald and everybody, and O'Hara. And she said she would be glad to read a couple of short stories. So I did a story called "The Pit Fight." It's an old story my daddy used to tell me a lot. It happened up in Camden. It's about a dog and a wildcat, and I did that. I think a lot of the motivation there was I always read stories. . . .I'll tell you exactly what did it. I read a lot of short stories, and I've always noticed that the authors would get to a confrontation scene where there is any action or physical fighting going on, and they would veer away from it, or they would handle it in such a way where you knew they were faking. Hemingway occasionally could bring it off, I thought, but I read a book by Humphrey Cobb called—oh, God, it was a Kirk Douglas movie about. . . .

Conversations: Paths of Glory.

Fox: *Paths of Glory*, exactly that. In there he is describing the protagonist meeting a German soldier. He was on his knees, and the line was: "I dealt him a knock-out blow." I said, "If this book is this good and he writes this badly about something like that, something is wrong with most writing." I'm very competitive anyway, and I knew I could handle stuff that had action in it. I had never seen enough of it in fiction or non-fiction. Liebling was very good at it; he did it comically, but he did it. He got to it and he did it and then he would finish off. So I did this story, "The Pit Fight," and then I forgot about it. Then about a month later Caroline Gordon just announced in class that there was a writer, and everybody looked around to see who the hell that was, you know, and she launched into reading this thing out loud. She's got a beautiful voice which does cadences nicely, and she read it very well and then got me aside and said, "You ought to think about doing this stuff seriously and getting out of sales and that sort of stuff." I said, "No, I wouldn't get out of sales because I'm making a lot of money." I didn't want to leave it. So she kept encouraging me—got me an agent, Annie Laurie Williams, whom I later changed to Max Wilkinson. That's about where it started. Then I think what happened was that I got the offer from Knox, and then Knox began sending stuff around to the magazines. And the magazines began calling. The *Post* called and *Harper's* and *Sports Illustrated*. So I got into them very quickly. In '62 I was writing for all those magazines, all at once.

Conversations: In one year?

Fox: It was less than a year. It was incredible.

Conversations: You never were an apprentice. You woke up one morning and you were a pro.

Fox: Yes, that's about it. I wouldn't quit my job in sales, though, because I knew this wasn't going to last. They said, "Will you do a book?" And I said, "Yeah. 'Southern Fried' might be a good title." They loved that title. I hate the title now—well, I guess I like it. But I figured this is the only book I'll ever write because this is a terrible mistake; this isn't going to last because I really wasn't a writer.

William Price Fox

Conversations: How old were you at this time?

Fox: About thirty-four, I guess. So I said, "Well, this will last one shot, so I'll just do all kinds of stuff. I'll just do virtuoso stuff. I'll do 'Pit Fight,' and I'll do people talking, and I'll do a lot of different things." So, in the book there are a lot of different tacks. There's a lot of black stuff in it; there's a lot of monologue; there's a lot of repetition; there's a lot of stuff just depending on cadence and rhythms. "I'll just show my ass," I said. "This will be a one-book deal and I might as well do everything that I can now." So I just did it all at once. I did the whole book in about four months, the whole thing. Then it came out. This is really weird. See, it had this cover by Jack Davis, and it was the typical Southern kind, you know, gal with her tits hanging out, and a dog with his rib-cage hanging out, and. . . .

Conversations: It looked like God's Little Acre.

Fox: It looked just like *God's Little Acre*. As a matter of fact, Davis was a *Mad* comics illustrator. I didn't like the cover but, you know, that's the kind of thing they wanted, and I figured, you know, they knew what they were doing. I didn't know anything; I signed the damn book Bill Fox even. And they said that wouldn't do; so we messed around and used my full name. But I figured that would be the end of it. They thought so too, because it was a highly regional book. Knox tried to sell it to the hard covers. No one would touch it. This was '62 when the country was very, very touchy about everything then. We were very distinct regions then. We still are, which is good. And he couldn't sell it to the hard covers. They said that it was too regional and wouldn't sell. Then it came out for forty cents, and all of a sudden within a month it got a big review in *The Times* and the *Tribune*. The *Tribune* was John Hutchens. He gave it a big, wild thing. It was one of the first soft-cover books ever reviewed that way. Meanwhile, Gold Medal had shipped all the damn books down South because they thought it wouldn't sell a nickel's worth in New York. The bookstores were jammed for a forty-cent book. Usually everybody wants to get good bargains. They had to ship the books back up North. They printed it several times, and then it went on from there.

Conversations: Your next book?

Fox: The next book. Let me see what happened. I got real good reviews. A lot of offers to do a lot of things, but I still wouldn't quit sales, because I figured it wouldn't last. I also kind of resented being called a Southern writer. I figured I could do anything, you know. I said, "I can do anything now." So I then did a book called *Doctor Golf,* which vanished on the press almost; it just didn't do a thing. As a matter of fact *The New York Times* reviewed it—one line in the books that were published for the day. It said, *"Doctor Gold"*—g-o-l-d—"Humorous articles about gold." Incredible. That book got super reviews all over the world. It didn't sell because it's out of print, but there are three or four fan clubs around that still read that thing. And they have dinners about it. People send me letters. It's a very inside book on golf. It's very hard to explain. Updike gave it a half a page last year in *The New Yorker.* He was reviewing a book on golf and he said the big book on the metaphysics of golf is *Doctor Golf.* Actually it wasn't metaphysical at all, just a very inside—well, I think, very funny book. Well, anyhow that came out and did terribly, but got good reviews. I also knew I could do anything I wanted. I could do New York or any scene I wanted. About that time I got a chance to go to Hollywood, and I decided with that money I could quit my sales job. So I quit my sales job, went to L.A. and lived there five years.

Conversations: What studios did you work for?

Fox: I started off with Filmways, worked under Paul Henning who owns several TV series. Then I worked for this Norman Lear, terrible guy. Norman Lear at Paramount. Then Columbia. And I worked a good deal at MGM. I did a thing called *Moonshine Light, Moonshine Bright.* And that was bought by MGM. I was asked to do the screenplay and I did the screenplay, and then they went broke, and it's still on the shelf. We're trying to buy it back now for somebody else, but they won't turn it loose. They have a curious thing out there. If a book has been out there for several years they keep adding more money to it, because it sits on the executive's desk and accrues more value than they put in up front. So now it's worth a lot of money as far as they're concerned. We can't get it back. It's a terrible damn thing.

William Price Fox

Conversations: Who's we?

Fox: PBS wanted it and I had a lot of offers from L.A. from other studios who wanted that. But now, it's too expensive to pick up.

Conversations: During the five years you were out there you worked for three different studios?

Fox: Four. MGM and a lot for Fox, an awful lot for Fox.

Conversations: That makes five. How many of the scripts you worked on were actually produced?

Fox: Maybe three, and those were all abysmal. The only movie I worked on that was produced was a real turkey. Called *Cold Turkey*, as a matter of fact. And two pilots: I did one for Paramount for CBS; one for Fox for NBC.

Conversations: Which were not produced?

Fox: They were produced for one-shot deals; they weren't picked up as a series. Most Southern stuff like that gets real crappy. What they do is—they still do it, but back then this was '66, then again in '71—they have a very hokey approach to the South. They'll say, "All right, this scene is going to be Southern so let's all have fun." So everybody starts running around bowlegged and slapping their legs and acting ridiculous. An awful lot like Li'l Abner. So my stuff really suffers on the screen. You wouldn't recognize it. And I minded that, but I liked the money.

Conversations: What was the money like?

Fox: Oh, God, I was making $3000 or $4000 a week there for a while.

Conversations: But it wasn't steady?

Fox: No, it was steady for a couple of months, then get nothing. Then I did *TV Guide* articles. I did about six of those profiles. I worked for the *Post* and *Harper's*, all the magazines. I was doing another book. I keep a lot of things going at once. I'm always fearful that something is going to stop, and it usually does. So I

52

get about six things going at once and assume half of them are going to drop out.

Conversations: And from Hollywood you went to Iowa?

Fox: No, I went to Europe for about four months for the *Post* and *Holiday*.

Conversations: You did travel articles?

Fox: Yes.

Conversations: How did you end up teaching creative writing at the University of Iowa?

Fox: Oh, Kurt Vonnegut and I are friends. I met him way back in New York when he was working for Knox and making no money; before he went to Iowa even. Knox was Kurt's and mine and John D. McDonald's editor. As a matter of fact, Sarah, my wife, was an editor at Fawcett. She was one of the editors for John D. McDonald's stuff. Travis McGee, McDonald's hero, got his first name from Sarah's mother's name. Kurt had gone out there—I think he needed the money, or he needed some time, and he went out there. He was in the advertising business and was doing science-fiction stuff and not making any money for that. He went out there to do a book. I think he did *Slaughterhouse-Five* out there. He had done *Cat's Cradle* and *Mother Night* and *Player Piano*. I think none of them made any money at all until later when the Seymour Lawrence deal came through and put him in hard cover. He went out there and taught for two or three years.

When he left he called me and asked me if I wanted a job out there. I couldn't decide when I came back from Europe whether to go to L.A. or come back down South or stay in New York. I didn't know what to do. It just happened that George Starbuck called and said, "I'm holding a spot open for you. You want to come out and try it?" So I went out and tried it, and I really liked it. Liked it very much. Nice place to work in.

Conversations: How long were you there?

Fox: I was there about seven years. What I did was combine fiction and screenwriting, and also did a lot of commuting to L.A.

William Price Fox

from there. I did two things out in L.A. I'd teach a couple of days and be on a plane or train—I took a train a lot—go out there and work, then come back. I did a lot of articles from Iowa.

Conversations: What were the rewards of the teaching for you—certainly not the money? You're still in it, obviously it means something to you.

Fox: Yeah, I'm still in it. I don't know, I think it means something because, you know, you can. . . .I've had a lot of success with students that had some talent, an awful lot. I mean like, oh, about twenty or twenty-five books, and several screenplays. I'm able to recognize talent most of the time. When they're too abstract I can't follow it.

Conversations: Students you taught have published more than twenty-five books?

Fox: Oh, yeah, at least.

Conversations: Isn't that unusual?

Fox: No, not really.

Conversations: Don't most kids who take creative writing courses vanish without a trace?

Fox: Yeah, but not at Iowa. Iowa is different because you get a very selective crowd out there. I had four in one class that published. And one of them was Tom McHale. And John Casey. No, Casey was not my student; he was Vance Bourjaily's, but he dropped in a lot. And McMillen. And this real good black writer named James Alan McPherson up at *Atlantic* now. He's from Savannah down here. That was my best student of all of them, I think. James Alan McPherson—very, very good writer. But I've gotten so I can recognize what I think is good and encourage it and tell them where the strengths are.

Conversations: Do you feel that it robs you of time or energy for your own work?

Fox: Oh, yes. No way not to, because you find yourself working so hard on it that it replaces something that you should be putting on your own work.

54

Conversations: Why do you do it?

Fox: It's the money, I guess, but it's also the security of your knowing you always have a paycheck coming in. That's probably it, I guess. And you always feel that the next book is going to be a disaster. You know you're not going to get anything out of it. And I've been commercial—I mean, not commercial in the sense of doing crap. I was offered a lot of money to do a book on Jackie Gleason. I get a lot of crap offers like that—biographies of morons from L.A.—I won't touch any of that stuff. And I won't do movies for people I dislike, you know, or cheap movies. I think teaching beats doing that. It's a nice crowd to be around, I mean, academicians in general. I kind of like it. I went to a speech the other day on Gullah which was very good. Yes, a university is a nice place. It takes care of all its crazies very nicely and its drunks. It's kind of a— a protective kind of thing—and it's one of the few places that can be that way.

Conversations: Would it be unfair to suggest that perhaps your feeling of comfort in academic circles now is a way of making up for the fact that your own education was long delayed?

Fox: Yeah.

Conversations: Well, would this be a form of compensation?

Fox: What meaning—

Conversations: Well, you feel you'd missed something—

Fox: By not being educated?

Conversations: By not having a normal collegiate experience.

Fox: Not really, because I wouldn't have wanted to go and take a master's and a Ph.D. I think that's—not a waste of time—but a waste of my time. Those years I spent bell-hopping, a lot of hustling down in Miami, and a lot of real good sales work in New York—I've met a wild damn set of people. Had I gone on and taken a master's and a Ph.D., I'd have been four more years in school. I might have been just dried up by that damn time.

Conversations: You came back to college when you were how old?

55

William Price Fox

Fox: I came back to high school in the tenth grade when I was twenty. That's even better. What I was doing up there was, I was playing ball for Columbia High. I wasn't big enough. I was trying to put some weight on. And my family are all bootleggers. When I came to Wardlaw, it's a junior high over here on Elmwood, they assumed I was going to be a bootlegger. They decided to give me manual training in woodwork, metal work, sheet-metal work, and all that sort of thing. All they wanted was to keep me out of jail and develop my skill with my hands. And, you know, that's fair enough. And back then—this was in the forties—they never tested anybody adequately. I finished Wardlaw and went on to high school, Columbia High over here on Washington Street. Same thing there; I was put right down in the damn basement making more pokers and whisk-broom holders, bread-boards....

Conversations: So you quit?

Fox: Well, I had a job at Western Union. I was a messenger boy; I was singing telegrams. This was during the war. They had about fifteen messenger boys, but I was the only one who knew the black section of Columbia. I know every damn alley which is a lot—down by the river, all those streets. I know a lot of people down there, because I grew up down there. And I was the one who delivered death telegrams in the middle of the night, that sort of stuff. I was a premium messenger boy. And I'd also sing "Happy Birthday," which a lot of them were reluctant to do. I'd do anything just to get the hell out of Bottom and not go to jail. I was trying to get some money ahead. Get some, you know, class or something.

Conversations: How old were you when you dropped out of high school?

Fox: About sixteen I quit. When I was seventeen I told the Air Force I was eighteen and I had been two years in college. They tested me and I tested very high which surprised me. I got in and I became a lieutenant in a year. You know, flying bombardier and navigator; I did some co-pilot work. And I was green as hell, and crazy. I would volunteer for guinea-pig missions; I'd do stuff that no one would do. They'd put me in a room and take all the oxygen out and watch my reactions—wild stuff only a kid would

56

do. In a way, I think a lot of us were allowed in back then because we were in such good shape that they could really work us over without our knowing any better. It was curious about that oxygen thing. I was put in this room and they reduced the oxygen slowly and watched my reaction. And I kept writing my name. That's one of the things, or to tie your shoes. The name is a very revealing thing. I wrote William Price Fox and my serial number. Then as the oxygen got less and less, I wrote William Fox; and then Bill Fox; and then, before I went under, I wrote Billy in the same handwriting I used as a kid. In other words the handwriting changed—just right back to the beginning.

Conversations: When you got out of the Air Force?

Fox: I went back to high school.

Conversations: You went back to high school again at twenty?

Fox: Twenty. I stayed there two or three months, and they gave me another test and let me come to the University of South Carolina on a probational basis. I came down here and they gave me some tests. What I got on the tests were very high in aptitude and very little interest in anything. Just no interest.

Conversations: A born writer.

Fox: Probably. They let me take what I wanted to take, so I took a lot of stuff. I took engineering first. I had taken subjects in chemistry and a lot of math. But then I had no money. So I had to go back to work in my officer's uniform, back at the goddamn grill I had left to go in the service. I was working out at Doug Broome's and Jack Sox's—that's where that *Southern Fried* sequence came from. In other words, ex-lieutenant working for ex-sergeant, right, and I'm going to college and I'm reading Jean Paul Sartre and all this crap. Working on the grill eight, ten, twelve hours a night and then going to school and then going to labs; I just couldn't do it. I tried to play some golf, too. So, of course, school suffered. I did very badly in engineering and I began taking courses that were easy, like anthropology, which is a snap, you know. Then I got into history which I really liked. I didn't like English because English is too hard. I liked history very much because there are a lot of stories in that, especially medieval history, a lot of that. I got ten courses in medieval history. And I took courses in early Christian heresies and wild damn things. I drifted more toward the professors I liked rather than the courses they taught. You know what I'm talking about? That may be the way once you're educated, I don't know. So I kept open, trying different things. I didn't know what I was going to major in until the last year, and then I got a teacher named Lafferty—died a couple of years ago—taught philosophy. And I'll give you an idea of how strange it all was and how ill-equipped I was for anything, a lot of things. I almost had a degree in philosophy, which I've totally forgotten all of, but he said, "You need a course in logic to get your major." He said, "There's no way for you to pass logic." He said, "There is no way for me to teach you logic and stay sane. So what I am going to do is, I'm going to give you a B if you'll just not show up. I cannot stand the idea of your being in this class in logic." He said, "Also it's going to spoil that beautiful naivete of yours." That's the kind of advice I was getting from taught people and, you know, I'm sure it turned out right. Had I been a real logical person I'd have planned myself better and probably done very little.

Conversations: So, you got your BA in four years?

Fox: Yeah, I got a major in history and a lot of philosophy. And then I was able to take a lot of psychology courses which are close to philosophy and just fake those damn people. You know, you just give 'em the same stuff. I didn't take college very seriously, of course, except for history. I liked that very much. But I had no languages, so I couldn't go on with that very much. I had no ability to learn Spanish or French. I couldn't do any of that. I just absolutely could not do it. So that was the end of the Carolina story.

Conversations: Why did you leave Iowa to come and teach at the University of South Carolina last year?

Fox: I'd been offered the job for several years and I kept putting it off. I really liked Iowa, but I found I was getting closed in by all those writers being around me all the time. Always talking writing. Every time you pass by a rhododendron bush somebody jumps out with another manuscript; I got really tired of seeing all

that. And also it is a small town. Listen, I'm from here. All my folks
are from here. You know, I began to miss this weather, great
weather for golf. Iowa is grim for golf. Iowa is a real academic
town; everybody is from some place else. No one is from Iowa
City, except maybe the meat packers and soybean growers out
there. I just got tired of it, tired of the Amish people. I don't know
them, but I get tired of that Midwestern. . . I get tired of
Midwestern humor, that's fair to say. I like it down here. This is a
funny damn place right here; it's funny down here, really funny.
And I like the blacks. I've always liked the blacks, and there
weren't many out there at all. I went to a black church yesterday.
And well, I just missed Columbia very much and every time I
come back here I feel good to get back.

*Conversations: Does coming to Columbia have an effect on your
work? Are you writing more; are you writing better; are you
writing differently?*

Fox: I don't know. I'm writing less; I know that. I'm doing so
many damn things: I'm riding a damn elephant in a parade and
I'm making all these talks, you know. I hate doing talks, but
people keep after me, and I'm too big of a sap to say no. I keep
trying to get in touch with different things. I just finished the first
act of a play. They wanted me to do a play for the Bicentennial
Year, which was due last year, but they're going to do it this year.
The Town Theatre play is based on *Southern Fried*. This
collaborator, Franklin Ashley, and I work together. He's pretty
good at music, and he's pretty good at playwriting, too. And we
worked on trying to make those stories—put them into a play
form but we couldn't do it. So we finally set it in one. . . .There is a
story in there called "Razor Fight at the St. Louis Cafe." We
gradually found ourselves using the St. Louis Cafe as a setting for
the play which is a black night club. Over a period of a couple of
weeks we realized there's no room in there for whites. It's an all-
black thing.

We kept going and discovered a lot of funny, damn
interesting things you can't do with whites but you can do with
blacks. I'll just give you an example. You see a black has a lot of
style, you know, in their comedy. And they can do a lot with
shrugs and the way they walk and the way they say, "Uh, uh," in a

William Price Fox

way a white can't. A white can but it's imitating black. You know, they can do neat parts and they can do so much neat stuff that I've never seen in a theatre. You take a show like *Guys and Dolls* or *Hello, Dolly!* and then give it an all-black cast, but it's basically a white part and the blacks can do it—and they can do it usually better than the whites. Pearl Bailey is awfully good in *Dolly*. But, I've never seen a black comedy written for blacks, except maybe, oh, Amos 'n Andy stuff, where you're actually writing within their language, you know. *Porgy and Bess*, but very few comedies though, when you think about it. Especially lately. Usually now a lot of black plays are too polemical about "Too long have our black brothers. . . ." You know, the very heavy stuff, the anti-white thing.

There ought to be something that's entertaining. I've never seen anything really good. *Purlie* was an idiotic play, I thought. I saw it on Broadway. They made fun of the whites in a stupid way. It's like black comedies; it should be done with some taste. You can do so much with just the shortest kind of set lines with rhythms. Rhythm goes great with black stuff. We got a scene where two hookers are waiting for a program. . . we got a guy and a black hairdresser sitting around and one of the girls is reading *Ebony* magazine. She says, "Jim Brown got married." The other one says, "To who?" And she says, "Some nobody." And the other one says, "Well, she's somebody now." And then the other little fellow says, "Jim Brown, does he sing or play ball?" See, that kind of stich a black can do, you know, and when a white does it, it's disparaging, right? But once you get into that night club scene with its characters, when you get them mellowed out where you like them and they like each other and they're able to relax, you can do that stuff, and you can do "Um, hum" and "Uh, huh" and walk off and come back and back. All the stuff, you know, that you never see on the stage. You can write that but it will never quite. . . .You'll never get those cadences. I use a lot of rhythm and people miss 'em, you know, unless you read real hard.

Conversations: What's the play called?

Fox: Well, it's called "Southern Fried" now. We might change it to "The Club 555." We got a guy playing poker, and he's real

60

nervous. He can't play for big stakes. These gals are looking at him, and he's real nervous and shaking. And one says, "Look at his eyes. Look at his teeth. Look at his hands." And the other one says, "Look at his feet. And look at that fool Monroe trying to count to five." Well, it might be a disaster, but it might be a wild—it's going to be a wild goddamn thing. It really is. I think it's maybe something quite new.

Conversations: Is this the first play you have ever done?

Fox. Yes.

Conversations: And the first musical?

Fox: Yeah, oh, yeah.

Conversations: Are you doing lyrics or just the book?

Fox: Book. Franklin Ashley and I are doing the book together; and then Franklin's doing the music. When I was in Nashville two weeks ago I was doing a piece for *American Heritage* on the Grand Ole Opry. I was up there with—this is a funny story—I was in Johnny Hartford's—the producer's—office. He kept a picture on the wall of Shel Silverstein, the cartoonist. I said, "You know Shel?" We got to talking. Shel's in Nashville, been living there eight years. We were good friends in New York, so I called him up and he came over and we spent three or four days together. Turns out he's written a hundred damn songs. He wrote "A Boy Named Sue" and he wrote a lot for Waylon Jennings, and a lot for Doctor Hook, and a lot for Bobby Bare—all Bobby Bare's stuff recently. I told him about the play, and it's incredible because about ten years ago Jean Shepherd called me up. He wanted to do *Southern Fried* as a musical on Broadway and he wanted Shel Silverstein to do the music. And we met in the Limelight for about a month, every night. Shepherd is one of those people that never stops talking. And I wanted to get something done. Jean would say, "What we're going to do is. . . ." And I'd say, "Let's do it." Finally I got worn out. I had my sales job, man, I couldn't afford to talk that much. So we broke up. There wasn't any antagonism; it was just that nothing ever happened. But we had a lot of great ideas that never worked.

So all of a sudden here's Shel and I in Nashville two weeks ago. Shel said, "Oh, I've got a hundred songs," you know, and he

William Price Fox

sat down and he played them. He plays guitar pretty well. And he taped, oh, about twenty songs. A lot of them are black that he's never been able to use and that he can rewrite and everything. So what he's going to do is give us. . . .Well, we're going to give him a part of the action. But he'll do the music.

Conversations: For "Southern Fried"?

Fox: Music, yeah. He's got some great lyrics.

Conversations: This Columbia production is a tryout?

Fox: Oh, yeah.

Conversations: Do you expect to take it up to New York?

Fox: Yeah. I think I'd like to. See, I've never heard anything quite like that before. We backed into it. We didn't have any idea what we were going to do. So that's the way I did that, yeah. But I like the idea of that black stuff, because, man, you can do so much rhythm. You'll notice that we dropped a couple of pieces from *Southern Fried* into it. This is really curious. I saw Philip Roth's *Goodbye, Columbus* on Long Island about three or four years ago, the play production. Three short stories, and they were terrible—just awful damn production. What they do is they'll step forward and somebody will narrate it, and then they'll move around. But it's a talking kind of thing. It flattens out and gets very, very dull. I've never seen anything on the stage adapted from a short story that worked. It's got to be written for the stage. So we tried to do these damn short stories from *Southern Fried*. The same thing happened in L.A. They kept trying to use the short story as *the* short story. You can not do it. You have got to do something else with it. You have really got to change that thing around.

So I very quickly saw that Franklin wanted to hold on and everybody up at the Town Theatre wanted me to do this, this, this. They said you've got to have this, and got to have this, and you've got to have all this crap. And all of a sudden I said, "Well, all we have to do is. . . .We're just going to have to use none of it. Just start a whole new fresh thing. Just do the night club and let it take off with new characters and go on." So we finally wound up with taking a character from "Fast Nerves," a gambler, that's all;

62

and we're using a sequence from "The Pit Fight" and one argument. That's all we're using from *Southern Fried*. So what it's been is a gradual taking away of the *Southern Fried* material and the new material. But the resistance has been incredible even within yourself. You want to hold on to this and hold on to this and all of a sudden you realize that by holding on to something.... It's like writing a novel. If you hold on to something and if it makes you ruin the whole thing around it, you've got to get rid of it.

Conversations: Are you temporarily not a novelist?

Fox: No, I've got one about, hell, about three-quarters finished. I finished the damn thing, but I didn't like it. I could have published the damn thing, but I decided not to, that something was wrong with it. The point of view was wrong. It just didn't have the thrill that I like. I mean it didn't have the thrill or the energy that I like. So I put it aside and now I'm back into it again.

It's about the circus. I did some time with them down in Florida. I followed them around for a month or so. I'd keep dropping in a lot on these medicine shows that are still down there—the old ones—they're still down there in Florida. I met a lot of that medicine crowd and I got very involved with those people. I had some chances to do a non-fiction book on them, but I didn't want to do it. I kept saying no. But I finally ended up doing a novel about them. The material is so thick that I couldn't get enough fiction into it. Do you know what I'm talking about? I got too much material and I couldn't handle it; and it got too heavy and fell apart. But now I'm backing up, and I'll use some of it. I've got a whole different attack on it now. What the theme of it is, is back about twenty years ago, maybe more than that, they kept trying this hustle every now and then to try and combine circus with religion. You know, to avoid the income and entertainment taxes. There's no reason why not. I mean, you know, Billy Graham does it all the time. It got too heavy. The point of view wasn't right, which was from inside the circus crowd, and I didn't know enough about it to handle it. So now I've backed up and had an outsider, much like myself, in sales coming into it for another reason. And that puts it into a different set of gears.

William Price Fox

Conversations: Do you throw away much of the stuff that you write?

Fox: Yeah. See, I don't plan stuff and that's one of my real problems. I don't plan anything. I do plan basically, but not really. I try to keep my options completely open, and that's a good thing and a terrible thing, and you can just waste your life doing it. But *Ruby Red*, now, was—that book was going to be about my uncle, Martin Luther Fox. He's called Spider in the book. I was going to write a book about him. He's an incredible character. I wrote at least 300 pages about him, then I introduced Ruby. Then about a 100 pages later I realized that she was better than he was. So I got rid of all his stuff and went with her.

Conversations: But you're going to try to salvage his stuff?

Fox: No, well, yeah. I will eventually, I guess. But I can't say I hate throwing it away. I just don't keep the stuff the way I should.

Conversations: Would you describe yourself as a bleeder?

Fox: No. No. Stuff comes very fast from me, and I get very high energy.

Conversations: Do you write on schedule?

Fox: No.

Conversations: Same time every day?

Fox: No, wish I did. I don't. I write whenever I can. But I can sit down anytime and write though. It's not as if I need—

Conversations: Do you write every day, or try to write every day?

Fox: Yeah, oh yeah. But I can write. . . .I used to write in the subways in New York—even the subways—in my lap. I'd get that ferry and go back and forth—you know that ten-cent ride to Staten Island, and go back and forth on that. I don't mind noise; I work against the wall. I don't like to work out in the open. I have no trouble cranking up, ever. But I try to keep myself open and not plot it, because I find my best characters come out of people that just kind of walk on, you know. And then I let them stay there a while and see how it feels. This is the kind of thing most people would plan in books, I guess. I guess that's why they write more books than I do.

Conversations: Do you have a career plan? Do you know what projects you still want to do?

Fox: I'm more interested in novels than anything else. And I want to see how the stage play goes. I think it's maybe something really nice—I may be mistaken though, I don't know. If it succeeds I wouldn't want to do a lot of plays. I want to do a couple of real big, big novels. I haven't touched any of my background at all yet. All my stuff that I've written about has been highly fictionalized and. . . .

Conversations: When you say background you mean personal or your family's connections with bootlegging?

Fox: Personal, and the family, in a way. I've always kind of been ashamed of that and now I'm not. I've never written about my dad or mother. My dad was an incredible character. Back in World War II he left us all and went into the service. He died last year. I've never touched on any of that in any of my war stuff, or I've never done myself at all. I'm just beginning to see what a weird bird I've been. What I'm saying is that I've got a lot of material that I haven't touched, because what I'll do is I'll get something started, and then I'll fictionalize everything so quickly that I wind up using very little of what's there. So, there's a ton of stuff I haven't even scratched. I mean that Miami Beach stuff. I was down there a year bell-hopping, and I only wrote one little short story about that. I was in Hollywood for five years, and I wrote nothing about that. So I'm very lucky having come to writing late. That's part of it, I guess. Another lucky thing is not taking advanced courses, you know, and reading too much and getting too smart. Another thing, I haven't been scared by writers. I think if you take too many courses and read a lot of Conrad, a lot of Faulkner, and a lot of Fitzgerald, you realize just how great they are and how puny you are, you know. I didn't have enough time. I just said, "Hell, I can do this."

Conversations: Have you been influenced by any writers?

William Price Fox

Fox: Not a soul. I never read anybody. There are passages of Fitzgerald I love. I mean the last three pages I think are great, you know, the meeting with Daisy—I love all that.

Conversations: In Gatsby?

Fox: *Gatsby,* yeah. His other stuff seems, I don't know, indulgent. There's no humor in it at all; it's not very funny, ever. I don't think Hemingway's very funny.

Conversations: A lady that heard you read recently said that your description of the Chitlin' Strut reminded her of the party scene from Gatsby. *But you see no direct influence at all?*

Fox: No, I'll tell you who I do like as much as anybody: I like Gogol's *Dead Souls* very much. It's one of my favorite books. My favorite book of all books—I've decided in the last few years what that is—is this *One Hundred Years of Solitude.* I've read it three times now. I don't know what in the hell he's doing, but he's just great. As a matter of fact, if I had read that book ten years ago or twenty years ago, I would never have written a line. That to me is so great. Just everything. He's funny; he's wild; he's got texture; he's sane; he controls it. He just does everything ten ways. But most writers, I don't know, they run out of material. I love McCullers; I love her *Member of the Wedding.* That's one of my favorite books. But then her other stuff I get very tired of because it's too talky. She tries to tell us too much and I'd rather be shown it through characters and action. I like O'Connor very much—Flannery O'Connor. I like Faulkner somewhat; I don't like him as much as Tennessee Williams. And I like Hemingway. I think I like Fitzgerald as much as I do anybody. Then Marquez, he's probably my favorite now. I think he and Gogol. . . .I don't like Twain at all. I doubt that I'll ever read him again. I think I read *Tom Sawyer* one time. That's kind of a dumb book, I guess. I like some stuff on the Mississippi; I like some of that.

Conversations: Do you think of yourself as specifically or mainly a Southern writer? Have you come back to return to your roots?

Fox: No.

William Price Fox

Conversations: Do you feel that it was no accident that your first book was Southern Fried *and that here you are, fifteen years later, back in Columbia?*

Fox: Yeah, probably. But I don't think it's looking for material because I've always never looked for material. I've always never gone out and looked for it, because, you know, I've always lived pretty precariously and lived with abandon. In other words, I'd never go out and look for material and write notes down. I heard a line the other night at the Elvis Presley thing. I can hear lines and I'll never forget them when they're good enough. You very seldom hear a good line. You'll get a lot of them down here; you'll never get any of them in that damn Iowa—I mean spontaneous lines. The other night at Presley this woman said, "Oh, I wish I could sew for him." Isn't that great? I mean, you can't write. . . .No one can write that well, right? I mean she expressed the whole thing there like that. I mean that's a great example of what some sixty-year-old fan would say.

Conversations: You were really uncomfortable out of the South?

Fox: Yeah, in a way, I was. You know, I was all right as long as I was on, talking. But then I got to listen and to react to it, and then talk. I didn't like that. I got a lot quieter than I used to be. I used to do a lot of talking. I was on Johnny Carson a couple of times. I was on one night for a half an hour. And this is very revealing and stupid, but that's the way it was. I was on first one night; usually they put writers on last. He wanted me to come on in a bell-hop's uniform. I said, "Hell no, I'm not coming on with any bell-hop's uniform on. I'm coming on as a writer." Big deal. I got on there, and it was just ridiculous, because we mentioned being a writer up front about twenty seconds. The agent was there and said to be sure and mention the book and all that stuff. We got into talking bell-hopping and talked about all of that for twenty minutes and never discussed that book at all. And later his fans were telling him to get that Southern bell-hop back on and all this kind of crap. Then, you know, I sat down and this agent stops and says, "That was a great act you did. You are a very warm human being." That's the way they talk up there, you know, everything is pronounced. I said, "That's terrific."

67

William Price Fox

They put McMahon on. He laughs at everything. One of the things about being Southern, you get up North and you can....If a situation is going a certain way you can make it go....You can get more Southern and no one can tell what in the hell you are doing, you know. You can say something that's absurd and they will think, "Well, that's a big Southern thing that only red-necks understand." I began putting McMahon on, because he's such a jerk he'll laugh at everything. He'll laugh at whatever time he thought it would be funny. And I don't like to be laughed at; I liked to be listened to. I don't do one-liners, right? I mean I don't do one-liners! Anyhow, he kept laughing. The s.o.b. will laugh at anything. I asked him why he was laughing, or why did he find that funny? Then the light went off and he jumped up to do a commercial. And I was talking to Carson about Carson getting McMahon. I said, "This guy laughs too much over here. I think if you could roll a can of dog food across there, he'd just fall down and we'd have something to laugh about." I've never seen a guy laugh so much in my life. When the show was over they asked me, "Can you do this act? You know, as a night club thing." I said, "What act?" See, they thought everything was rehearsed. Anyhow, what I am saying is I did that damn talking stuff and I got so involved with bell-hopping that I never mentioned that I was a writer at all, so nobody even knew it.

Conversations: Let's get back to your classroom work. How do you teach creative writing? What is your method in the class? Do you make the kids read their stuff aloud? Do you make them read good stuff? How can you teach a kid to write?

Fox: Well, I do what I did in Iowa. I get a short story. . . .I make them write something, try to get them to write something that is close to themselves. You know, that's usually a person you've known. Then I'll Xerox it up and give everybody a copy of it. Then I'll read it, or if they're not embarrassed they'll read it, or somebody else will read it. They can remain anonymous if they want to; it doesn't really matter about that. And then I'll go over it close, you know, not so much for the story but just to see if the writing is any good. You can tell if the writing is any good in the first paragraph where you see the first connections and how the choice of words works. I also lean pretty hard on attitude—

whether it's condescending or arrogant or smartass. You can spot that very quickly, too. Usually the first page you can spot everything that's going to happen in that story. I try to get them saying, "Oh, boy, watch for it." And then what I do is try to undo a lot of their learned rhythms. They've read so much Conrad and Updike and all that, they write like that. They'll talk beautifully down here; they got great speaking voices. Did you ever notice that? Great, and then they'll get to a page they've written and it sounds like Conrad, doesn't it? They start writing like Conrad, and I try to get them out of that.

Conversations: How?

Fox: Well, I show them where their Conrad influence and memorizing ends and where they begin. Usually after about two or three pages they'll relax: they can't mimic anymore and they'll move into something that's theirs. And if you have them writing about something that is domestic—about, you know, their relations at home or something or getting into school or something tight with them—usually they will get loose from whatever it is they are mimicking—Conrad, Updike, Mailer, or Joyce Carol Oates. Eventually they'll get loose and you can see a few lines that's theirs.

Conversations: And this is how you spend most of the classroom time just going over the kids' work?

Fox: Yeah, well, their voices, if they've got a voice. I work on that, too. Usually they do. Then I encourage them to use it. And the way to encourage that, I find, is to have them write a story— meaning by story, a diary of a couple of days. You know, real short, tight sentences. Or to write a letter to a best friend. You know, a relaxed letter. In other words, to undo all those long words.

Conversations: You don't lecture at all. It's all laboratory?

Fox: Well, yes, but I'll do my talking within that. I do an awful lot of talking. Then I read. I'll show them stuff like the fellows I mentioned, and I'll show them how good that is and how bad that is. They love to see what I think is bad, because they think that a lot of writers walk on water. Take a story like James Joyce's

William Price Fox

"The Dead"; it's a classic story. Show where you think he's full of crap, you know, where a line doesn't fit.

Conversations: Where?

Fox: Oh, when he describes her shoes, or when he calls the shoe a member of the pair, or all the alliteration that's misplaced, or the repetition. The words could have been chosen a little more precisely. Once they can get so they can see that these things aren't carved in bronze, they get a little more speed up. I mean they aren't in awe of writing; most of them are petrified by writing. I don't know why that is. Most of them look at a page and it's like a J. Arthur Rank movie gong going off, and they get into this serious. . . .None of them write comedy. It's just incredible. You very seldom see a comic writer. I don't know why that is.

Conversations: Are they pompous?

Fox: No, they're not, though. You get them out of the class and there's nothing pompous about them at all. They get on that page and get pompous. You get them out in the damn night clubs and you've never heard better comic stuff. I don't know what happens to them. But anyhow, I try to get them to recognize that they've got some hope where there's some talent there if they can find their voice. If they can't find a voice then there's no way. Also try to get them to experiment with different layers of experimentation. In other words, just do a mess and not try to give it any form; just get loose and get so they can write. A good way to teach kids drawing is to give a formal drawing and put another thing on top of it, and you notice that other layer's going to kind of get muddy. Well, a teacher who doesn't know a lot will make a kid stop a drawing when they think the subject has been done. They'll take it away from him as a finished sheet rather than letting the kid stack up stuff and go through the process. In other words, I try to get him familiar with writing rather than reaching for some conclusive thing to hang up, or show off, or sell. I'll say I want a page of just rambling. Give me one long periodic sentence, you know, that will go on forever; a run-on sentence, just to see what happens, with no ending; just keep on going. You know, something to break whatever fear that's got a hold on them about writing. You try to break it if you

70

can. They're all hung up on finishing something rather than learning.

Conversations: Are you able to help the good ones get published?

Fox: Yes, quite a bit, yeah. I have a couple here so far in magazines. I've got four right now in L.A. doing movie work. They're pretty good. That *Bingo Long* movie was a student of mine back in Iowa. I set the whole thing up for him, book and everything. Hell, it was my material from Satchel Paige. I interviewed him and gave him all that tape. He did a book and then the movie. That's a pretty good movie. They're all interested in media now for some reason. That's a terrible thing. Stupid. They want to become filmmakers. That's the worst damn field in the world. And, as filmmakers they don't do any writing, they just do filmmaking. So, Jesus, once a week I have my class of English go over there and we will write scenes and shoot them with portapacks, you know, and play them back. Some of the documentary kids are pretty good. We did one documentary on car auctions, and they did a couple on the Chitlin' Strut, and one kid did a sixty-minute movie on Norwood. It's working out pretty good over all. But it's sad, because filmmaking is so hard and if they ever do get into it they've overlooked the main ingredient, the story.

Conversations: You feel that part of your job as creative writing teacher is to launch the kids?

Fox: Oh yeah. All of them want to be published in all the magazines.

Conversations: How do you do that? Do you put them in touch with agents and editors?

Fox: I'll call the agent and I'll call the publisher. The ones that are good I'll do anything I can to get published.

Conversations: Would you say that a creative writing teacher who can't help the kid get going isn't doing his job?

Fox: I would say yes; I would say he was not doing his job. It should be his place to get his students started. That's the hardest thing.

William Price Fox

Conversations: Part of the qualifications, then, for a teacher of writing is contacts?

Fox: Yeah. There's much more, but that's basic. They need so much help. I've got a couple of kids writing for the *Record* down here, you know, book reviews. And the *Sandlapper*. Just anything that will get them started. Yeah, I've usually got about ten that are doing small things around, but you have got to start small, you know. See, Iowa spoiled the hell out of me because, my God, I had a girl and one of the first stories she wrote was in *The New Yorker*. A lot of *New Yorker* stuff, a lot of *Harper's*, and a lot of *Vogue*. It's been a big adjustment down here realizing this is undergraduates and graduates. You see at Iowa I had students up there in their thirties and forties that had been publishing a lot, too. This can make a lot of difference, you know that. They'd just come back a lot of the time to get revitalized and to change their styles. It was much more professional. I think a teacher should be able to place work. Yes, very much so. That's why I keep involved with ETV and the papers down here, and I've got a good feeling with the newspaper editors and movie producers. I make damn sure that anything I've got that's good from students gets placed. That's one of the things that I do well because I know the trade pretty well. I also know the editors, I mean, like at *The New Yorker*, damn well. Jeffrey Ward at *American Heritage* was an old editor at *Audience* I worked for. As a matter of fact, I've gotten five students published in that magazine, at least five. One of them has got a book coming out this month, and another student of mine is doing a review of it for the *Columbia Record*. So it all ties together after a while. You just got to know how to do it all. And you can call a lot of favors in after a while, but that's how everything works. Right?

Conversations: Are the markets drying up?

Fox: I don't think so. I think some dry up and some don't. I was up at *American Heritage* the other day and Jeff Ward said, "We're paying $1000 to all the writers now." That's big for *American Heritage*. "But," he said, "we're desperate for writers; we've got no writers." And the irony of it is that most people just think that everything is sewed up. *The New Yorker* often is sewed up because they have a lot of staff writers, but they say the same thing: They're always looking for good writers, that there are no good writers around. Like I tell my students that the writers like Tom Wolfe and Joan Didion and Gore Vidal and Norman Mailer and the really better, better article writers cannot afford to write articles. They're too interested in writing novels, big books, and movies where the money is. When you live so, pretty high, you can't afford to do articles. You can't afford to write for *Esquire*; there's no way to write for *Esquire*. You can get three articles a year in. That's only $4000 or $5000 and, maybe, that's all you can do. So that market is always open for students. It wasn't when the *Post* was operating and they paid big money. Then it was different. Then a short story sold for. . .I made $17,000 for a long short story.

Conversations: For one long short story?

Fox: Part of a novel, but it was about thirty-five pages. We did it in two parts, but it was big money at the *Post*. Back then, boy, O'Hara wrote for it; everybody wrote for it. Now, Emerson is down here teaching, right, and the *Post* is gone. The highest-paid market now is probably *The New Yorker*. Actually, *National Geographic* is probably pretty big but they want you to spend more time in the field. But the market is always open for students, especially magazines.

Conversations: What about book publishing?

Fox: I think less so, because what you've gotten into now is the soft cover. Money now is the soft cover. Bantam will not publish anything less than a quarter of a million at a crack. They cannot afford to buy a new work. What they'd rather do is buy something like an *Exorcist*, something pre-made, and just run it out like john paper. It's a big production. The costs are up so high and the presses are so big now and so fast. . . .The big outfits like Dell, Fawcett, and Bantam are geared so big; I mean they're putting so much stuff out now that they can't do small ones. At the same time people like Anchor and Vintage can do small printings—these odd-sized books, you know. An odd-sized book will do well in a bookstore in Columbia, a university bookstore, but they'll never get on the racks because they don't fit, first of all. Did you know that? All those wire racks are built for that little Bantam-sized book. I mean there's some hard facts out there; there's some hard facts out there that you got to come up against. I think Lippincott tried a couple of years ago to do a soft cover with the hard-cover jackets, and it didn't work. I don't know what they are going to do. But they keep working stuff out. Somebody ought to design a hard cover that would sit on those racks, because the racks are what control it. But how are you going to fault them? They have got to move that damn stuff out. When I was in sales we used to try to sell packages for hosiery, and you're limited by the way the shelves are built, right? It's that simple. You know, you've got to find out where the limits are and work within them. There's nothing wrong with that. Like *TV Guide*—you work for them and the articles are 1500 words, and you have to come within twenty words. Once you set those limits up, you can have a lot of fun within those limits.

Conversations: What do they pay for 1500 words?

Fox: Oh, I think it's $1000 but, boy, they're hard words though. The shorter they are, the harder they are a lot of times.

Conversations: Do you regret the passing of the pulp magazines? They paid a penny a word, but they gave writers a place to get published.

Fox: Yeah, I guess that's all gone. TV has replaced all that. And TV scriptwriting is just awful; I'd rather write anything else, I think.

Conversations: Would you describe yourself as a regional humorist, as a regional writer?

Fox: I guess I would, but I'm not a regional humorist. I like to think that I am doing more than that. This fellow from *Time* magazine came out a couple of months ago and interviewed me for them. He wanted some journalistic one-liners to describe the South. Everybody is trying to do that. You know, "If grits ain't groceries, and odd things poetry, then Mona Lisa was a man"— that kind of stupid alliteration that means nothing. But they want one-liners to describe what is a very complicated and very fragile thing down here. You can't do that. You wouldn't believe how difficult it is to describe anything like the South. He said, "Well, how would you describe it?" And I said, "I can't describe it. No one in their right mind can tell you exactly what it is because there are too damn many things. And if I could describe it you couldn't print it in New York because it doesn't transfer." He said, "Well, give me an example of what I can't print in New York." I told him about how when a black person asks for something over a counter they will be very clear and talk almost Trinidadian. They won't talk like Sea Island Gullah—Sea Island Creole, it's called. It's a beautiful language. It's as complicated as English, with African rhythms and English usage. Anyhow this black goes out to eat. When a black man orders, he orders very carefully so he's not asked to repeat himself. They'll say, "What did you say, boy?" And he's got to say it again; then he gets in real trouble. The Southerner can be a real mean son of a bitch. I mean, that's the lowest when they do that, and they're professional at it. This little red-neck character is behind the counter and the black says, "I would like a sliced barbecue and a orange drink." The girl says, "What size orange drink?" And he's not ready for that, right? He says, "Huge." The *Time* reporter says, "You're right, I can't print that." Not because you can't say that in print; you can say it but it won't mean anything. See, some humor is like the sweet corn down here, you can't ship it.

My favorite local thing is the way you'll hear a story in L.A., and you'll come here and you'll hear the same story. Any good story they'll make it happen in Columbia; if it's too good to happen in L.A. it will happen here. They'll say, "Bill, you won't believe this." I'll say, "What's that?" And they'll say, "I saw this down on the corner of Main and Gervais. A blind man. His seeing-eye dog was pissing on his leg. I noticed he was trying to feed this dog a fig newton. So I got up close to him and I said, 'Mister, do you know that dog is pissing on your leg?' And the blind man says, 'I sure as hell do, and the minute that I find his head with this fig newton I'm going to kick his ass.'" That's one of the funniest damn stories around, but I heard it in Hollywood. But see, here this guy sees it on Main and Gervais. In Columbia they do that. They bring stuff right down here and then they'll, you know, make it a Columbia story. There's a lot of that around town, an awful lot. But the "huge" story, you cannot write that: it doesn't work on the page; it doesn't look right. You can't do glides: you can't do the way a black will glide down a sentence.

William Price Fox

The line comes down like that and you can't write that way, you know that? Unless you do it like E. E. Cummings, and that's no road for fiction. But you can't get that slide at all, so you've got to get the equivalent of that which is very hard to do.

Conversations: How do you do it? What you have been describing here are all kinds of oral patterns that you can't get on a printed page. And yet you are a printed-page man.

Fox: Well, I try to do it and I just hope that people who know my work. . . . What I detest is that speed-reading because they miss all of the stuff; and I do a lot of that ricky-ticky stuff.

Conversations: Are you saying that you need Southern readers who will be able to supply the rhythms?

Fox: Often, often you do, yeah. What you'll do is often the material will force the rhythm. There's some dumb old thing in *Southern Fried*: "The reason I traded that hog for a dog was for the same plain and simple reason I can't go running no fox with no hog." You know, there's no way not to get a rhythm out of that, right?—by the words. And often the words themselves will force a rhythm. I never thought this thing out too much. What I try to do is not really try to write for the reader, but for myself. I don't make any concessions to make things clearer; I don't make them necessarily to be fuzzy. I just try to do them right on the head, I must say. And then when I try to explain stuff, I caught hell, you know. Like I did a piece called "The City Gal and Johnny Cash," and I made up this little beginning about driving across the mountains. The cab driver says, "When the sun hits that building over there, that looks just like Athens." And I say, "Georgia?" He says, "Come off it man—Idaly." And I wrote I-d-a-l-y; and then I dropped into the damn story. I got a ton of damn letters from people saying tell Mr. Fox that Athens is really in Greece, right? Or, what in the hell do you want to embarrass the magazine for. I could have put *ha, ha,* or an asterisk. You know, I know it's been there for 1000 years and all about Hector and Priam and all. But the minute you start doing that and being clear. . . .I think that when a writer begins to become clearer to everybody he loses most of what he's got. So I try to write not for Carolinians, but for myself, really. And a lot of the stuff has got a lot of New Yorker rhythms. There's a lot of Jewish inversions and stuff and I do a lot of black stuff. Lot of people thought I was black when I first started writing.

Conversations: How would you describe your work at its best, when it's really going good? What does it achieve?

Fox: I don't know, it's partly energy and a lot of leverage.

Conversations: What do you mean by leverage?

Fox: There's a lot going on underneath it; there's a lot going on underneath it. The one thing I do well is I got to undercut stuff. I won't want to hit it on the head too hard. I'll get to it, and I'll mention it, and then I'll get off. I don't want to belabor it too long. I do that a lot. I've got a very good ear for dialogue—people talking on different levels. I'm a pretty fair storyteller. I'm not very deep on the big message, but I guess my stuff kind of oozes through. I'm saying the messages or the attitudes are coming through without me flagging them.

Conversations: What do you do better than other people? What do you do best?

Fox: I can describe things. I can pick out the detail that works, usually. See, I worked so hard in growing up, and I know how a damn kitchen operates—I've seen how it operates, so I know a lot of those small details. I was on the street a long time before I started writing. I know that a Coca-Cola stopper at the end of the light string is better than nothing. I really feel that, I mean, things shouldn't be unfinished; things should be tied off neatly. I mean there should be points. I like to give people specifics. I like to build things with a lot of energy. . . .But there's some specifics there about throwing salt on the duck boards to keep you from slipping, that's the kind of stuff that I like. I love that kind of stuff.

Conversations: Inside stuff?

Fox: Not only inside but stuff that locks the scene down to the page. Details where the reader. . . .Where I know what I'm talking about, and I want you to know damn well I know what I'm talking about. I'm not writing something about a brain surgery operation, which I'm not about to write about. I write about

William Price Fox

what I know. I write how a jail cell is. I write about stuff I really know, and I am able to get what I think is important to me to be told. Like if you're driving a truck or a bus and you slow down, just slow down, something is wrong with that sentence. If a dog crosses the road and you slow down there, it's a whole different dimension. Everything should have some kind of thing going on. Writing isn't always like that, but it gives you a texture. I like to think I can do little, small things, you know. Like in *Ruby:* she's sitting there and she's real pissed off at everything; and rather than talking about her being pissed off, that comes out in the dialogue. I don't go into her head and examine what she's thinking. I'd rather have it come out in the dialogue and in what she does. She's stirring a cup of coffee with a lipstick stain on it and, rather than raise a lot of hell about it, she turns it around and drinks it left-handed. Now that doesn't give you a hell of a lot— but it adds a little bit to it. I like little bits like that. It shows what she's going through at the moment, what she's like at the moment. Another time she'll raise hell about that thing being there, but right at that particular moment she does that with it. I don't really work on that; it just comes. But when I get it, usually it's the stuff that I don't cut. Stuff I know that's going to hold up.

Conversations: Isn't that just accurate observation?

Fox: Well, yeah, maybe that, but it is also locking up particular observations at a particular moment. I mean, observation by itself can just be observation, a report, an analysis. It's got to be locked into an actual scene that is going on at the right angle. Everything is angle; everything has got to come in at the right angle. I mean, you could have a lot of observations that would bore your ass off. Most of them do, but I like the locks, the separate locks—the ones that hold that particular scene to the page and make it different and make it work. A line like in "On Top of Old Smokey"—you know, "He'll tell you more lies than the crossties on the railroad and the stars in the skies." Now that locks it down and it works like a bitch.

Conversations: The information, the material, the observations—we keep coming back to that. Perhaps, writers don't like to think of it, but every writer is inevitably writing for a select readership of people who know enough to respond to his technique and material.

Fox: Exactly. People like, you know, people like Michener, Robbins, and Uris are writing for a big cross section of the country. And they are very successful and they are probably very good, but I can't read that stuff. It's just dribble; I think it's awful. I couldn't write it. I'd get bored not doing something brand new.

Conversations: Who's the best writer now working?

Fox: Marquez. Gabriel Garcia Marquez. I may keep on reading that *One Hundred Years of Solitude* forever.

Conversations: How about in English? If you weren't William Price Fox, who would you like to be?

Fox: Marquez. No one else. No, nobody. Marquez either. He's already done it. I'm still learning; I'm just getting into gear. I don't want to be anybody else because I like my own stuff, you know. I like stuff that is funny; I really do. I find very little funny stuff going on in the work of most writers—except Marquez. Kurt Vonnegut's funny occasionally. I can't think of anybody else. Not Malamud. I like Malamud's early stories, *The Magic Barrel*, those are good stories. I liked *The Assistant* very much. It's very heavy, but very good, and very well worked. I like Kingsley Amis's first book, *Lucky Jim*; that was good. No, I don't want to change with anybody else. You know, that's weird isn't it? I think certainly not a real big pop-writer like Michener. I think if anybody writes something with that broad an audience in mind, it's going to be pretty sorry. Unless they've got something really unique. I remember I was once asked to do a book which turned out to be called *Fail Safe*. Somebody asked me if I wanted to do that book. I said, "No." I was just getting started writing, you know, and I had enough sense. . . .Well, I was stupid—I should have done it and I'd have been very wealthy. But see, I didn't like the material—generals and all that A-bomb stuff.

Conversations: What are you going to write tomorrow morning?

Fox: We're going to do a reading of this stage play tonight. Then I'm going to start working on some more of that. Then I'm working on this *American Heritage* piece on Nashville, and I may

William Price Fox

go to the Masters for *TV Guide*. I always go to the Masters every year because I play in the writers' tournament over there. I'll cover that for *TV Guide* and then when that is over edit a *Travel and Leisure* piece. I've got a PBS documentary. I'm working with Richard Leacock on a half-hour show on the Chitlin' Strut. Then I'm going back to work on my novel. I may get back to it this weekend. I keep looking at it and liking it. I really like what I've got now; I really do. It's about a salesman in New York. I'll tell you what happened in New York. I was in sales on Park Avenue, and I couldn't think of a goddamn reason for getting out of that job and going into writing. You know Park Avenue, 300 Park Avenue, that's the old Postum Building. If you stand in front of the Pan American Building looking to the north that first building on the left is the Postum Building. It's a great old office building and I was on the sixth floor. In my office I had two windows, an air conditioner, some shelves. Looking straight out on Park Avenue across the street, I could see the Triboro Bridge and all of that stuff. Across the road they were building the Bankers Trust Building and I said, "Goddamn it, when I can't see the sky and Queens I'm going to leave." But every day it would get higher and higher. And I'll be goddamned if I didn't time my life so I quit that job as the last floor was being completed. Incredible!

Jill Krementz

*John Gardner, at the age of 44, has achieved success in two careers:
as a distinguished medieval scholar*—The Complete Works of the
Gawain Poet *(1965),* The Alliterative Morte Arthure and Other
Poems from Middle English *(1971),* The Poetry of Chaucer *(1977),
and* The Life and Times of Chaucer *(1977); and as a critically
acclaimed novelist*—The Wreckage of Agathon *(1970),* Grendel
(1971), The Sunlight Dialogues *(1972),* Nickel Mountain *(1973), and*
October Light *(1976). As a teacher and writer, Gardner has focused
his attention on the nature of man and the democratic values that
he feels are enduring. He believes that the forces at work in
Chaucer's age are the same forces shaping the modern world. Recently
retired from teaching, Gardner lives in Cambridge, New York.*

John Gardner

This interview with John Gardner was conducted in June 1977 by C. E. Frazer Clark, Jr. over late breakfast at Detroit's just-opened Renaissance Center. They were the only people present. Their table was in a concrete outpost above an artificial pool, the bottom of which was already covered by coins. The immense vaulted interior of the Portman-designed building made the people walking along the other levels seem insignificant. Gardner was offended by the dehumanizing architecture, the complete separation from the outside world, and the overwhelming sense of the concrete buttresses surrounding him. His thoughts easily turned inward.

Conversations: You've had the best of two careers: scholar and writer. Which came first?

Gardner: I guess writing. I don't think they are very different. Insofar as scholarship is really different from sensitive reading, I think it's bad scholarship. It's true, there's a certain amount of benefit to a certain kind of literary scholarship which has nothing to do with books, as you know, like watermarking things. But really what I've done in medieval studies is try to understand poems. I did an analysis of *Beowulf* which I think is absolutely right. I think it is the first analysis of *Beowulf* to account for the whole poem. I think most people have accepted it, generally, as right. But I didn't come to it in the usual scholar's way, among medievalists at least. I came to it by trying to understand the poem, simply. Very few people do that. Usually what scholars do is to take a particular approach—like they decide they are going to take an exegetical method. They read all of Augustin and people who died hundreds and hundreds of years before Chaucer and then see what they can find of Chaucer that has the best of it. Or they decide they are going to study nominalism and see what they can find in Chaucer that has nominalism, you know. And they look at the poem through a kind of jeweler's glass, specially tinted with nominalism, and specially tinted with Augustinism. The result is they get half-truths which they blow into complete distortions and falsehoods. I think what a real scholar does is the same thing a real reader does: A real reader of contemporary fiction lives in the modern world, soaks it up; reads a Bellow book and thinks about the application. And I think that in the same way a real scholar has to absolutely soak up the Middle Ages. He reads all the history he can read—not because it's his job, but because he loves to do that. He reads all the philosophy of the times and previous times, because he loves it. If you happen to find an old English poet knowledgeable in Greek literature, which you do in Cynewulf, you notice it because you know the Greek literature. In other words, I think the only real way to be a scholar is to just be a whole man. If you try to be something else, and I think modern education almost forces you to be something else, then you're going to be a bad scholar.

When I went to Iowa graduate school they still had the Ph.D. program which was English literature from the beginnings to William Faulkner, who, of course, was living at that time. Then later they began to say, "Well, we can't read all the criticism this way, so we're going to have to have a specialty in the nineteenth century." We could read all the books; we always could read all the books, from Homer, for that matter, to Faulkner. But we couldn't read the criticism. And it became more and more important that you knew what some third-rate person said about Germaine Bree, who said something about you know, some novelist. It became important that scholarship no longer be total. I think that's when everything began to go badly wrong. When I was in John McGalliard's class in Middle English—Chaucer class, I think—he asked me to do a paper on the Arabic background of a Spanish poem which has to do with *Parlement of Foules*. I said, "Professor McGalliard, I can't read Arabic." And he said, "Well, you've got three months." So I did it. I didn't know that I could do it and I did it. Kittridge regularly assigned things like that. Those old guys. But what happened is that we got into the criticism business. I think it's a terrible thing to read lots and lots of criticism. I don't think we really need to read any, but I know that's a radical kind of feeling. But if one is going to read American literature, I think one should read American literature, from the least known. . . . That's how you know what the big guys are doing. Poe was reading it all, so why not us?

Conversations: And writing criticism about it.

Gardner: Sure. If we spend all our time reading criticism, then we can't get that background.

Conversations: Is it unusual, in your view, for a medieval scholar to also write modern novels?

Gardner: There's Tolkien. I don't know—actually, it used to be. In the old days medieval scholarship was a scholarship of vicars, you know, and dilettantes—wonderful dilettantes. And, of course, they all wrote novels. All the nineteenth-century people, except for Furnivall, wrote fiction, and all of the early twentieth-century medievalists. One doesn't usually think of, for instance, C. S. Lewis as a medievalist, but he is, of course, and his main scholarly field is that. Charles Williams is a medievalist. But in the medieval field it's more the rule than the exception to be a novelist and scholar. It's kind of weird.

Conversations: Why is it do you feel, and I'm making an assumption you may not agree with, that so many scholars today don't write?

Gardner: I think it has to do with that same thing I was talking about before: the scholarship becoming—I don't know how to say it exactly—but, well, a specialty in the sense that it's a gimmick. When a man begins to approach literature, not for a full understanding of it, not for full human understanding of it, but maybe to get ahead in the profession, or maybe because he believes you can understand literature through one narrow prism, like with Frye's formula for tragedy, comedy, romance, and so on, you get a different kind of man. One kind of man is willing to cut novels into one small piece; another kind of man wants the full effect. Let me use a different example: what John Hull does, what you do, what many scholars, if you still want to use that word—humanists—do with a writer is to soak themselves in him. Like I think you probably haven't read anything but a Hawthorne book or a book about Hawthorne for a long time, because it seems to me that your whole consciousness is deep in Hawthorne. Well, John Howell, my friend at Southern Illinois, reads Hemingway and Faulkner, Hemingway and Faulkner, Hemingway and Faulkner. Lately he's been reading a little Gardner, but that's because he's my friend. But he knows everything Hemingway and Faulkner ever breathed. He knows what they wrote on the backs of postcards, and he knows exactly what Faulkner was reading when he was writing "The Bear" and so on. He's sort of become Faulkner. Bergson has a business about the intellect and the sort of total personality. John Howell and you, I think, are the kind of scholars who learn by becoming a person, by just absolutely steeping yourself in the person. The result is that you get an intuitive and brilliant and wise scholarship, as opposed to the intellectual scholar who gets certain facts. He clicks them off and he arranges them in columns according to some predetermined system of arrangement.

One of the reasons I'm not teaching medieval literature anymore is that I can't stand to read the criticism. About 90% of it is wrong and bad—bad methodologically. So I think that when people begin to be strictly academic, in the worse sense of that, of course they are not going to write books. They don't care about the things that are in books. They might as well be surgeons, particularly the kind of brilliant surgeons who cure people's brains or fix their eyes and don't give a hoot about the patient. The patient is, as far as they are concerned, a tomato—which is okay. I mean I need that in my surgeon.

Conversations: A great operation though the patient didn't survive.

Gardner: Right, right.

Conversations: Well, obviously you care about books and from what you say you're going to do more writing and less scholarship. Is that true?

Gardner: Yeah, I'm going to do a lot of scholarship—wish we had some other word, but we don't.

Conversations: Study?

Gardner: Study, yeah. That is a much better—that's a wonderful word. I'm working on a book—I've just finished a book called *Thor's Hammer: A Literary Manifesto*, which is coming from Basic Books, which is a statement about the aesthetics of fiction. And I'm now working on a fairly long-term project, a second book, which is simply a description of what all the major contemporary writers are doing. I don't want to praise or condemn, I just want to make it perfectly clear what Mailer does, what Bellow does, and so on. And I want by means of this to suggest the possibility of a whole new ranking of people—not that ranking is important. Ranking is, in fact, a very bad thing in fiction, but it's important if people are already ranked. If Richard Locke can say that the greatest American writer is Norman Mailer, then somebody has to come along and say, "Wait a minute." It's not that I want somebody else in Mailer's slot; it's that I want that slot abolished, you know, and certainly I don't want Mailer to be thought of as a more important writer than very sensitive younger writers, who can't get into reviews because Mailer's there in the way like a huge old cow.

So the book I'm doing now is—I'm taking, in fact, Richard Locke's list in *The New York Times* a week ago, and I'm going to talk about all those writers, everyone that he talked about. But I'm also going to talk about all the ones miraculously he skipped. He's talking about literature since 1955 and he doesn't even mention Jerry Salinger! It's true, Salinger didn't do very much, but we know that he's got stuff sitting in that house. I mean we know that he's been working on that novel for a long time; we know he has like a dozen stories at least; and we know that they must be wonderful. And we do know that he is one of the great artists of our time. One can't just pass him in silence, while raising a Tom Pynchon into a sort of wonderful trapeze artist gorilla or something, you know. I mean I'm for him, but—you know. So I think that's going to be a work of study that I certainly will enjoy, and it will be long and difficult.

I've been doing some of that this year. I spent one week rereading everything of Italo Calvino, and then reading his *The Castle of Crossed Destinies*, his new book. I'm only going to talk in my book about American fiction, simply because you've got to stop somewhere, but it's a joy to take a week and just steep yourself in a guy that you're familiar with, that you've read before. It's an amazing kind of thing and I read—I spent a week reading all of Tom Williams's stuff, because he brought out this terrible, terrible book, *Tsuga's Children*. It's a silly, sentimental, schlocky book, although he's written very respectable books. And I was interested in sort of getting the total picture, where this awful book could come from—I think I know. That's what I'm going to do with the whole thing now.

Conversations: Let me ask you a different question. I've heard teachers complain that the students don't read. They don't own books; they don't seem to want to read. Do you find that? And if you do, why do you think it happens?

Gardner: Well, you know, I can't really answer that. I haven't been in a normal kind of situation. At Southern Illinois University a great many of the kids we had were pretty desperate kids. They were ambitious; they were keenly intelligent; they were ignorant. I had a lot of black students. They were farm blacks and some were from South Chicago, and they very urgently wanted to get out of their fathers' sort of rut. They were as pushy as any Jew you've ever heard of, or any young Italian or Irishman in New York. And the biggest problem I had with those kids was if you mentioned Camus, you know, in a side connection, they'd come in red eyed in the morning because they would have read Camus. And they were slow readers. Some of those kids read with their finger, but, by God, they read their book. One time white kids wanted to close Southern Illinois over Cambodia or something like that—it did close one time. But the black kids locked arms and chanted. They wouldn't let the school be closed. Well, those kids don't read in the sense that I read as a kid, just sort of devouring books, but they are reading everything that they can read, you know, so it's simply not a problem.

When I taught at Bennington College it was obviously not a problem, because Bennington College is the only real arts college I've ever heard about. They teach science, but it's a service. That is to say, a poet or a sculptor can't really be a contemporary poet or sculptor if he doesn't know about Einsteinian relativity. So all the science courses are really science for the layman and this kind of thing—not that they're called that. And in that kind of school people do read, at least the people that are in English. They read all the time.

Conversations: Literature matters to them.

Gardner: Yeah, sure. At Williams College I never had any problems because that's one of those middle-class, in my judgment—you know, I may be wrong about these colleges, and I apologize in advance if I am—but in my judgment it's one of those middle-class colleges which intends to turn out doctors, lawyers, college presidents. And it does that by putting people through hoops. You know, you read 275 pages by next Monday. I don't think that it's complicity really, but it all turns out to be that way; that is to say that the professors who end up happy there are all professors of that ilk. And, of course, those kids read. I don't think they read for pleasure, but they read an enormous amount because of the assignments.

Skidmore College had a very bad program in English, in spite of the fact that it had some good teachers, because it accidentally selected out bad students. I looked at their catalogue, and in their attempt to be liberal—and they are very liberal at Skidmore—they put in courses in the English department: two courses in black literature, four courses in feminist literature, six courses in American literature, one course called Masterpieces, and one called Shakespeare—the only figure course that they've got. They're bending to the students: "What do you want kids; we'll do it." A good kid in high school, a person who would be a literary type, a writer or reader, looks at the Skidmore catalogue and throws it away. He goes to another school. So they've got a sort of natural selection process which is calculated to get nonreaders—I mean it's not calculated to, but it does naturally get them.

I guess what I finally have to say, and I guess what I'm saying, is that colleges really are more different than we think; each does have its own personality. And certain colleges will attract heavy, heavy readers. I was just visiting at Queens. That's an interesting place, because, you know, it's a punk school: sort of suburban, sort of ghetto, it's right between the two; on one hand is Syosset and the other is Queens. And the kids walk around with books sticking out of both back pockets of their ratty jeans,

John Gardner

or pushed up into the arm like we used to carry cigarettes, in the sleeves of their T-shirts. And every place you look there are learned graffiti. That kind of school obviously reads. San Francisco State, where I taught for a while, people read. At Northwestern I don't think people read particularly; I think they went to movies. So I guess the culture is very mixed.

Let me say one thing about that, though. When we say people aren't reading anymore, let's remember the temptation is to think, "Ah! They're all watching television!" But John Jakes's new book, *The Warriors*, has an initial printing of 3,000,000 copies and it's going to go through four, five, six, seven printings. He is wiping out television like crazy. He's not a fool. Scholarly people have a tendency to say that there are these serious artists, you know, and then there are these dumb hacks out there. John Jakes is not a dumb hack; he is a man who loves American history, who knows an enormous amount about it. In fact, during thirty years or twenty years, whatever, as a PR man, he spent all of his time for pleasure reading American history, everything that he could find. And then suddenly he got the great idea of a soap opera in which he sort of moved this family, the Kents, through all the great moments. He has these incredible things like the whole Gettysburg Address printed in a novel with interruptions: "Sam Kent perked up his ears," you know, and things like this. We may laugh at it as bad art, but it was never meant to be art; it was meant to be a sort of wonderful, loving sashay through soap opera history. The history is authentic, and the feeling about the event is good, I think. It's true; as soap opera it is very good. Okay, this is writing. It's neither fiction in the highest sense nor is it nonfiction in the highest sense, but it's something people really do read, you know.

We've got to remember we're in a democracy, and if we really believe in that principle, and I really do, we're going to have to accept some funny values. We're going to have to finally end up admitting that the best artist we ever produced, the most impressive all over the world, the most influential on all arts, is Walt Disney, of all people. He's the man who brought the animated cartoon and music together for the first time—spectacularly. He's the man who created the myths for us so that Americans are now the owners of the idea of the animated cartoon, in spite of the fact that the Czechs are better at it. We own it because Walt Disney did it, and we are the owners of the fairy tale. The Germans made them up, and the Germans knew what to do with them, but we own the whole field of the fairy tale now. When I want to do an American opera I immediately think of fairy tales, because what could be more American than Snow White, that great American fairy tale, or Pinocchio. Actually, the Italian Pinocchio as a story is wonderful art, but Walt Disney's Pinocchio is wonderful democratic art.

We're a lot better than we think. I think people are reading a great deal; it's just that we might not approve of what they are reading. On the other hand, our grandfathers didn't let their kids read H.G. Wells, right? Jules Verne was very bad taste. Nobody read Fielding except aristocrats, you know, but not ladies. Richardson was, of course, the worst kind of pulp; in fact, he was John Jakes without the history.

Conversations: Is your feeling for democracy one of the things that prompts you to explore and maybe try all of the different forms of writing? You've done fantasy; you've done novels; you've done scholarship; and you're talking now about plays and other things. Are those linked in some way?

Gardner: That's an interesting question, because it makes me look at what I've done in a different way. It really is true that one of the very powerful influences on my childhood was the political feelings of my grandfather and my father and my uncles and so on. The women in the family didn't really give a hoot, you know, but the men were always talking politics. They always hated the Democrats but were really Democrats—they were farmers and they didn't know they should have been Democrats, anyway. . . .

Conversations: Where was this?

Gardner: This was in western New York. My grandfather had a big farm. Two of his sons, my father and Uncle Harris, took over after he died and split it into two farms and so on. I'm not sure that's exactly right; I guess my father had split off earlier. Anyway, they talked about it all the time, and I really do love the idea of democracy. I do absolutely believe in the people-king. I think that the people's judgment, every time it's been heard, has been wonderful. Jimmy Carter is yet to be proven, but there's no question that he's the people's choice. Nixon is said to have won by a landslide; nobody went to the polls—no landslide. Only five out of 1,000,000 go, you know, and four of the five vote for one man, it's not a landslide. But I like the popular presidents; I like them very, very much. I liked Harry Truman; I loved Eisenhower, maybe some awful things happened in his administration—nevertheless. . . . I loved John Kennedy, and I think, again, he was the people's choice in some remarkable ways. So yeah, I think that it is true that my feeling about being able to shift from form to form has a little to do with the democratic feeling.

It is certainly true that I am extremely offended when people talk to me about writing as a sort of noble cause and they look up to the writer, you know, as some sort of shaper. Well, I think writers do shape people's feelings, but they also express views. I don't like that idea of the writer as king, the romantic hero, and I hate the Byronic figure. I really like the sort of Balzac, the man who appeals to many people. Sam Clemens is one of my very favorite writers, you know, because he really does express feelings that my father-in-law, for instance, would have expressed had he been a writer—a Missouri man. And I think that if you feel that way. . . . For instance, a lot of "serious" writers in America, I think, would be embarrassed writing a book of light children's verse, embarrassed writing a TV series on Boswell, embarrassed doing an animated cartoon, certainly embarrassed to write light, little parodies of fairy tales. They probably would be embarrassed to write an epic poem, because it's obviously going to have to be an anti-epic and can't be. So maybe it is a democratic feeling.

Conversations: What do you think the function of literature is in a democratic society?

Gardner: I was going to go on with the other question hoping I could say one more thing and you really do bring it to exactly what I want to talk about. You know, the Folger Library. In my opinion, it is the greatest monument of all for democracy, better than all the statues and buildings that have ever been put up. Folger's idea was exactly the idea: These are the books that created America. He's got everything: he's got Galileo to the works of Shakespeare and so on. It's the idea, free and clear, of no limits: "I am my own judge"—you know, that wonderful last line of Vergil's: "I make you your own priest." That's what democracy has to mean. There's no aristocracy of intellect or anything else. The result is going to be what it was for Thomas Jefferson, pain and misery, because you're misunderstood, or fools use that freedom for their own aggrandizement at your expense. But it's young hope for me. And that's what democratic means. It's having all the movies out.

This, by the way, does not mean that I wouldn't censor pornography because I would. I think that pornography shown in the privacy of somebody's own home is okay. I think, probably, there are situations in which it is okay. But as an open and blatant corrupter, and I think it is a corrupter, I'd be against it. I don't want to develop that much, because it's not an interesting subject, but the liberal idea that we should let everything happen is a bad idea.

What one has to say is that the real nature of a democracy is that it's an adversary system in which all the different points of view shout to be heard. And the majority determines, you know, what we are going to do. I think the reason the system works most of the time is that when a particular group is hurt too much—as blacks have been hurt too much, for instance, and Indians have been hurt too much—they begin to shout louder, and people of fair mind begin to say, "Wait a minute; we've got to help these guys." Pretty soon the majority is on their side, even though they are a small minority. I don't think you just give in to every little minority. If a group comes along and wants liberation for the gorilla, or a group comes along and wants freedom of murder, whatever, the majority has got to say, "No!"—not only no, but "You can't do it, and if you don't like it get out." I absolutely hate the idea of democracy being confused with absolute liberalism—license, complete license. I think a civilization is dead the moment it believes that all values are equal. They simply aren't all equal. What we have to do is struggle in a democracy to hear all sides with a certain amount of fairness. We have to keep the press as open as possible. I wouldn't go back to the blue laws, by any means, for movies or books or anything. Maybe I'm just slow to change; maybe I'll finally come around to total license, but I don't think so. I think

93

the real function of democracy is to hear all the ideas, to listen to the possibility of all the life-styles, to allow every life-style that doesn't cause any harm to anybody else, and to resist with all your might that which is harmful to the individual in the society. Every time I say those things in universities, I get boos. I don't care. I'm an upstate Republican—what do you expect?

Conversations: As you think about your own work and what you're planning and what you're going to write, what do you find that literature means to you now that you've come as far as you have? What are you trying to do? What purpose does it serve?

Gardner: I think basically what literature always does is not so much apply new values, which is what science kind of does, as reassert traditional values which have worked and question traditional values when they seem to be risky. I think the real purpose of literature is to discover open-mindedly and bravely what is healthy and what is unhealthy for individuals in this society—to expose what is unhealthy for what it is, and to expose what is healthy for what it is, and never to cheat on the argument. Like if I really want a particular value to be healthy, and I begin to lie in my drama so that I make it healthy, when, in fact, it's not that healthy, then I've written bad literature. I've written cheap propaganda. I think that churches, for example, are in the business of conserving values, conserving ritual values, and I'm all for it. Hurrah for churches! They are kind of an anchor on society. So the Pope can't say, "Okay, guys, you can all take contraceptives now," because a whole mystic aura has been gathered around the sex act and reproduction and so on. It's a ritual feeling that is no longer appropriate to the world, because of population and so on. But to just throw that ritual feeling out is to throw into doubt all the ritual feelings that make us what we are. So the Pope always has to go slow. I think any intelligent Pope must be happy that there are the Berrigans out there gnawing at the edges and making it easier for him. Meanwhile, he's still the papa and he has to keep the rules.

But artists are the opposite. Every novel, every true novel, is a complete reassessment of all values. I often say to my classes that every novel begins in one of two ways: "A stranger came to town," or "She got on a train." There are no exceptions, really. The stranger may be cholera, or a wife gets cancer or something, but some disruptive force comes into the community and throws the community's values into panic. And then they have to decide which of those values will hold, which of the values of the stranger are more valuable and so on. Or you leave Alabama for Chicago and you're in a new situation where you have to test all values. You can't write a novel that isn't like that. The sort of wonderful thing is that so many thousands of novels do begin with one of those two, the only two, possibilities and manage somehow to get all the way through without reassessing a thing—and that's incredible.

But art is always reassessing, and for me that's the main function of art. But it has to be quickly added that the reassessment is of no interest and no value if it's not dramatically valid, if it's not thrilling, or interesting, or amusing, or in some way captivates the reader's attention and feeling. And that, of course, means that it's going to deal with characters, because that's one of the things we're deeply interested in by nature. That, of course, means that it's going to be psychological, whether or not it ought to be. It's going to deal with action, because that's what keeps us going. Finally, the way you reassess values—what the novel really does is reassess values—but the way you reassess values is the entertainment function, and it becomes more important for the success of the novel than the basic purpose of the novel, and that's when you get into trouble. A great artist keeps the balance between what he's really doing, which is reassessing values, and the way he makes it interesting and valid, like close analysis of character and situation. And then, of course, the more you think about close analysis, the more you get into technique, the more you get into trickery, and pretty soon you're off in the lunatic fringe where a lot of people are these days, doing nothing but technique, and nothing but tricks and gimmicks. And that's bad, because the very center of the art, which is moral, is rotted out. You've got to be committed to values first and foremost, and that's what I think novels are, and painting, sculpture, and music.

John Gardner

Conversations: I'm sure everyone always asks who you consider your principal influences. Who had a significant influence on your early writing career?

Gardner: Oh, sure. The main influence of all is my family, my father and mother. My father is a wonderful reciter of poetry and does sermons and makes things up. And my mother can also do that, but she was an English teacher and she loves poetry of all kinds. They love Shakespeare, so I heard a lot of Shakespeare, but I didn't hear it in a context that made it sound academic or strange. I learned it the way Joe Papp learned it, you know, "These are good plays, Joe," right? And they were. That shaped me in a funny way in that it led me to a love of the metaphoric and the indirect and the beautiful language and so on. I think probably besides the writers that my parents most liked, which were Sir Walter Scott, Shakespeare, Dickens, and so on—all nonrealists—the other influence that was huge on me was Walt Disney movies. I liked other kinds of movies: I liked Alan Ladd, OSS movies, *The Great Gatsby* that Alan Ladd did, and Roy Rogers, and Gene Autrey, but I always knew that these were sort of just entertainment.

I always knew that when you went to *Snow White* you were going to art. My parents didn't know that. In fact, I used to get the Mickey Mouse comic books. I don't know why. . . because I kept thinking somehow in a comic book I would see what I saw on that screen, and it never happened—a silly Donald Duck, Bugs Bunny, all those various Walter Lantz and Walt Disney characters, except for Walt Kelly, who really was an artist. But what I saw on the screen was art to me, and then, of course, when I found out in college there was Chaucer and that there was Homer—*The Odyssey* is just the greatest animated cartoon ever, and *The Iliad*: when Achilles is going out to battle and his horses turn around weeping and talk to him, that's Walt Disney, you know. And then Melville was a great love of mine, was when I was in high school and is now. Still, Walt Disney! You think about Captain Ahab, when they finally go after the whale, opening the trapdoor and out come five Orientals, and he had these Chinamen chasing the whale. That's straight Disney; everything in Melville is straight Disney—marvelous stuff.

That's, of course, why Disney is great. Disney was highly original in what he did, which was to bring a certain group of animators together and conceive a certain kind of movie. But every great artist is a sort of potent moment in which powerful influences that are all around him come together in one man. Everything that was in Melville—I don't even know if Walt Disney ever read Melville, and I'd be a little surprised if he did, although he probably did—but he's got it. Look at the feeling that Poe got when, out of a certain moment in history, angry, angry Poe jelled it into all the modern forms: he invented the detective story; he invented the pirate story; he invented the doppelganger story; he invented the Kafka story, you know, the story without a beginning. All of that rage, all of that love of ghosts, and spookiness, and Platonism, it's all in Disney. Disney is a sort of focus, like the point of a jewel, for all kinds of things. At the moment Walt Disney arrives we know that Americans are great artists. He influenced Calder, you know. Calder went in a different direction, but it's marvelous.

Well, those kind of influences were the strongest. One other was that my family loves music and listens to a lot of it. I used to listen to the Texaco opera things, and then Saturday nights if there was an opera in either Buffalo or Rochester, we'd go to it. Opera is, in a funny way, also animated cartoon; it's really an old-fashioned animated cartoon. I think the opera kind of comes out of the singing puppet show, but operas as they're done now are really animated cartoons. It's a very weird kind of thing. You think about opera productions before the Second World War: They were pretty authentic—this was before Rudolph Bing at the Met. They were pretty traditional stagings; they were very much like eighteenth- and early nineteenth-century stagings in Europe. After the Second World War when Bing took over, they turned into animation stagings. Suddenly a whole new view of opera came about, so that, for instance, before the war Tosca stands like a puppet singing after the firing squad scene and then jumps off this little parapet four feet high, and you have a sense that she's jumping off the cliff. That's enough, right? You don't see where she goes. After the war you have a production in which there is a thirty-foot wall and a four-foot wall downstage right and you've got professional catchers. Tosca throws herself over the cliff and she falls and falls and falls. It's a whole different world. I love the opera. It's the queen of the arts. I like it the best of all. I love to write libretti, and I love to have a good composer set them. I know that if that stuff survives it will out-rate my novels. It's good stuff.

Conversations: Let me bring you back, finally, to the condition of modern fiction. In capsule form, what do you think are the major limitations of today's fiction?

Gardner: I think the major limitations of the fiction which is being most promoted are the failures of most writers to deal with what fiction essentially deals with: Aristotle's idea of actualization of the potential which exists in character and situation. There is an increasing concern with things that are side matters in fiction, not at the center at all, trivia. For instance, technical tour de force, or what I call performance fiction—fiction which you read because you wonder what can he pull off next, although you're not learning anything from it. It's just stand-up comedy, sort of wonderful decadent art. Or fiction that is subverted to the purpose of the essay. This can be very great fiction. For instance, Solzhenitsyn is a great writer; he's a great journalist; he's using the novelistic form because he can get to people that way. If he were an artist in the classic sense of artist and concerned with beauty of form and power of expression and so on, he'd cut two-thirds of what he says because a few examples would do it. He knows this. I'm not saying anything that would be a surprise to him. But it's very important to Solzhenitsyn that he get the whole story out, and so he's willing to drag down the plot, to confuse characterization, and so on in order to get out the whole tragic story of modern Russia. That's wonderful journalism; it's super stuff; but it's not great art. I mean, Shakespeare didn't take all of Holinshed; he took the best and he made things up and changed things and so on. Solzhenitsyn is not free to do that because of the nature of his program. In lesser hands, like in the hands of Ed Doctorow, the subversion of fiction for essay is even more annoying. And then there's the kind of fiction which Bill Gass has been involved with, and I hope he's not going to be in all his career—he may not be in the tunnel, although what we've seen of the tunnel so far, it seems to be the case—fiction in which it's art for art's sake, absolutely divorced from reality, from any real problems, or from analysis of real values. I think all those kinds of fiction are a mistake. It's okay to have a few examples of it, and it's a pleasant sort of diversion, but when there are no essential writers, or, at least, the establishment recognizes no essential writers, there is a problem.

The other problem in contemporary fiction, of course, is that in a capitalistic system there are so many powers pushing at you and cheapening what you do. The Beatles come along with a brilliant and original idea about music. Instantly some capitalist thinks up the Monkees, who can't even play their own instruments, but who look like cute kids. They dub voices and they give them that and they package a product—which destroys the Beatles. Rock and Roll music is dead, absolutely dead, because it's cheap and easy to produce shoddy imitations. *Shane* comes along. It's the first serious, great Western, a symbolic movie of character. Instantly somebody comes along with an imitation, and, of course, it's hard to watch *Shane* anymore because the imitations have so beclouded it. It's hard to look at the paintings of Raphael anymore, because cheap silly ministers have used imitations so much—bad copies of Raphael in their Methodist programs and so on. Good art is always in competition with bad. In a capitalistic system, where money is the thing, when it takes a writer ten years to write a serious, important novel and it takes a company two months to produce an imitation, you've got a problem. I think that is the biggest problem American artists face. I don't know what you do about it, except I think that you go to war with the capitalists; that is to say, you beat them at their own game. John Jakes was saying jokingly, but I think it's an interesting idea, the only way that we are ever going to win against those bastards is that we get the Astrodome. I said, "That's great! Let's do it; let's do it! We go like Yevtushenko, and we'll speak to millions and make them cry, then we'll tell them how bad his fiction is and give them the names of the good writers." The good writers are there; they're all around us, wonderful writers. It's just amazing that they can't get above the sort of thought trap.

It's funny—when you read a Charles Johnson novel you can't believe that people can write this well these days. It's just astonishing. Or you look at Mark Halpern, the guy who did *A Dove of the East*—a wonderful writer. He's got like six stories or seven or eight in that book, and every story is in a different style. First story, I don't remember the order, but the first story I read is a contemporary Jewish tale—in the old sense of tale—set in modern Israel, about a man who murders the devil. And it's a wonderful—it sounds so authentic you think an Hasidic rabbi did it. The next is a delicate, sensitive story about a girl crossing the United States in the nineteenth century on a train—it sounds like Tolstoy did it. This man can master any style, and yet the style is not the master of him. The stories are moving, thoughtful, deep stories. There he sits, you know. He should be on the front page of *The New York Times*. People should be screaming, "Wow! We have a new genius!" But he's buried under mountains of Mailer and Nabokov and other people who burned out, if they ever had any fire. Beating the capitalist system is the big issue. That's why I'm starting a radio program. Now I really honestly think. . . .

Conversations: You're starting a radio program?

Gardner: Yeah, I'm trying to get going a five-days-a-week, one-hour-a-day program on the arts, in which what we do is praise the unsung heroes of music and ballet—although ballet is not a problem, because the wonderful thing about ballet, for reasons I do not understand, is that it's all good. This is just a moment for ballet. Everything from the New York Ballet to little places in Norman, Oklahoma, are really good. It may be because ballet is all texture, and what we're good at is texture.

Conversations: Well, another thing you must object to, then, is commercialism—if we can use that word to substitute for capitalism. Commercialism is also responsible in large part for the difficulty young promising writers have in getting published, because publishers are reluctant to take a risk.

Gardner: Sure.

Conversations: They'd rather publish something by a recognized figure that would guarantee a return than to gamble.

Gardner: Right. In fact, even if publishers want to publish the young unknown, if it's a big publishing house they have a hard time doing it. It's even an unkindness to the unknown writer, because the salesmen just won't sell them. The salesman's job is to get in and out of the bookstores as fast as he can. And if he's got six famous names—Updike, whatever, you know—and one unfamous name, he's just not going to sell that book. He's just going to let it go, and it will die. Reviewers aren't going to review an unknown; at least, it is a lot harder to get them to. So that finally the unknown has no choice but to publish and slowly make his reputation with little publishing houses. On the other hand, of course, there is a bright side. That situation is encouraging the starting of small presses and small publishers, and it's encouraging university presses to go into novel publication and so on. And I think that's going to be great. Why don't we just have two separate communities: the commercial one, if you like, and the real one. If the real one begins to be heard about, which it will—you know, years ago nobody ever heard of the Jabberwock Press. Now, because of Douglas Wills and a few people like that, it's pretty well known—not the way Random House is known, but it doesn't deserve to be known that way. Yeah, I think it's awful for young writers now.

Conversations: I get the feeling also that the fate of a book is often decided before it has an opportunity to meet its public. The advertising bucks, promotion bucks, are determined in advance against the product without any necessary regard to what the real reaction is.

Gardner: When Bob Coover won the Faulkner Prize for *The Origin of the Brunists,* his book was pulped before publication date. They didn't know it was going to win the Faulkner Prize. When it won the Faulkner Prize, the publisher was in terrible embarrassment because they couldn't even send a copy to anybody. They didn't have copies for reviewers. It was a grotesque mistake. He never did do as well as he should have on that book because by the time they got more books manufactured. . . .

Conversations: Do you have anything on your mind that you would like to share with readers of Conversations?

Gardner: I do have one thing that I think readers should be aware of: It's very important that they take a part in the process.

John Gardner

Readers complain there's just nothing very good to read. Once in a while they run across a good book by some unknown or somebody famous, for that matter, and they think: "Well, there was that book." Mostly they run across bad books and are discouraged and so on. I think that readers should tell publishers that. I think that one should make it a normal policy after reading a particularly good book or a particularly bad book to write a letter to the publisher. The publisher doesn't think much about it if he gets one, or two, or six, or 100 letters—he thinks a little when he gets 100. But, for instance, when John Updike did *A Month of Sundays*, which is an annoying book because it's Presbyterian neo-orthodoxy carried to a really pornographic extreme, or when he published the book just before that which was a kind of wicked book, nobody wrote to Knopf about it except me. I think readers should say, "This is a terrible book. What do you think you are doing? What kind of dummies do you think we are?" People in the commercial world—I like to say the capitalist world. It's not because I'm a Marxist; it's really because Republicans make this fine distinction between free enterprise and capitalism. That's how we divide ourselves from the Rockefeller Republicans. Anyway, I think that one has to take part in that whole process. Stop them. The commercial world keeps underestimating people. The kind of nonsense they think people like—it's so stupid. Like *The Saturday Evening Post* was a wonderful magazine; it published wonderful people. Then it began to think people wouldn't like this or whatever and got crazy theories.

Conversations: Made assumptions.

Gardner: Yeah, and suddenly the fiction got bad and then the pictures got bad. I was talking to George Hughes, one of *The Saturday Evening Post* illustrators, and he explained what happened. Completely by accident *The Saturday Evening Post* shifted from a men's magazine to a family magazine. The reason for the accident was that looking for wonderful thrilling stories, it began to publish Mary Roberts Rinehart. Mary Roberts Rinehart was, of course, a woman, and the readership picked up. More families read it, not because it included a woman's stories, but because those stories were wonderful stuff, in the old

Saturday Evening Post tradition. So some stupid somewhere at some desk said, "Aha! Picking up the women. Maybe. . . . " So then he started doing women's fashions. Nobody at the *Post* knew a damn thing about women. As long as they left them alone and treated them as merely intelligent human beings, they were selling like crazy, but as soon as they started thinking, "What do those women want?" they underestimated women and they killed the magazine. George Hughes got so he couldn't paint for them anymore because he was constantly asked for an image of women that he didn't understand—basically because, of course, it was a made-up image by some stupid editor. That kind of thing happens all the time, that kind of underestimation, and the only way that you can protect yourself as a reader, you know, the only way you can protect yourself from the commercial people underestimating you is to tell them what you really think. When these dumb books come out—pompous, pretentious, dirty, whatever they are—you write a letter. I've belabored that, but I really wish readers would stop getting cheated.

Conversations: How do you want to be remembered?

Gardner: As the greatest librettist of the twentieth century.

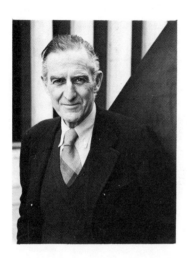

Brendan Gill, journalist, critic, and novelist, was born in Hartford, Connecticut, on 4 October 1914. He graduated from Yale University in 1936 and immediately began to write regularly for The New Yorker; *he has done so ever since, writing hundreds of pieces for the magazine and serving in turn as its film critic (1960-67) and its drama critic (1968 to the present). He has published two novels,* The Trouble of One House *(1950) and* The Day the Money Stopped *(1957), a collection of short stories,* Ways of Loving *(1975), and several personality studies, including* Tallulah *(1972),* Cole *(with Robert Kimball, 1971), and* Happy Times *(with Jerome Zerbe, 1973). His reminiscence* Here at The New Yorker *was a big best seller in 1975. He published a study of Lindbergh in 1977 and is currently working on another of Stanford White.*

Brendan Gill

Brendan Gill was interviewed by John Baker in Gill's incredibly cluttered office and workroom in the same building that houses The New Yorker *offices (but one floor below them). It bears the legend "The Word Factory" on the door, and inside Gill types and researches among piles of papers, old books, and magazines, dispensing drinks to his visitors from old chemical retorts. He is an inveterate party-goer, as well as being, in his critical capacity, a regular first-nighter at the theatre. On the evening of the interview, which took place between 5 and 7 P.M., he was planning to attend at least three of four parties, including two authors' parties and a dinner party.*

Conversations: At what point did you decide that you would like to be a writer?

Gill: Oh, that was when I was a child of maybe eight or ten. I already had in mind having half-a-dozen careers. I wanted to be an architect; I wanted to be a lawyer; I wanted to be a doctor. Wisely, I had already rejected the priesthood. I had some feeling then, I think, that writing was the most general of all the areas that I could go into. It committed me to the least, and required the least discipline and preparation.

So I was writing wretched little poems in the local papers in Hartford, Connecticut, when I was ten or eleven, and they'd be signed "By a Ten-Year-Old Boy." Or sometimes it would be "Brendan Gill, A Ten-Year-Old Boy." Contemptible! But I was published early and therefore early infected. The disease being incurable, by the time I was twelve I was the editor of the little grammar school newspaper and the literary magazine; *The Noah Webster Trumpeter* it was called. At country day school I was editor of several publications, then on to the *Yale Literary Magazine.* There was scarcely a time in my first twenty years when I wasn't editing some magazine and writing most of it myself.

Brendan Gill

Conversations: Were you a voracious reader as a child?

Gill: Oh, yes. I think reading is almost an affair of the glands: somatic manifestation of the perturbations of puberty. Most people I know did the bulk of their reading in their earliest years. It's from the time you learn to read until you're about thirty that you ransack books, or whole libraries. Few people that I know do much impassioned reading after thirty.

Conversations: Or if they do it's simply things they feel they have to read because they're current, but they don't read things that form their thoughts or life.

Gill: My father was something of a genius. He had been brought up in the 1880s in a little town in Connecticut at a very good academy and had thousands and thousands of lines of verse in his memory. He used to reward his children by asking us to memorize, as he had done, Shakespeare and Cowper and Scott and all the rest. He bribed us to do it, paying us a dollar a line. Imagine the fiscal wantonness of the man!

Conversations: Even a sonnet would keep you going for a week.

Gill: Of course! Financially, I was sitting pretty, for this was back in the 1920s. He himself had had to do all his memorizing for nothing. He had been a poor boy, and he loved spoiling his children. He was also eager to get results. He knew that cupidity was the road to a well-furnished mind, as it is to practically everything else.

Conversations: How many Shakespearean plays did you memorize at that rate?

Gill: Oh, I had thousands of lines of verse in my head, and I'm a great nuisance to my children and grandchildren because I can still recite them, with or without gestures. What it amounts to is having a portable library with you wherever you go. I don't have to carry a very heavy book bag aboard a plane; I have books enough in my head. We've enjoyed today, for example, a flawless blue sky, and I've been thinking constantly of Yeats's lines: "Suddenly I saw the cold and rook-delighting heaven / That seemed as if ice burned and was but the more ice." I like having that ice ready to hand.

Conversations: Back to school days. Obviously you wrote a great deal while you were at Yale.

Gill: Yes, I was always writing and was also intending to be a lawyer. I haunted the courtrooms in New Haven. My family were all lawyers and doctors, so I kept that as a possibility. I've also had a lifelong preoccupation, architecture; that is a profession one has to start moving toward very soon, and I didn't want that. So I went on being a writer, writing short stories and poems—mostly poems. Poems, too, I think are somatic manifestations. It's a natural part of one's adolescence to become a poet. If you're a real poet, you survive adolescence and go on to the hard work of maturity.

Conversations: Have you published any poems in your maturity?

Gill: Yes. I've published a few poems in *The New Yorker* from time to time over the years. In fact, the other day I got a letter from a young woman who had written down a love poem of mine from *The New Yorker,* and she asked me if she might incorporate it into her wedding ceremony. I was honored, for little as I approve of marriage, I approve of ceremonies. One publisher at least has wanted me to bring out a book of verse, but I haven't enough. I think in old age I'll succumb to the temptation; one succumbs to every folly with age. I wrote a book of poetry that came out when I was an undergraduate. It's called *Death in April.*

Conversations: That's a very undergraduate title for a book.

Gill: April and death—of course! My poem won a prize at Yale, and the condition of the prize was that you had to publish what you had written. It turned out that the prize money and the publication costs of the poem were identical. Still, it's a nice book.

Conversations: Is it worth much of anything to a book collector?

Gill: Oh, yes! Very gratifying, that. Thank God for small editions. Soon after *Death in April* I started writing short stories, and that was how I arrived at *The New Yorker.* I continue to think of myself chiefly as a fiction writer, but the fact is that I've earned my living mainly as a journalist.

Brendan Gill

Conversations: You submitted stories to The New Yorker *when you were still at Yale?*

Gill: Yes. Those were rejected, but then in the fall of the year of my graduation I had my first acceptance from *The New Yorker*. That was 1936. Mercifully, I have continued to be published in the magazine ever since, though sooner or later we superannuate ourselves. As we lose the old know-how the likelihood of continuing to have short stories appear in *The New Yorker* becomes increasingly remote. I don't fear that; I welcome it.

Conversations: How do you mean exactly?

Gill: In other lines of work people are retired simply by age. But a writer being an artist retires himself by inability. The creative faculty diminishes with age, along with sexual potency. You can mark this decline in most writers as vividly as you can mark the loss of their hair or the increase of their wrinkles.

Conversations: I think of you as still astonishingly fecund.

Gill: Oh, naturally I consider myself the exception. Doesn't everybody? The last beat-up poor devil crawling in on his hands and knees here at *The New Yorker* is under the misapprehension that he is young and full of promise. But given that we live that lie, it's also the case that I appear to have more energy than almost anybody I know of any age. It's an accident of bloodlines.

Conversations: But you spoke a moment ago as if you felt that it was more and more difficult to place stories in The New Yorker.

Gill: I wasn't speaking personally. I was saying that all writers, all artists, retire themselves through failure, and it will happen sooner or later that my work will be less welcome than it is now. I mean to be as good-humored as possible about it when my time comes. Our editor, Bill Shawn, and I have often talked about the fact that one must retain at least the appearance of sweetness toward life as one's powers diminish. Obviously, one seeks to blame one's increasing failure on the world; Thurber in age, for example, when *The New Yorker* started rejecting his work, had to assume that *The New Yorker* was proving to be a much worse magazine than it used to be.

Brendan Gill

Conversations: What about E. B. White, who last year published his very successful volume of letters?

Gill: Andy has never seemed embittered by age; by my lights, he's behaved very well.

Conversations: He still does those column ends in the magazine, doesn't he?

Gill: Yes—what we call newsbreaks. And they're still fresh and lively.

Conversations: I wonder if White hasn't been much heartened by the reception his volume of letters received?

Gill: How could anybody fail to be heartened by it? He has what I call an honorable modesty: He knows his own value. But I'm sure he welcomes this expression of interest in him as a writer and as a human being. One never knows as a writer whether one deserves much attention as a human being. I think you have to measure up to a certain standard as a human being in order for your letters to be worth reading. Many people can create a work of art of some value, whether a short story or a poem or a painting or a composition in music, whose letters are trash; other people ravish our minds even with trifles. Stravinsky, for example, had a mind so exquisite that much of what he wrote and said was as interesting as his music.

Conversations: How would your letters stand up? Are you simply a scribbler of notes and so forth?

Gill: Never a scribbler! Sometimes I have written letters that people have kept, and I have not been ashamed to have them kept. Still, I'd prefer that all my letters be destroyed. In this I'm like Henry James, who, whenever he said anything in his letters that was of any value whatever, would write at the bottom of the letter, "Burn this!" That was the sign, of course, for the recipient of the letter to save it.

I don't believe in leaving epistolary traces, though I'm not above envying the traces when I see them elsewhere. I never fail to read other people's published letters.

Brendan Gill

Conversations: When you're writing a letter, do you exert as much care in its composition as you would, say, if you were writing for The New Yorker?

Gill: Not quite, though I am a rewriter by nature. In my job as Broadway critic for *The New Yorker*, I do an awful lot of rewriting. The first page of my copy I might type over twenty times, and maybe the second page ten times, the third page less.

Conversations: How much would you change it each time?

Gill: Perhaps only a couple of words. But I like making every page look perfect. Luckily, I enjoy the physical act of typing.

Conversations: You told me once that you leapt very easily to The New Yorker *when you were, I believe, twenty-one years old, and you assumed then that this was how it was always done. But when I interviewed John McPhee recently, he told me that he worked for years before* The New Yorker *took any notice of him at all.*

Gill: Ah, but it's easier to write fiction at the beginning of one's life than it is to write fact. Fiction is the air one breathes. The kind of factual writing that John McPhee does so brilliantly isn't something that you'd expect to be the handiwork of a twenty-one year old. He is the master now of a style and of an intensity of apprehension that means that if he writes about oranges or the Pine Barrens of New Jersey or the making of a birch-bark canoe or even the eating of debris off the forest floor, all those things become equally fascinating. I don't think any writer could have made them fascinating at twenty-one. Nevertheless, John Updike could write fiction for us at twenty-one with no difficulty: writing short stories, wonderful things that were like fireworks spinning around inside his head. Those fireworks were as likely to be set down on paper at twenty-one as they would be at forty-one or at whatever age John is by now. What McPhee served may seem a long apprenticeship, but it's something besides an apprenticeship. It's a getting ready for all kinds of other things that are going to take place. Think of Ted Hoagland, for example—how could he possibly have said in youth the remarkable things that he's able to say now? Age is indispensable to writers like Hoagland and McPhee.

Conversations: You broke into the magazine with short stories. What was the predominant theme in your stories in those days?

Gill: Family matters. I think that the editors of *The New Yorker* were interested in my first stories because I was writing about an Irish Catholic background that they knew nothing about. It had for them a sense of great novelty. I was writing about nuns and priests, and nobody around *The New Yorker* knew anything about nuns and priests, except that Ross was terrified of them. Every time the magazine would print a short story containing the expletive "Jesus Christ!" a couple of nuns would be in the corridor trying to bullyrag Ross into cleaning up the magazine.

I soon used up my capital of novelty because, although I was of Irish Catholic descent, I really knew very little about Catholics. My family had moved away from what Richard Rovere described once in reviewing a novel of mine as "the Irish Catholic lower depths." We were more or less assimilated into the Protestant way of life. Fairly quickly, I had to turn to something else. I suppose the chief theme of my writing in one disguised form or another has been the fear of abandonment. That's what my two novels have been about, and, I think, three or four of my most important short stories. And that is almost too easy a theme to account for; plainly, having lost my mother when I was seven, I was likely to transform my feelings about her death into whatever art I was capable of making.

Conversations: There's never been a time when you felt that you'd said all that you wanted to say in any particular genre and you couldn't see your way ahead as a writer at all?

Gill: I think in fiction one often feels that. History usually fails to contain a record of a writer's false starts, but the writer himself remembers with anguish the number of works he has begun—the striking ideas that have proved intractable in literary terms. Looking back on one's life, one observes a veritable graveyard of brave chances taken in vain. It's a wise cunning on the part of living writers not to talk too much about their failures.

Conversations: Your career seems to break into sections. First, you publish a couple of novels, then you publish a number of personality studies, and then you publish a book of short stories.

Brendan Gill

Soon you'll be publishing a book on architecture—as I recall, a biography of Stanford White.

Gill: My latest book, which is about Lindbergh, commemorates the fiftieth anniversary of his flight across the Atlantic. It's what I call a meditation on Lindbergh and not a biography. I feel very close to Stanford White; I enjoy writing about him. Like me, he loved going to parties. Unlike me, at any rate so far, he got murdered at one.

Conversations: Anyone else you're interested in writing about?

Gill: Frank Lloyd Wright, who was a good friend of mine. There are a few people like him who had some effect on the world in the 1930s, and whom I happened to know. I knew Eleanor Roosevelt, though I didn't know Franklin, and I'd like to write about both of them.

Conversations: You're not one of those who scorn her as a conventional liberal?

Gill: No. I think of her as heroic. She grew up as well as she could inside the terrible crib, the almost coffin of her life.

Conversations: Coming back to the early days at The New Yorker, how long was it before you worked at, say, "Talk of the Town," in addition to writing stories?

Gill: After I had had some short stories in the magazine, I started doing "Reporters at Large." I went from there to doing "Talk of the Town" and then to being an editor. For many years I did a lot of "Profiles" and "Reporters at Large" and hundreds of "Talk" stories, nearly all of which have fortunately gone out of my mind. Every so often I have to look up something in the library, and I'm astonished to discover that I was the author of it.

Conversations: Was there a conscious New Yorker style in those days? Everybody thinks there's one now, of which you're, perhaps, a prime exemplar.

Gill: There never was one then and there isn't one now. I think in the early days there was more worry about writing a conventionally correct English than there is today.

Conversations: What seems to me to be lacking from most American periodical journalism is a sense of delight in the very act of writing. Reading Here at The New Yorker, *I was constantly struck by your relish in dealing with words.*

Gill: There may well be some literary showing off in the book, but then I believe a writer ought to have the capacity to show off. Some of our best writers are people who are able to operate at the top of the tent without a net; they turn wonderful somersaults up there.

The writer himself doesn't necessarily feel as much pleasure in the act as the reader does in observing it. I have never been clear with Joe Mitchell, for example, whom I think of as our best writer, whether he was at any moment in his life actually happy in the act of writing. It may simply be that the consequence of his misery in the act of writing is our joy. Mitchell's suffering is a condition I haven't experienced myself. I work as intensely as I can, but I rejoice in the labor of it at least as much as I do in the results. It's a matter, in part, of writing as labor. I like physical activity, even to the point of digging ditches. Similarly, I like the act of writing longhand, and I make an effort to achieve an attractive penmanship, though many admirable writers are content with an ugly scrawl.

Conversations: I know exactly what you mean about the physical work. I was talking to John Cheever awhile ago, as everybody else seems to have been doing in the last few weeks, and he spoke of the same thing—the pleasure of chopping wood, how he could happily spend the whole afternoon at this, and the best way you could get to know a man, he said, was to have him on the other end of a two-handed saw. Then you know you have to combine, or find his rhythm; otherwise you won't last. He would gain people's mettle simply by inviting them to help him saw a log.

Gill: E. E. Cummings died chopping wood. It may well become a literary tradition. One of Frost's greatest poems is about chopping wood. Perhaps for writers it serves as a therapeutic gesture: something they are capable of doing that is both skillful and mindless. White has also written about it.

Brendan Gill

Conversations: But White, of course, lives in Maine.

Gill: Up there they need more wood than we do.

Conversations: Indeed. But he's in a situation where such practices are automatic, whereas I think of you, rightly or wrongly, as an essentially urban person.

Gill: Yes, I do very little wood-chopping here in New York. It's very hard to find a tree my size on 43rd Street. Nevertheless, we have fifty acres of woods up in Connecticut, where we live in the summer. And we do burn our own wood, bringing it down to the suburbs where we live in the winter. I may mention that nothing is more irritating to the amateur woodsman than putting an iron wedge into a great big stump and then bringing a sixteen-pound sledge down onto the wedge and seeing it disappear into the heart of the stump.

Conversations: Somebody should write a piece about the physicality of American writers, and the things they take pleasure in. I think you would have an extraordinary number of them who exult in one form or another of physical exertion.

Gill: McPhee is, I believe, a great tennis player.

Conversations: He is indeed—tennis, squash, anything that's rapid, hearty exertion.

Gill: I think games-playing is very different. It's hard to imagine our great nineteenth-century writers playing tennis. Melville, James, Poe—the only nineteenth-century writer I can think of offhand who was extremely physical was Walt Whitman. He really did, it appears, walk as much as he boasted of doing.

Conversations: Can we get back to the development of your career at The New Yorker?

Gill: My writing had gone from one step to another on *The New Yorker*. In the early days, my career consisted of accommodating to the various needs of *The New Yorker* rather than of accommodating to what one might call my emotional needs. Now, or ever since my late forties and early fifties, I have been trying to turn back in a direction closer to what is needed by me emotionally. At *The New Yorker*, there are so many ways to achieve one's goals; for example, I could review movies, review plays, review books, and write short stories and poems.

Conversations: How did the opportunity to review books first come about?

Gill: Shawn invited me to try my hand at it. I can remember the first book that he asked me to review was an abridgement of Toynbee's history, which was then at the very height of its fame. I read this abridgement, and every single fact in the book that I had personal familiarity with proved to be wrong. I couldn't believe my eyes, because Toynbee was a godlike figure to me then. I didn't dare to write a review of this book because I couldn't believe that I was right and he was wrong. But that's how it was: he was full of howlers. After that rocky start, I settled down comfortably enough to reviewing my betters. I did reviews of various English writers whom I was interested in. People like Henry Green and Ivy Compton-Burnett, whom publishers were trying to launch in this country but who never really caught on to any great extent. I rarely did reviews of books that I didn't like. It was mostly the question of Shawn's knowing what my tastes were and saying, "Would you like to do this?" and I would say yes or no.

As for movie reviewing, like almost everybody else in our century, I've always been interested in movies. Shawn asked me if I wanted to be a movie reviewer when John McCarten moved over to reviewing plays, after Gibb's death. Of course I said yes; I believe in saying yes to anything Shawn proposes. If he asked me to jump out of a window, out I'd go.

After six or seven years of movie reviewing it was the question of somebody's taking McCarten's place, and Shawn again said, "Would you like to try reviewing plays?" Again I said yes. I'm convinced of the value of circulating jobs in this fashion, and I would think that the time ought to come fairly soon when somebody else would be allowed to be the Broadway Drama Critic for *The New Yorker*. It's a marvelous job, and I'd be eager to go on with it until I was 110, but I'd regard it as very unwise on the part of management to permit me to do so.

Conversations: Why do you think it would be unwise? Simply because you feel you would lose touch with what the contemporary playwrights were trying to say?

Brendan Gill

Gill: Yes, yes. I feel strongly that this is the case with many of my fellow reviewers. It's very hard on brilliant young playwrights of twenty-seven and twenty-eight to be reviewed by people in their sixties and seventies. Again and again I'll find that the old folk are disgusted by things that are not disgusting to my children in their twenties. For that matter, not disgusting to me. Directly or indirectly, the older reviewers really do ask: What is the world coming to? That's not the question the reviewer is supposed to ask in the presence of a work of art, whether successful or unsuccessful. Ideally, I think plays by thirty-year-olds should be reviewed by people roughly of the same age. Ken Tynan was a brilliant reviewer in his twenties; so were Bernard Shaw and Max Beerbohm. Some of my contemporaries grow old in what is called harness, and that is a very good expression for it. They protest that actors are not speaking clearly anymore, when, in point of fact, the reviewers are simply growing deaf.

Conversations: You don't feel that there's a sort of mature wisdom that they can bring to bear on playwrights?

Gill: It's a possibility in principle, but I rarely observe it in fact.

Conversations: What sort of standards do you bring to bear first on your theatre criticism? What do you look for, essentially? I've often felt that you look for a quality of wit and lightness of spirit.

Gill: Well, first of all, like everybody else, I make the distinction between criticism and reviewing. I've always felt strongly that what I do is reviewing and not criticism. I perform a fairly primitive journalistic function; I try to convey some sense of the play to a large number of readers whose chief interest is: Do I or do I not want to go to see this play? In the case of books, it's always been easy for me to attempt a second function; that is, to address the author of the book and let the reader look over my shoulder as I carry on this seeming discourse with the author. For some reason, this is difficult for me to do with playwrights. Be all that as it may, there hasn't been very much opportunity in my life to do genuine criticism; I've contented myself with reviewing. But someday I'd like to write at length about Charles Ives and how I think he got to the point he did. If I do that piece at all, it will have to be in age and retirement, when I can set down 20,000

116

words or so at leisure and afterward look around for some benign editor willing to publish it.

Conversations: Are there other things like that in music and the other arts that you wish you could write if only people would let you do so?

Gill: Well, Shawn is willing to let me try a "Profile" on Moliere. It would be something of a surprise to readers of the magazine to open it one day and find that we have a 300-year-long dead man in the book. It's imaginable that if I were to write about Ives, Shawn would find some means of putting that in the magazine. We have all kinds of curious headings under which pieces can appear these days, including simply "Recollections," which can embrace anything.

Conversations: You couldn't imagine writing a book on Ives? Say, 50,000 or 60,000 words?

Gill: My ideas about him aren't valuable enough for that. They have mainly to do with his background as a nineteenth-century figure in Connecticut, not with his music.

Conversations: Was there any problem for you in making the transition between theatre and movie criticism?

Gill: None that I was aware of. They're both forms of art that I've been interested in since childhood. I still write about movies in a magazine called *Film Comment*, which is published by the Film Society of Lincoln Center.

Conversations: When you began writing film criticism, back in the fifties, movie reviewing wasn't taken as seriously as it is today?

Gill: Not at *The New Yorker*, at any rate. Our drama critic, Wolcott Gibbs, despised movies and McCarten had no very high opinion of them. He thought critics like Farber and Agee and Parker Tyler were daft. Speaking of Agee, I think it was characteristic of the state of movie criticism in those days that Agee would tell the truth in *The Nation*, and in *Time* would tell a half-truth. *Time* was his livelihood, *The Nation* his pulpit. Agee managed to perform that feat of journalistic sleight of hand with perfect equanimity.

Brendan Gill

Conversations: An astonishing thing—he didn't really ever falsify anything, and yet. . . .

Gill: The art of leaving things out! Gradually it became the case here in New York that everybody wanted to be a movie critic. I think perhaps nowadays everybody wants to be a movie maker rather than a movie critic; that's a lot more difficult to achieve, not least because of the money problems involved.

Conversations: In your opinion, the best of contemporary movie critics is. . .

Gill: Pauline Kael. It was quite a shock to everybody when she came East, this vivid, passionate person, to show us how to speak our minds! And, of course, Dwight McDonald was writing admirable movie criticism a long time ago, though without Kael's evangelical imprimaturs and obstats. She is the first woman pope.

Conversations: Twenty or twenty-five years ago there were few books on movies, isn't that so?

Gill: Yes, and now they come streaming out, in a constantly increasing cataract. I'm puzzled to know who buys them all. I have scores of them here in this office, threatening to displace me.

Conversations: It seems as if everything that Kael or Simon or Sarris or Haskell writes immediately appears between hard covers.

Gill: It's ironic that all this intellectual excitement over movies comes at a moment when fewer and fewer movies are being made. Maybe two hundred movies will be made in America this year. And many of them are being made only in order to end up being shown on television. Movie-theatre-going is an activity that will diminish radically in the next few years, and it is being encouraged to do so by the industry itself, which sees far more money to be made selling its so-called product to TV. The nature of the product is bound to be altered by its eventual destination; a very dangerous situation.

Conversations: Doesn't this place an added burden on the movies that are left? I mean, as occasions for criticism? Do you think a lot of basically rather ordinary movies are being overly interpreted and being regarded far too much as signs of the contemporary Angst?

Gill: *Angst* were already an endangered species when I was a child. The last *Angst* died on Haystack Mountain, in Norfolk, Connecticut, in 1917. The fact is that standards of criticism having gone up, bad movies are given a much harder time than they used to be. The industry complains of adverse criticism just as Broadway producers do, and to the same idle purpose. No outsider can kill the movie industry; if it dies, it will be a case of suicide. Magazines also have a natural life span; if they don't commit suicide, they die of old age. In my lifetime, scores of magazines have vanished. It was their destiny to do so. So with newspapers as well; people mourn their loss in principle, but in actuality most of them were terrible.

Conversations: Do you see a great deal of television or do you feel it should receive serious attention? Michael Arlen writes about it in The New Yorker *from time to time, and very well and very seriously. Is it something that interests you as a cultural phenomenon and that you would be interested in writing about, or not?*

Gill: I never seem to be able to watch it for long. With the best goodwill in the world I'll turn it on intending to see such and such a program that I've heard praised, and in a few minutes I'm impatient. I get up; I walk up and down; I have to look away. There is some singular out-of-tuneness between me and the tube. It could perfectly well be my fault and not its fault. The only things that I've ever watched with great respect on television have been actual events: funerals, Senate hearings, inaugurals, and the likes of that. A great tragic event, like President Kennedy's death and funeral, is transformed into a work of art by TV; we respond to it in aesthetic terms and are moved as if by some age-old great ritual or play. But when TV attempts to create a work of art, something goes wrong. Drama, music, dance— they are all altered for the worse. Even Merce Cunningham cannot survive being reduced to a tiny dancing doll.

Conversations: It is, then, essentially a matter of scale?

119

Brendan Gill

Gill: Only partly. The intrinsic unreality of the image—particles of light at the end of a tube—also poses problems. Movies share the unreality, but in a movie house one is encouraged to suspend disbelief by being a member of a large group in a dark place: a Platonic cave, which our living rooms are not.

Conversations: Is this something that you think the people who make television programs have taken into sufficient account: the fact that they are seeking to establish contact with maybe two or three people sitting in their own living rooms?

Gill: I don't know what they would do with it artistically if they *did* figure it out. Obviously they have figured it out with regard to commercials, because commercials are very successful: four to a minute and all causing us to go out and buy something. *Hamlet* couldn't do that! The commercial is designed not to appeal to an audience but to an individual. It isn't a shared activity. Neither is book reading, or not often. And the one thing people didn't expect about television was that it would increase book reading. The fact is that something is going on on television that causes people to turn to books—people who wouldn't have bought books before, and who now buy them in enormous quantity. You get Bronowski's *The Ascent of Man*, for example, selling hundreds of thousands of copies.

Conversations: Absolutely. Alistair Cooke, Kenneth Clark....

Gill: And it could only have come from television. So television assuredly does something useful to people's minds. It's much more respectable intellectually than what we supposed snobbishly ten or fifteen years ago, but I don't begin to understand the process.

Conversations: Haven't you appeared from time to time on TV?

Gill: Oh, I like going on television! It's a great lark. On public television, I moderated a program called "Behind the Lines," which was a serious study of how well or badly the press was handling the news. It was an experiment well worth carrying out.

Conversations: Dead now, isn't it?

Gill: It had received a grant from the Ford Foundation for, I think, $200,000, which by the nature of TV was gobbled up in no time. Nobody expected us to become self-supporting and we weren't and so we vanished, without a trace. But the need for such a program remains. What puzzles me about TV, even after having worked in it, is the hold it has over the young. They feel a genuine affinity for it; it is literally part of the air they breathe.

Conversations: Isn't that bond an expression of laziness? Something is in your room, and you can turn it on, and that's it?

Gill: No, no! An explanation of that sort is never a likely one; it's what our parents said of us with respect to listening to the radio, and it was what their parents said of them when the first funny papers came into the world. Every generation assumes that the generation that follows it is manifesting intellectual laziness.

Conversations: But in a home that has several other media of communication, where people can turn on the radio, or play records, or read books—why is it, then, they turn on television?

Gill: Well, I think in my family it is still books, but maybe all writers think for self-defensive reasons that in their families it's still books. An enormous number of books get read in my family, and I'm glad that some of them are mine.

Conversations: How do you rank the different sorts of writing you do?

Gill: First, poetry; after that, short stories; and after that, I would think novels; and then reviewing. There is a kind of taint of self-satisfaction in playing God in reviewing which has a tendency to diminish it, or ought to diminish it, in one's own eyes. It's very pleasurable to be passing judgment on the work of one's peers; one must be skeptical of oneself continuously for indulging in this voluptuous satisfaction.

Conversations: Do you feel that publishers have been fair in what they have chosen to take of your output, since you've been essentially a magazine journalist over the years?

Gill: Oh, yes. If I'd had the gumption and intelligence to write more novels, they would have published them. I have had a very good relationship with all my publishers, and I've had more publishers than most people, because the different kinds of books I've written have quite naturally had different kinds of publishers.

Conversations: You did have a big best seller with Here at The New Yorker. *Did you get any feedback from people who had been at* The New Yorker *over the years and who felt that you had traduced their role? I've seen a certain amount of criticism that suggested that here and there you were, shall we say, pursuing your own line, and that you were ignoring contributions by this or that author—that it was all a bit overpersonal?*

Gill: I established in the opening chapters the principle that it was a highly personal view of the magazine. By calculation, everything in the book was something I had known at first hand. I put in very little history; for example, I said almost nothing about the first ten years in the magazine, about which I knew almost nothing. I reported only what I had heard and seen and tasted and smelled. That's one of the reasons that I had very little to say about the younger writers on the magazine, even, say, about John McPhee. For though McPhee isn't young in the world's eyes, he's young in the eyes of *The New Yorker*, and young to me.

Some of those so-called younger writers felt that they were being unjustly left out of my account; that it wasn't *Here at The New Yorker* but "Here as it used to be at *The New Yorker.*" Not knowing them well, I had no anecdotes to recount about them; I knew nothing about their private lives. It happens that the people I was close to in my generation were in many cases raffish and disorderly characters. The younger members of the staff, whether or not they're raffish and disorderly, may well feel that there is another book to be written about *The New Yorker*. To my eye, there's very little nonsense taking place these days in the corridors of the magazine; very little dishevelment, intellectual or emotional, as compared to my day. Still, I hope for the best. I bequeath them my title for the book, on permanent loan. Actually, it wasn't my title; I'd never have had the nerve to pre-empt it. After reading my manuscript, Shawn kindly suggested the title, and I was very grateful for it. Shawn is a genius at inventing titles, as well as at other things. He then generously contributed a long passage to the book, describing Ross in his terms. Several thousand words about Ross by Shawn are a priceless addition to any book.

Conversations: Were you surprised at the extent of the book's success?

Gill: Shawn and I were both astonished that so many people were interested in the magazine. And my vanity was tickled because there were places in Arkansas, for example, where many more hundreds of copies of the book were sold than there had ever been *New Yorker* subscribers. Naturally, I was quick to deduce that there was more to the book than merely information about *The New Yorker*. Also it's true that several thousand people wrote to me to tell me how much they had liked reading about my marvelous father and my cranky Uncle Arthur and even about my hedonistic philosophy, rough-and-ready paganism that it is.

I hope that if my latest book, *Lindbergh Alone*, should prove to be a success, it will be not only because Lindbergh has been the most celebrated figure in the twentieth century, but because something in my meditation about him is of value to people without regard to his fame.

Conversations: Who have been the authors who have meant most to you in your life, the ones you keep coming back to?

Gill: The great nineteenth-century people I live with and by are Whitman, Emerson, and Henry James. And the twentieth-century figure that I live with and by is Yeats. He teaches me how to grow old and be ever more joyous and then get ready to die. I suppose the greatest American poet of my lifetime is Wallace Stevens, who was a friend of mine. He's not a man, however, of whom you readily say, "I live by him." One stares up at him, aghast with admiration, but one doesn't learn from him; one is content to listen to his intricate song.

Conversations: Which of your contemporaries do you particularly admire: Cheever, for example?

Gill: Oh, yes, but Cheever and so many others have been associates of mine on the magazine and my admiration is mingled with personal feelings. I think of Updike and Gallant and Cullinan and Salinger and O'Hara, who wrote over 250 stories in *The New Yorker*. An impossible man, O'Hara, but one whose work I remember with delight.

Conversations: Which leads me to ask how you would like to be remembered?

Gill: The waited-for note of necrology at last! Well, in the first volume of a charming new publication called the *Marianne Moore Newsletter*, the editors publish a letter to me from Miss Moore, which she wrote to me back in the sixties and which I had entirely forgotten. In the course of the letter, she said, "You engender an insatiable appetite for life." Now, I should like above everything to be remembered for that ability, to whatever infinitesimal degree I may be thought to have possessed it. The words are too numerous to fit easily onto a gravestone, but I console myself with the thought that gravestones have gone out of fashion; it is enough for me that MM uttered such praise.

Edward Gorey was born on 22 February 1925 in Chicago. He attended the Art Institute of Chicago and the University of Chicago before entering Harvard, from which he graduated in 1950. After working for a short time at Doubleday, Gorey began illustrating his own texts and has emerged as one of America's most respected illustrators. He recently designed the set for a Broadway production of Dracula, which is to open this Halloween. His books include The Unstrung Harp (1953), The Listing Attic (1954), The Hapless Child (1961), The Wuggly Ump (1963), The Gilded Bat (1966), Amphigorey (1972), The Loathsome Couple (1976), and, most recently, Edward Gorey's Dracula (1977).

Edward Gorey

Edward Gorey visited the Manhattan apartment of interviewer Robert Dahlin for their conversation on 20 April 1977. Gorey preferred that location to his own apartment in prestigious Murray Hill, where he says he "lives in squalor among lots of cats." The mood was informal, Gorey wearing tennis shoes, blue jeans, and many rings.

Conversations: How did you get started doing art-word combinations?

Gorey: I really don't know. I mean it all just sort of came. I started out writing plays.

Conversations: Oh, I didn't know that.

Gorey: Yeah, well, nobody has ever seen any of them, so to speak.

Conversations: You did work on Dracula, *didn't you? Or did you just design that?*

Gorey: I designed *Dracula* for Nantucket three summers ago, but ever since then it has been off again on again. They wanted to bring it to New York after Nantucket, but it turned out that the producer there had not gotten rights for anything but summer stock, because it hadn't occurred to anybody that there was a possibility of anything else. And then an old fan of mine named Harry Rigby, you know, *No, No, Nanette* and everything. . . . Actually I met him maybe about a year before, and we were going to do something together, but it never panned out. Anyway then he heard that I had done the *Dracula*, and without telling me he went out and got the rights for New York. He didn't really care all that much for the production on Nantucket. The producers up there wanted to bring it in off-Broadway. And Harry was having delusions of grandeur. It happened that Josh

Edward Gorey

Logan's wife had played the French maid in the original production back in 1927, so Josh Logan was presumably interested in directing it. This whole nonsense went back and forth for a long time, and then everybody's rights lapsed, I guess. Then somebody else named Bruce Mailman got hold of the rights, and he would call me up every couple of months. Like this week Christopher Lee and Hayley Mills were going to be in it, and next week it was Peter Cushing and I don't know who, and so forth. That never became anything. Finally John Wulp, who had produced it on Nantucket, got the rights back last October for Broadway. So now I'm redesigning the whole thing, and it's presumably coming into New York on Halloween.

Conversations: Terrific timing.

Gorey: Yes. Well, it was supposed to go on this spring, but that didn't work out, partly because I haven't finished the sets and costumes yet. Every day or so they call up and scream, "Where is something more for something or other?" and so forth. Up until this morning I understood that it was going to go to Westport for a week in August; then it was going to be at the Kennedy Center for six weeks, I think it was; then it was going to be in Boston; then it was coming in on Halloween. Well, when I spoke to somebody or other this morning, "Oh, no, we're not going to Westport; no, we're not going to the Kennedy Center—Roger Stevens called up and said he didn't want us at the Kennedy Center. So we're going to Baltimore for four weeks or something." I suspect it will be a major miracle if the whole thing ever takes place. Anyway that's all I'm doing.

Conversations: Does this Dracula *stem back to when you were first beginning to write plays?*

Gorey: Oh, God, no.

Conversations: You didn't work on that one as a writer a long time ago?

Gorey: No, no, no. I'm just designing this. They're calling it my production, which I think must make the director feel a trifle idiotic; it's the same director as we had in Nantucket. Frank Langella is going to play Dracula, supposedly.

128

Conversations: Terrific.

Gorey: Except he sounds like a real pain. I've only met him once—he was quite charming and everything, but I keep hearing these things. See, it's got to be totally realistic, because he can't work in anything that isn't a totally realistic set; and he wants a follow spot all the time, and various things. Fortunately I will not have to cope with it. Of course, the producer, John Wulp, is very nice, and he is shielding me as much as possible from all this nonsense. He keeps telling the coproducers, "Don't get him upset. Don't do this or that or he won't do this or that." It's the first time I've ever really designed—well, it's the first time I've ever designed a Broadway show, certainly. Everybody tells me that once they get it into the studio you have to go stand over them with a club to see that it is executed properly—which I don't quite see how I'm going to do, because I won't even know whether they are executing it properly if I look at them.

Conversations: When did you begin writing plays?

Gorey: I started writing plays when I was in the Army for no very good reason that I can recollect now. I've always drawn. I never knew what I wanted to do when I was a child. After I was in the Army I ended up at Harvard in a sort of inadvertent way. I was drawing and writing, taking creative writing courses; you know, the whole bit.

Conversations: Were you trained as an artist?

Gorey: Not really very much. I used to take Saturday classes—I come from Chicago originally. I took Saturday classes at the Art Institute in Chicago from time to time. I actually went to the Art Institute for one term after I got out of high school, then I switched over to the University of Chicago. But I was promptly drafted—so much for that. My first publisher saw some of my drawings and stuff and got interested. I didn't have anything that would make a book at the time.

Conversations: Who was your first publisher?

Gorey: It was Duell, Sloan & Pearce, which is no longer in existence. Mr. Duell and Mr. Pearce—I don't know what happened to Mr. Sloan—both died. At the time they published me they had a brief affiliation for a couple of years with Little, Brown, so that the imprint read Duell, Sloan & Pearce/Little, Brown. My first two books were with them. They didn't make any money, nor did you get paid much attention. Great piles of those books were remaindered on 42nd Street for nineteen cents several years later.

Conversations: What were those?

Gorey: *The Unstrung Harp* and *The Listing Attic*. God, I wish I had those copies now. I remember I bought fifty of each when they were remaindered for nineteen cents, and I don't know what happened to them. I wouldn't have thought I knew fifty people, much less fifty people I was planning to give away a book to. I have one battered copy of everything I've done at this point. I've got an apartment that consists of nothing but books; on the other hand, I don't collect. It's a mania to buy books. I can't go out without buying a book. But it would never occur to me to collect. I collect authors, because obviously I want all their work, but this business of first editions and that whole thing doesn't strike me.

Conversations: How did The Unstrung Harp *and* The Listing Attic *come about then?*

Gorey: Well, *The Listing Attic* was the limericks I had been writing for years, but I never had done any drawings for them.

Conversations: Did you plan to publish them?

Gorey: No—I don't know. I don't know what I thought I was doing. I mean why was I writing plays that obviously couldn't be put on? They were like ten pages long and demanded the technical powers of the Metropolitan Opera stage to get put on, what with the special effects and everything. I remember I started writing *The Unstrung Harp* to order, except I don't know if anybody gave me the idea for it. They just said give us an idea for a book that you think we might find feasible. Why they found that feasible, I cannot imagine at this late date. Just about that time I moved to New York, after I had been living in Boston for 2½ years. After I got out of Harvard I came down to visit New

York and was offered a job at Doubleday and turned it down at first, because I didn't want to live here. I wasn't starving to death.

Conversations: In the editorial department?

Gorey: No, it was in the art department. I started out as an artist in the art department, then I switched over to being a book designer. I was there seven years in all.

Conversations: Do you remember how you came to the attention of Duell, Sloan & Pearce?

Gorey: I had an English teacher at Harvard, John Ciardi, the poet, and I got to know him fairly well. He knew Merrill Moore, the psychiatrist and poet. I think Merrill somehow introduced me to Mr. Pearce and Mr. Duell in Boston. They saw some of my drawings and were interested, Mr. Pearce, especially. As I say, they asked me to try and think up an idea for a book. And I guess I did, because they published it in the fall of '53—which meant that I came to New York in January of '53. So I must have done the book before I came here. But anyway they published that in '53. Then *The Listing Attic*, which was the limericks—I had enough for a book. I showed them a couple of sample drawings, and so that was the second book. And then I didn't have anything published for nearly three years, when Doubleday published two books of mine. Which is only the beginning of a lurch from one publisher to another.

Conversations: Your books are, I think, an acquired taste. You have to get to know them to understand the way you work. Is that why you changed publishers?

Gorey: No. I never changed publishers; they always changed me, as it were. They all thought they were going to make more of a splash with whichever particular book they were doing at the time. And then they'd do like one or two, and the splash didn't arrive. So they would say reluctantly, "Well——" So for awhile there I went from Duell, Sloan & Pearce to Doubleday to. . . . Well then I got sort of overlapped. I was a partner in relation to this children's book reprint venture called Looking Glass Library. We did one of mine there, but then at the same time I did four books with Ivan Oblansky. The less said about that experience the better.

Edward Gorey

Conversations: But very good ones. Isn't The Hapless Child *from that association?*

Gorey: *The Hapless Child* is from that, and *The Curious Sofa, The Fatal Lozenge,* and then *The Sinking Spell.* Then I worked for Bobbs-Merrill for a year, and they published one book of mine. Then somehow I was at Simon & Schuster for four or five books. My editor there was Bob Gottlieb, but he went over to Knopf and did not take me with him. There seemed to be a lot more—oh, well. Then my present editor at Dodd, Mead was at Meredith, so I published three or four books with Meredith. Then I went to Dodd, Mead where I am at present.

Conversations: You've been there for a while, actually, haven't you?

Gorey: Yeah, actually Peter Weed there is the only editor who has really kept me on for a long time. And then, of course, the anthologies were with Putnam's.

Conversations: One of your books was published by the Fantod Press.

Gorey: Oh, that's me. I published, let's see, I guess fourteen of my own and will continue to do so at intervals. I've been doing it for a long time, because there were periods when I had all sorts of things that hadn't been published. Finally I ran out of stuff.

Conversations: The last two books have come out rather quickly, The Broken Spoke *and now* The Loathsome Couple.

Gorey: Yeah, well I didn't even intend *The Broken Spoke* as a book. Part of it was done for *Sports Illustrated,* and there was part of a show that I had at the Graham Gallery a year ago Christmas. And my editor, Peter Weed, at Dodd, Mead, said, "Can't we make a book out of it?" He's always taking things and turning them into books, *The Awdrey-Gore Legacy,* for example. I did that for *Lampoon* and didn't think of it as a book, particularly. Then also there's a guy named George Bixby, who has the Albondocani Press; I did a couple of small books with him. He never prints more than 300 copies of anything. He's a rare book dealer, too.

Conversations: Instantly valuable.

Gorey: Yes, that's the whole point. Of course, since I've more or less been connected with Gotham Book Mart—I don't know how many years ago, seven or eight maybe, when I did *The Sopping Thursday* for them—since then I've been sort of a cottage industry with them. It's all very artificial, I think. Who am I to complain? But I think it's helped my reputation enormously, because anybody wanting anything of mine goes to the Gotham. They put out those catalogues.

Conversations: And he has that little shelf of your things.

Gorey: Yeah, and all the rest of it. The fact that there has been this one place kind of beating the drum, I think, helps a lot.

Conversations: What does it feel like to be a cult figure, which I think you certainly are?

Gorey: I'm afraid so. I'm not sure.

Conversations: Do you live in fear that some crazed fan will come out of the woodwork or something?

Gorey: Well, no. It's a little odd, because I'm never sure whether.... See, I've been going to the New York City Ballet ever since I came to New York, virtually every performance. So there are endless numbers of people who know me—don't know who I am, but, you know, know me from the New York City Ballet. So if I'm caught someplace else, voices will come out of the dark saying, "What are you doing here?" And I think, "What do you mean what am I doing here?" Sometimes they won't even explain. Then usually they'll say, "Why aren't you at the New York City Ballet tonight?" or something. And when the New York City Ballet was on strike, people used to come up and commiserate with me in the streets and say, "Oh, you poor boy! What are you planning to do?" Also, there is no use denying that my physical persona is about as eccentric as you can get.

Conversations: Oh, well, I think you've got some way to go before you get that eccentric.

Gorey: I mean, for instance, I walk a lot, and I'm always walking in the same places and everything. So people again who do not know me just recognize me. But then, of course, there are the people who do know who I am. It's always flattering to have someone come up and say, "I love your work." But, on the other hand, what do you say after "Thank you" and that sweet smile I put on them? After all, I've been doing this for twenty-five years almost. So now it's: "Oh, you've been one of my childhood idols for as long as I can remember." You know what I think? "Am I really that much older than you are, whoever you happen to be?" I've decided that, as somebody's pointed out, the older you get, it's very difficult to tell how much younger anyone else is. I mean I can't really tell the difference now between people who are fifteen and people who are thirty-five. When that first started happening, it did rather flabbergast me.

Conversations: What book set you into this category?

Gorey: I think *Amphigorey*, in a way, because that's the first. . . .

Conversations: But that's so recent.

Gorey: It isn't all that recent. It must be out about five years now, because *Amphigorey Too* is coming out in paperback this fall.

Conversations: Who's doing that?

Gorey: Berkley. Obviously, you know, a lot of people saw it who had maybe just seen one or two of the books before. And, of course, especially *Amphigorey Too* has all the stuff that was privately printed.

Conversations: Do you start out with a notion of what you are going to do or for the whole of a book?

Gorey: No, not really. I think you have to sit around waiting for the initial idea. I don't think you could just sit down and say, "I'm going to write a book about such and such." You've got to get the idea from somewhere, wherever it seems to come from outside. It always seems to me that there has to be some little seed or something that. . . .

Conversations: Do you remember what would have been the seed for The Hapless Child *or* The Curious Sofa?

Gorey: *The Hapless Child*—I happened to know what that comes from. It was a French movie dating, I think, about 1905 or 1906, called *L'Enfant de Paris*. I can't remember the director. I only saw it once. At one point the Museum of Modern Art started to go through its entire collection on Saturday mornings. You could subscribe to it. For years we'd just sit upstairs on Saturday mornings, and we'd watch all these movies that hardly ever get shown otherwise. I know that the movie starts out exactly the way *The Hapless Child* does. *The Hapless Child* deviates quite early. But I've always been a passionate moviegoer. I've been very much influenced by old movies, and a lot of my books do derive, in one way or another, from old movies. That one I remember. I was quite impressed; I can remember sitting in the dark and thinking, "Oh, what a zippy movie." Actually it was, I think, the little girl in the movie who was kidnapped and taken down to the Riviera and was finally ransomed at the end. The plot was entirely different.

Conversations: Did it end the same way?

Gorey: Oh, no, no, no. It had to have a perfectly happy ending. I think maybe the business about the father returning was from the movie. But it had a totally happy ending. As I say, it was just the opening part of it which somehow set me off, and I remember jotting down a couple of salient points in the dark. *The Hapless Child* is the one book, I remember, in which I was on about drawing number five drawing wallpaper and I thought, "I'm so bloody bored drawing wallpaper. I can't stand this." So I put the book aside for about five years. Then suddenly I felt, "Well, I better finish this up." So I went back to drawing wallpaper and finished the book.

Conversations: I must say that's the one thing that's true about your art: there are a lot of lines there.

Gorey: Yeah, but a lot of people draw a lot more lines than I do. Somehow I think I manage to give the effect of having drawn more lines than I have or something. I'm not really all that intricate. I mean I'm intricate, but there are other people, I think, who spend a lot more time at their drawings than I do.

Edward Gorey

Conversations: I suppose it's not a valid question to ask you how long it would take you to do a drawing. Every one must be different.

Gorey: The complicated ones are somewhere between a whole day and part of the next maybe—one or two days. I work reasonably rapidly when I'm working, which sometimes is very little.

Conversations: Do you develop it as it goes along, or do you have it pretty well mapped out by the time you sit down?

Gorey: The one thing I did learn very early was that I had to have the text completely written before I could do the drawings.

Conversations: Oh, you do write the text first?

Gorey: Yes. I mean I can start by doing the drawings, it wasn't that. It was if I started doing the drawings, I'd never finish the text. I had to know how it was all going to come out before I could. . . . That is one of my problems now: I mean I have something like fifty or sixty texts waiting for illustrations. Then I have God knows how many more that are partially written. I will probably finish those since I have. . . . Well, as a child I can still remember things that I didn't finish, and feeling so guilty about it. So I haven't for twenty-odd years, I don't think, started something I didn't eventually finish.

Conversations: Do you block out the artwork?

Gorey: No.

Conversations: As you're writing a text you must have an idea of what you're going to use for illustrations.

Gorey: No. I trust myself enough so that I don't have to say to myself: Will this make a drawing? I think my subconscious takes care of that. When I'm writing occasionally I'll have a momentary block, or I'll think, "What made me think I could do a drawing for this particular sentence," but I can usually solve it. I can quite often by doing a drawing of something completely different so that it will make a counterpoint.

Conversations: You said you work pretty quickly. Are you disciplined? When you're on a project do you get up in the morning, sing a song, and go to the table?

Gorey: No. I will do practically anything rather than sit down and work. With the slightest reason to go out of the house, the day is shot.

Conversations: A malady common to many writers.

Gorey: Success really does nothing for one, I've decided, at all. I used to think, "Oh, God, if I only didn't have to illustrate these dreadful books for other people"; not necessarily that they were always dreadful books, but they weren't my own. Sometimes I quite liked the book, but I thought, "I can't illustrate that," and ended up doing a terrible job. In other books that weren't really very good and that I didn't particularly like, I ended up doing a fairly good job, or at least I thought I had. It didn't make any difference whether I liked it, or disliked it, or how I felt at the time, or anything else. But just think—how marvelous to work only on my own projects. Well, now basically that's all I do do. And yet it's even worse somehow. I must say *Dracula* is not a project I ever would have taken to my bosom if they hadn't offered lots of money. Not that I have anything against it; it just doesn't interest me very much. I mean I'd much rather. . . I keep telling everybody plainly what I really want to do is to design sets and costumes for Gilbert and Sullivan or something like that. So far no one has taken me up on that. I have done a couple of ballet sets. But now I expect *Dracula* is going. . . and I also am doing a *Dracula* book, which I'm not really sure I want to do. But then they offered me so much money I couldn't turn that down.

Conversations: A book based on the play?

Gorey: It's all sort of lunatic. I haven't started on it yet, because I have to get the sets and costumes done. What it's basically, in theory, going to be is kind of a synopsis of the play in my own manner, but I suspect it's going to get further and further away so it will not bear any relation to anything. Presumably the backgrounds of the drawings will look like the stage and the costumes will be the costumes of the play. I'm certainly not going to try and reproduce the people, especially since nobody knows who will be in it anyway.

Conversations: Dracula must be in the public domain. You can do whatever you want to.

Gorey: Well, *Dracula* the novel is in the public domain. The play dates back to '23 or '27 and may still be in copyright. But, of course, the play is not really like the book. The play is the original one that Bela Lugosi did before the movie ever came out, way back in 1927, I guess it was here in New York. It's actually a quite good play. Hopefully they're not going to camp it up too much. Of course, there are all these Dracula books out now, you know.

Conversations: Oh, yes. Interview With a Vampire.

Gorey: I have no fewer than three advance copies of that book for some reason.

Conversations: They're trying to tell you something.

Gorey: I've never supplied. . . I hate these little blurbs from people. It always just puts my back up completely, so I've always refused to say anything, anything. Even my nearest and dearest friends who write books wouldn't dream of asking me. But I think I've got three copies of that book, and I can't see why they keep sending it to me.

Conversations: Well, I guess it is that you are a noted macabre, of sorts.

Gorey: Which I don't really believe in either so much.

Conversations: What do you mean you don't believe in it?

Gorey: It sort of annoys me to be stuck with that. I don't think that's what I do exactly. I know I do it, but what I'm really doing is something else entirely. It just looks like I'm doing that.

Conversations: What are you doing?

Gorey: I don't know what it is I'm doing; but it's not that, despite all the evidence to the contrary.

Conversations: Do you see yourself as a teller of moralistic fables?

Gorey: I don't know what anybody else's point of view really is, of course. Actually the content I always sort of let take care of itself, because I don't think one has any control over that anyway. Usually what sets me off is the kind of formal aspect of it. I can't think of a good example of exactly what it would be like. I can think better in terms of ballet: It's like doing a ballet with only a certain kind of steps. Obviously nobody ever says I'm going to do a ballet in which nobody does such and such. Like there's a section in a Balanchine ballet where the girl is manipulated by four men and never touches the ground. I'm sure that when he started out to do it he didn't say, "Well, I'm going to do a piece where the girl never touches the ground." But obviously, since he works very fast anyway, he probably got it all done and suddenly realized that she hadn't touched the ground. Sometimes I will take about equally from life, or from other artwork, or another book. I'm very, very catholic in my choices—sometimes it's dance; sometimes it's movies; sometimes it's other books; sometimes it's pictures. It may be verbal; it may be visual.

Conversations: Inspirations?

Gorey: Yeah. I tend to be very imitative, so if I see something I like, I think, "Oh, I'd love to do something just like that." Well, no matter how hard you try to do that, of course, eventually you wander off on something completely different. The original impetus may be something totally goofy. I remember, and I really still don't know what the connection is, *The Wuggly Ump* started from a book about that size. I don't know what the text said because it was in German; it was by Christian Morgenstern. But it was a little Easter book with rabbits and eggs and God knows what else. What that has to do with *The Wuggly Ump*, do not ask me. I think about the only thing that is left is that the books are the same size; the pictures are the same size.

Conversations: The Wuggly Ump is sort of unusual. Most of your books aren't in color, are they?

Gorey: No. I can work in color, but I don't often. Partly the reason I've never worked in color to begin with is that since I was working at Doubleday I knew only too well that if nobody knew who you were or anything, they weren't going to publish books in color. A lot of my books were intended as children's books and they would not publish them as such, which I always thought was very shortsighted. I said, "Well, my adult readership will buy it anyway. You might just as well publish it as a children's book." That's the only one that's ever been published as a children's book.

Conversations: So your inspiration comes from any number of things and this will be the kickoff for a whole book?

Gorey: Yeah. Unfortunately, as the years have gone, I can now practically conceive a book in about three minutes, which is all I need. I used to worry endlessly about what if I dry up? What if I never have another idea? While I would not like the feeling of never having another idea again, I can certainly do without very many more, because obviously I'm never going to finish up the ones I've got.

Conversations: You've got a long time to go yet.

Gorey: Well, one hopes. But I work, for the night is coming. I still have this whole backlog of stuff which I feel sitting up there waiting to fall on me if I don't get it done.

Conversations: Then you must plot easily, I guess. I mean if you can call. . . .

Gorey: Yeah—if you can call it. . . . I'm a firm believer in plotting. I know that sounds sort of silly, but I'm a firm believer in the plot as the underpinning of everything else. If you don't have a plot you're in trouble. Or at least if you don't have a plot you ought to have something else in mind to substitute for it.

Conversations: Do you revise as you go along?

Gorey: Yeah. I have to get the first sentence right or I can't do the second, and so forth. I can cover several hundred pages with versions of the first sentence. Actually I write easier than I used to. I mean I used to have to agonize. I also discovered that sometimes the revision just gets you nowhere; you might as well go right back to what you've done in the first place. Occasionally I will get stuck. Also I learned quite quickly, since I was working as a publisher, to think of my books as either thirty-two pages or sixty-four pages.

Conversations: You arrived at a certain number of gatherings and that sort of thing?

Gorey: So that basically my books are either fourteen things long, or thirty things long. So I can, without batting an eye, just automatically kind of scribble down the skeleton of a thirty-drawing book or a fourteen-drawing book.

Conversations: You're more of a cat person than a dog person, but you have more dogs than cats in your books.

Gorey: I left cats out of books for a long, long time. I don't know, maybe I was superstitious about putting them in or something. Even now I don't. My anthropomorphic cats are really something quite different from regular cats.

Conversations: When you are creating, do you find it easy to create characters—for instance, the people from The Loathsome Couple?

Gorey: That's a bad one to take, because that manuscript had been sitting around for many, many years. Mr. Gottlieb said he didn't think it was funny. He didn't say this to me; he said this to a mutual friend, or my agent—I guess she showed it to him. I thought, "Well, it's not meant to be funny." I suppose it was obvious that it was based on the Moors murders, which disturbed me very greatly for some reason. I'm a great aficionado—that's the word everybody uses—of true crime.

Conversations: You must have read—who is it?

Gorey: The Emlyn Williams book on it, I guess.

Conversations: Yes, and then wasn't there a woman who wrote about it?

Gorey: Oh, Pamela Hansford Johnson wrote that sort of dodge, which I sort of agree with, as I remember, about one of the reasons the murders were committed was because of all the nasty things the murderers had been reading.

Conversations: Pornography, right?

Edward Gorey

Gorey: Well, in a way, that book is kind of equivalent to *The Curious Sofa* because I had read very little pornography in my life. And if you will notice it, *The Curious Sofa* begins the same way as *The Story of O*, which is what finally set me off—where I think he picks her up in the park and puts her in a taxi after that. But I once remember spending an absolutely paralyzingly wet Sunday afternoon in Chicago reading *The Hundred and Twenty Days of Sodom* by the Marquis de Sade in French. I got so bored; I was really ready to blow my brains out after wading through that. But I always wonder how people can manage to write pornography. The first couple of pages are fun, but after that I just get. . . .

Conversations: There are only so many variations.

Gorey: Well, there are only so many things that you can do and so forth and so on. And so *The Curious Sofa* I wrote over a weekend and did the drawings.

Conversations: Over a weekend?

Gorey: Yeah. I just sat down and I really wrote it as fast as anything I've ever written, and I did the drawings just about as quickly. You know, there were two printers that turned it down.

Conversations: Not because it was pornographic?

Gorey: Well, no. One of them said they simply wouldn't do it. The other said that if we would remove the word "pornographic" from the cover they would print it. I think, in a way, *The Curious Sofa* is possibly the cleverest book I ever did. I look at it, and I think: "I don't know quite how I managed this because it really is quite brilliant." I don't like it, but you know, I'm really quite fond of its cleverness—the fact that everybody's names are totally indistinguishable. People used to approach me to illustrate pornographic novels after that. And I would say, "Have you looked at that book?" The men are totally indistinguishable from the women; everybody is seen from behind. That's the whole point: I think it's really about a girl who's got an obsession for grapes more than anything else.

But *The Loathsome Couple* was the same sort of thing. I resisted writing it for quite some time, and it really is one of those things I had to get off my chest. I sat around with a manuscript for a long, long time. The *Soho Weekly News* was always saying they would print anything. I thought, "All right, print this." And so I did it and I purposely made the drawings as red and a certain gray and dull and, you know, sort of unpleasant, uncharming as I could and everything. I was looking at it again, and it really is even more unpleasant than I thought.

Conversations: I don't have a great affinity for children, so that may be why I enjoy the book.

Gorey: Well, after all, I've been murdering children in books for years. It's much more personal to me in a way, I suppose, than a lot of the others, because I really read those books about the Moors murders. Somehow it stuck in my mind: This is really one of the great unpleasantnesses of all time.

Conversations: So The Loathsome Couple *is more of a sociological comment?*

Gorey: I guess. I don't know what it is. I was looking at it, and I thought, you know, what is this all in aid of, exactly. I remember thinking of some of the little jokes, or what seemed like jokes to me; like the meal—I spent a long time figuring out what they should have to eat.

Conversations: Artificial grape soda was first.

Gorey: There were lots of versions of that until I got it right down to my likings. And I saw in them a lot of myself, like the comment, "Even as a child she had thick ankles and thick hair." I kept thinking, "Had I better remove that sentence?" I couldn't quite. I finally decided to leave it in, but I'm not sure about it even now. I know one is always supposed to throw away one's best lines.

Conversations: What do you mean?

Gorey: Well, you know, if you've got something really spiffy you should throw that out because the rest is obviously not up to it. Quite often I have discovered this to be true. Since my things aren't all that long, quite often I throw away the first sentence and start with the second, as it were.

Edward Gorey

Conversations: Then you have all these brilliant lines you can scrape together into another brilliant book?

Gorey: Yes.

Conversations: Are there things that you would change now if you were to go back and redo?

Gorey: I doubt it. I always feel that whatever you did at the time was obviously what you had in mind. I hardly ever reread any of my stuff anyway, in any real sense of the word. When I was putting together the anthologies I had to sort of look at them, but I don't. . . . I used to worry about repeating myself, but I thought, "Well, I can't sit down and read my collected works every time before I start anything, or else I'll go crazy." So now I just hope that it's something slightly different from anything else I've done before.

Conversations: Do you have a favorite book?

Gorey: I tend to like the ones that make the least obvious sense. I'm very fond of *The Nursery Frieze*. And I'm very fond of *The Untitled Book*, at least I think I am; as I said, I don't look at them. I've always rather liked *The Object-Lesson*, because that doesn't make any sense. Those kinds of things are harder to do than almost anything else, so I feel I've done them reasonably well. I haven't done anything of my own that I didn't believe in. And I don't think the amount of work you have to put into anything has got anything to do with it. As I say, *The Curious Sofa* took me less time than anything else I've ever done. I do tend to sort of write the things that would make as little sense as possible. I've always been sort of fascinated by that; you know, Flaubert's idea of writing a novel about nothing. Most minimal art drives me absolutely crazy. In fact, most of what I do would drive me crazy in anybody else. I can find myself getting very upset by somebody else doing the same thing, I think.

Conversations: Is there something that has influenced you, like writing a novel about nothing?

Gorey: Well, that's one of those tag lines that has always stuck in my head. It's more an example. *The Object-Lesson*, for instance, really grew out of Samuel Foote's poem called "Grand

Panjandrum.'' It's a short eighteenth-century poem. He was a playwright, but he tossed off these ten or twelve lines. I cannot really repeat them to you, but it's a complete nonsense poem. The thing was that somebody said they could memorize anything if they heard it once, so he tossed off this total nonsense. I don't know if the person managed to repeat it or not, but anyway it turns up in anthologies of nonsense verse and children's verse. It makes no sense at all. Randolph Caldecott has done illustrations for it which are quite wonderful. Anyway, as I say, I purposely sat down with the object to write a piece that made no sense. That took me a long time to do. There were endless versions to that I had floating around somewhere.

Conversations: Is there any humorist or commentator or artist that has influenced the way you have developed? Or do you take your ideas and strike out on your own?

Gorey: I think actually the biggest influences on me have been things that are totally indirect. I mean I've been going to the New York City Ballet for just under a quarter of a century now, almost every performance. And George Balanchine's choreography has had—it's totally impossible to put into words—but somehow the way he works has influenced me a great deal. The way he works with the dancers: in a sense I'm trying to emulate his thinking. From the authors that I admire most I'm totally different; I mean Jane Austen is absolutely my favorite author in all the whole world, closely followed by Lady Murasaki and Anthony Trollope. I'm a great admirer of great, long nineteenth-century English novels. Nineteenth-century engraving, of course, has had an enormous influence on me. My work doesn't really look like that, but it obviously derives from that.

Conversations: In this combination of pictures and words, how do you see yourself—as an artist, or as a writer, or as an amalgam of the two?

Gorey: Well, I suppose, really, it's a combination of the two. In a sense I think of myself as a writer more, but that isn't true either. It's not that I'm just illustrating my own work.

Conversations: So you would want to be remembered as a writer of interesting little books?

Edward Gorey

Gorey: Well, yes, I suppose. Up until about, let's see, it would be about three years ago, I guess, I hadn't done any drawing that wasn't for a book for over twenty years, probably. I hang on to all the drawings for my books anyway because we were hoping that Mr. Brown at the Gotham Book Mart could sell my archives and I could retire or something or other. In any case, I probably have all the drawings for my books. And so when the question of having a show at the Graham Gallery came up, I had to do all new stuff. That was the first time I had done any drawing just for the sake of drawing for a long time, I'd say for over twenty years, and it was fun to do. But even then my mind tends to work in such a way—well, like the last show that I had. I did this one drawing just sort of off the top of my head and suddenly a whole book came to me, which eventually I will do. I just tend to think in series of things that will turn into books.

Conversations: Also, despite your love of ballet, I think you've only done one book about it.

Gorey: Well, there's The Gilded Bat, and then I've done a thing for the New York City Ballet called The Lavender Leotard. I do things like postcards and posters and buttons and things for the New York City Ballet Guild. I'd like to do a ballet alphabet book. I like alphabet books, you know; they're already ready-made, shaped, too. I've got a few alphabet books I've never gotten to.

Conversations: What are you trying to do in an alphabet book?

Gorey: The Fatal Lozenge is the first one.

Conversations: This would certainly, I would think, characterize you as someone with a bit of a macabre. . . .

Gorey: Well, yes. This was a very early book and at that date I was not above trying to shock everybody a bit.

Conversations: Primarily you just wanted to entertain?

Gorey: I guess so, sure. I don't know, I really. . . . I've always thought this business about audiences and everything is so much something or other.

Conversations: What do you mean?

Gorey: One of the things that's always made me sort of see strange colors is when people would say, "Oh, we've broadened the audience for ballet"; or "Somehow if everybody did this, there would be a bigger audience"; or "We must get to the audiences." Oh, poof. If people want to read something, they will read it. It all just seems to me that one's relations to an audience is absolutely incalculable, and about half of the population spends most of its time sitting around trying to decide what will go in the movies, or what will go on Broadway, or what will go in ballet. I must have seen every movie in New York, and at about 99% of them I think, "Who do they think is going to go to this. What did they think they were doing?" Even the ones where, you know, there's obviously sort of a basic gimmick, like *The Exorcist* kind of thing—movies like *Audrey Rose* and *The Demon Seed.*

Conversations: Do you have an idea who your audience is?

Gorey: Well, I can only go by the people that come up to me. There are obviously a lot of college people and even some high school ones, I think. And I suppose they are more "sophisticated," whatever that may mean.

Conversations: I would think some of the books would be too sophisticated for a high school group.

Gorey: Well, people who have been reading my books for a long time often say they've seen their children around the house with them. I obviously have a certain following with small children. Someone I know said quite seriously that *The Curious Sofa* was their child's favorite book. I don't know what the child thought was going on. Of course, I was a very precocious reader as a child. I learned to read by myself when I was about 3½ or something. I can remember reading *Dracula* when I was about seven, and it scared me to death, but I can't imagine what I was getting out of it. A lot of it must have been totally over my head. I remember reading all the novels of Victor Hugo when I was about eight, which is more than I can do now. I started trying to read one a couple of years ago. Tedium, dear God. I still remember Victor Hugo being forcefully removed from my tiny hands when I was about eight, so I could eat my supper. They couldn't get me to put him down.

Edward Gorey

Conversations: I'd hate to have to explain The Curious Sofa *to a child.*

Gorey: Well, I would too, but I don't know. . . . Well, any of the other ones for that matter.

Conversations: What book has been your most successful in terms of sales or attention, aside from Amphigorey?

Gorey: Well, I think probably *The Curious Sofa* and *The Hapless Child. The Broken Spoke* apparently has done quite well. And a lot of people said they liked it better than anything I'd done for a long time. That, of course, always makes me instantly nervous.

Conversations: I have the postcard that Dodd, Mead sent out for your party on my bulletin board, and I also have the invitation you drew for a party for Allegra Kent.

Gorey: That was fun. It was held at a place across from Lincoln Center. I guess it's a health club; there's a swimming pool, and I guess it gets rented for various things. But there's the most fantastic view clear over to the New Jersey flats, and the setting sun, and the airport, and the Statue of Liberty. . . just absolutely fantastic.

Conversations: How did you get involved in doing the invitation? Was that just out of friendship?

Gorey: Yes. I know a lot of ballet dancers, but I did not know Allegra Kent. She's always been one of my favorites but I'd never met her. One day my phone rang and this chirpy little voice came over the phone, "Hello, is this Edward Gorey?" I said, "Yes." She said, "This is Allegra Kent." And I thought, "Oh, sure, Honey. Now tell me something new." Anyway it was very ambiguous what she said. She said, "I've done this book on water exercises and I want to send it to you." I thought she was sending me manuscripts because she wanted me to illustrate them or whatever. So I was sort of startled by this, because I have always worshipped at her shrine. Then I thought: "This is the kind of joke that people usually pull on people." I was talking to somebody a day or so later and I said, "Oh, listen. I had the goofiest phone call a couple of days ago." I told them about it. They said, "Oh, that was Allegra. That's very Allegra." Indeed,

148

about a week later the book arrived. Then she started sending me notes and things. She does things like write a note and then stitch it up inside a paper bag and mail it. I was just crazed, but it was very amusing. And I got a letter from Washington, and she said, "Would you, could you possibly do a drawing for the invitation for a party being given for the book?" And I said, "Oh, sure I'd love to." So finally I met her. Funny—I ran into her on the street one day and said, "Oh, listen, Allegra, I think it's time we met."

The party was very strange. There were very few people from the ballet there, like five people. I had gotten invited on the strength of having done the invitations and stuff. Anyway, everybody was standing around, and I said in one of my best loud flippant voices, "Who are all these people, do you suppose?" There was this middle-aged lady, whose husband came up and said, "Oh, well, listen, we're old friends of Allegra's." I made it worse: I said, "Well, I didn't mean *you*." But everybody looked very odd.

Conversations: Ms. Kent's book is about exercise in water.

Gorey: Yeah. You put on these little, tiny water wings, which you clamp on to your wrists and your ankles, and you overcome gravity. She gave us a demonstration in the pool. The pool was filled with camellias stapled to water lily petals. Somebody told me later that a favorite thing to do was to staple camellias to water lily petals and float them on the water. Oh, dear.

Conversations: Are you doing more book jackets now? I notice you did Michael Stewart's novel, Belle, *didn't you?*

Gorey: Yes. The book's quite good. I thought it was extremely entertaining and very sinister. It's kind of like a really evil version of *Auntie Mame.*

Conversations: Do these dust jackets come to you from the publishers?

Gorey: Well, Michael Stewart got in touch with me because he didn't like the original jacket they put on the book and was willing to pay for another one. I didn't know him but he liked my

Edward Gorey

work. I haven't for a while, but I used to do book jackets a lot. I don't do them as a rule.

Conversations: How many languages do you speak?

Gorey: I don't speak any. I majored in French at Harvard, but my French is absolutely atrocious.

Conversations: Some of your limericks are in French.

Gorey: But they are very inaccurate. Edmund Wilson castigated me wildly for them. He was always castigating me for my prose. That's why when I finally dedicated a book to him, it had no text. I thought, "That will fix you, Edmund. Now what will you be able to say?"

Conversations: Did he castigate you in a review?

Gorey: No, no. The poor man did that one piece on me in *The New Yorker* once after I had had only four books published, and everybody's been quoting from it ever since. He was a very sweet man. He always intimidated me terrifically. I finally first met him at a New Year's Eve party when we both got wedged behind the same sofa. I don't hear very well in noisy places, so I couldn't hear most of what he was saying. He was very formidable anyway, though very nice. And the last time I saw him at the Princeton Club, deafness had ensued for all of us. I was trying to figure out what he was saying; and he was trying to figure out what I was saying; both of us were trying to figure out what the third person present was saying. This was not too long before he died.

Conversations: Do your books get attention?

Gorey: In a word, no, very seldom. Occasionally somebody will write a brief review. *Amphigorey* got noticed.

Conversations: Right.

Gorey: *The New Yorker* once reviewed, I think, *The Vinegar Works*, and made some nasty remark on the strength of the title. That was all I needed from them. They've never mentioned me since.

Conversations: Does that bother you?

Gorey: No. I always think it is nice when one finds one's name mentioned in passing, so to speak. Because if everybody knows who you are, I feel that's the greatest compliment you could get. Not that it happens very often; I could count the number of times. I remember once Edith Oliver at *The New Yorker* said that somebody looked exactly like Edward Gorey's drawings. Also in *The New Yorker* somebody in a brief review said something like, "He was one of the connecting links between someone-someone and Edward Gorey and somebody or other." As I say, it happens very seldom.

Conversations: Did Putnam's anticipate the attention that would be given to Amphigorey, *the first big collection?*

Gorey: Well, Mr. Targ, I'm sure, would say that he did. You know, I had resisted ever having any of my stuff reprinted.

Conversations: If it goes out of print, it goes out of print.

Gorey: That was my first decision in the publishing world: If it goes out of print, it goes out of print. Now I kept getting these poignant little letters from fifteen-year-old children in Kansas saying, "Oh, I just spent $45 for a first edition." Then all of a sudden Mr. Targ approached me and said, "Can we do an anthology?" I thought, "Oh, well, what the hell." I still haven't allowed any individual reprints or anything. And that's funny because I have this Swiss publisher, Diogenes, and they publish me a lot. They publish me both in German and English, depending. So in a sense some of my books have been reprinted individually. And then they offer me these little amounts of money.

Conversations: That's always nice.

Gorey: Yes.

Conversations: Addison-Wesley is reprinting three books that you have illustrated.

Gorey: Which, you know, I was very much against. But I couldn't really figure a good reason for saying no. I like it in a sense, because I always liked those drawings I did for Lear. That was one of the few things that I had done that I wanted to do. It was my idea to do. I am under contract to Mr. Targ to do *Alice in*

Edward Gorey

Wonderland, if I ever get around to it, which I feel is going to be, God knows, a major project, because I would like first to do all the poems in the books as miniature books almost. Instead of just say one drawing for "Jabberwocky," I would like to illustrate it as a complete, you know. . .

Conversations: Entity unto itself.

Gorey: Yes. Then, there will be the total trauma because it was one of the first books I ever read. I think it's probably been an enormous influence on me which I don't even recognize at this point. I know it so well, having read it so often. And the Tenniel illustrations are practically sacred. Actually, I don't think I would have agreed to do it, but I saw one of those books—it was kind of a compilation of various other illustrators of the Alice books. I hadn't realized how many people had tried it and how awful many were. Some are just unbelievably awful. Mervyn Peake did one back in the late forties, I think, which I was quite an admirer of. It was very much different from the Tenniel, but I realized that somebody else could do the Alice and make it valid. I so hated those Ralph Steadman drawings I couldn't. . . . Why he decided to take on the Alice, I don't know. But I thought probably I would also like to illustrate more Lear sometime.

Conversations: But primarily you want to continue doing your own sort of book?

Gorey: Yeah.

Conversations: Have you written any books that are all text?

Gorey: *The Black Doll.*

Conversations: What is the origin of The Black Doll?

Gorey: Oh, well, I was hoping to make it into a movie sometime. It was very seriously intended as a movie. I tend to drift my way through existence, and if I had decided to direct myself a little more than I ever did, I think I probably would have worked in the theatre more. I was connected with this thing called The Poets Theatre of Cambridge while I was at Harvard and afterwards. I loved it. It was kind of a goofy amateur theatre where we all did the very arty plays, and so forth. It was great fun,

152

but when I came to New York I didn't particularly care for the equivalent of it. Nobody has ever asked me to do anything particular, so. . . .

Conversations: Do you think The Black Doll *will ever be produced?*

Gorey: I don't know. There's a very nice young man who is not terribly professional about the whole thing, I don't think, but who has had an option on it now for two years.

Conversations: That takes it out of the market for somebody else to do it.

Gorey: Well, if I ever get the rights back, I think I'll just hang on to it and see if maybe I could do it myself.

Conversations: How long a film would it be?

Gorey: I think it would probably be short. I have a friend who directs soap operas and things like that for TV. At one point we actually made a half-hour movie which is still sitting in a vault somewhere. Somehow we ran out of impetus. The film is all made; it was all cut; we edited it; we had everything but our finally corrected print of it and the work print got lost. The master negative is still in the vault. I sometimes think of dredging it out to see what it looks like. This was all about ten years—a little more than ten years ago.

Conversations: Did your love of the performing arts induce you to write The Black Doll?

Gorey: I don't know. I was working on *The Black Doll* while we were making this half-hour movie. Now the cost for everything has gone up to such an extent. I would still like to do it sometime. The trouble is that I have delusions of grandeur in the sense that I would like to design it, direct it, the whole schmeer.

Conversations: Why not?

Gorey: Well, why not, indeed. Except that I don't have the rights anymore. If the certain man that has it now. . . . I don't think it's probably going to get off the ground ever. He's one of those people who has lots of money, but doesn't want to put up his own money and hasn't found somebody else to do so.

153

Edward Gorey

Conversations: Why did you publish some books under a pseudonym?

Gorey: I wanted to publish everything under a pseudonym from the very beginning, but everybody said, "What for?" And I couldn't really explain why I wanted to. I still don't know exactly, except that I think what you publish and what you are are two different things. I don't really see that much connection.

Robert Hayden was born in Detroit, Michigan, on 4 August 1913.
After a very early interest in poetry, he published his first volume,
Heart-Shape in the Dust in 1940. In 1941 Hayden entered graduate
school at the University of Michigan, where he studied under W. H.
Auden. He began a twenty-two-year teaching position at Fisk
University in 1946. There he initiated the Counterpoise series, which
commenced with The Lion and the Archer *by Hayden and Myron*
O'Higgins (1948) and included Figures of Time *(1955). In 1966 his*
Selected Poems were published. In 1976 Mr. Hayden took a leave of
absence from his teaching duties at the University of Michigan to
serve as poetry consultant to the Library of Congress. He is the first
Afro-American ever to hold that position.

Robert Hayden

*Robert Hayden was interviewed on 7 May 1977 at his hotel room in
Columbia, South Carolina, at the Carolina Town House by Richard
Layman. Mr. Hayden was in Columbia to receive an honorary
degree from Benedict College. The interview took place in the
evening at the end of a very long and trying day for the poet. He
had very graciously consented to spend an extra evening in
Columbia to be interviewed for* Conversations.

*Conversations: I heard a story recently about a high school
student in Columbia, a boy who had written a poem that was
going to be included in his class anthology. He said, "Yes, you
can use it, but don't use my name. My daddy would kill me if he
knew I was writing poetry."*

Hayden: Oh, yeah, yeah.

*Conversations: You have said that your family was poor and
hardworking, with no education, but that they sacrificed and
helped you to go to college. How did they feel about your choice
of profession?*

Hayden: Well, they certainly didn't interfere with it. They didn't
understand too well what I was doing, but they wanted me to get
an education. They wanted me to use my talent in some way, and
they never objected to my writing poetry. They didn't know very
much about it, as I say. They knew that I wanted to be a writer,
and they never objected to it. They were concerned that I find
some sort of work to support myself and all that. But there was
never any difficulty at home about my writing.

*Conversations: When did you decide that you were going to be a
poet? Sounds like you started quite early.*

Hayden: I did start quite early. I learned to read before I went to
public school, and I began trying to write poems and stories and

plays while I was down in the grades. I told about this the other night in my talk at the Library of Congress. I remember that when I was in the grades the teacher gave us a list of words for spelling and told us to put the words into sentences. I made up a story out of the words instead of just putting them into sentences. When I was in what was called in those days intermediate school, which today we call junior high school, I was trying to write poetry. By the time I got into high school I felt that I wanted to be a poet, and I was devoting all my time to it. I was reading poetry all the time and trying to write it, not knowing very much about it and not really having too much encouragement, but feeling very deeply that I wanted to write in that way, that I wanted to write poetry.

Conversations: Was there a place to publish in your high school?

Hayden: I had a short story in the school annual, and I had a brief sketch in the school paper. In both instances, they were not poetry. But I did have work in the school annual and the school paper.

Conversations: So when you went to college, you knew what you were going to major in; you knew what you were going to do?

Hayden: Well, yes and no to that. I wasn't quite sure about myself as a poet. I loved poetry, and I was trying to write it and always was reading it. But if I must be honest, I didn't have the kind of faith in myself that other young people seemed to have had. Certainly the student poets that I work with all have faith in themselves, and I didn't have that kind of faith. But I did like English, and I had done very well in English courses in high school. When I went to college, interestingly enough, I majored in foreign languages, with a minor in English. I had poems in the college paper. I went to what was then the Detroit City College; later it became Wayne State University. I had poems in the school paper and I came to be known as a poet. I never had any courses in creative writing as an undergraduate student.

Conversations: Were they available?

Hayden: There was just one, as I recall. Somehow or other my schedule never permitted me to take that one course in creative writing. But I did do some writing in my freshman composition courses and in other English courses. Though it wasn't poetry, the instructors thought I showed talent, and occasionally I would read a paper in front of the class, you know, that kind of thing.

Conversations: You said you were reading a lot. What were you reading, do you recall?

Hayden: Well, as a child I read, I suppose, mostly the things that most children read. Even though my family was poor and completely uneducated—that is my foster parents; my foster parents reared me—my own mother had an interest in books and so on. She was living in Buffalo, and from time to time she would send me books. I remember she sent me *Black Beauty*, the story of a horse, and *Beautiful Joe*, the story of a cur. Strangely enough, I read *Uncle Tom's Cabin* and I read *Robinson Crusoe*.

Later on, when I was in high school, I was in the sight conservation class because my sight was so very poor that I was taken out of the regular homeroom and put into this very special homeroom where our reading was supervised. We were not permitted to read small type, and we wrote on manila sheets of paper and used big, thick pencils—to this day I'm addicted to big, thick, black pencils and so on. But one of my sight-saving teachers used to read my assignments in English to me, and I remember that we were to read a book and report on it. I chose George Eliot's *Romola*. That had a tremendous influence on me, remember I was in high school. In the first place, I learned words that I had never known before. To this day I can remember how intrigued I was with the word "loggia," and the names of things, like the "Ponte Vecchio," and so on. I lived in that book; I just loved it.

And then later on—I guess I was out of high school or in my last year, I've forgotten—I read Hawthorne's *The Marble Faun*; and I read *The Last Days of Pompeii*; and I read Papini's *The Story of Christ*; I read *Toby Tyler, or Ten Days at the Circus*. And those books stayed with me. Hawthorne's *The Marble Faun*—I've tried to read it since; I tried to read it several years ago and I didn't get very far with it. But I was about seventeen or eighteen when I read those books.

Robert Hayden

Again I lived in *The Marble Faun*; I thought it was a marvelous thing—the atmosphere and the poetry in the novel and the mystery that Hawthorne worked out there in which one of the characters looks like Donatello's *Marble Faun*. He doesn't have the pointed ears like the marble faun and maybe he is, if not evil, at least amoral or something. Well, that and *The Last Days of Pompeii*. I loved those books, partly because they took me completely out of the environment that I lived in, and they appealed to my imagination, because they were full of strange and wonderful things that I'd had no direct experience with.

Conversations: Brendan Gill has said he thought that all of a man's reading was done by the time he was thirty; that is, all the reading that would influence his development.

Hayden: Well, I don't know whether I agree with that entirely. I've read books after that period that meant a great deal to me. I think some of Henry James's novels, particularly the nouvelles, like *The Aspern Papers* and *The Turn of the Screw*. Those meant a great deal to me, also. But I think I know what Brendan Gill means: that the books you read before you're thirty have a different kind of influence upon you, different from the influence that books after that have on you, because they help somehow to shape your sensibilities. They help somehow to stimulate your imagination. In a sense they help to form, perhaps, your aesthetic sense, and they help to form the particular kind of creative mind-set that you're going to have later on. So maybe that's true.

Conversations: Who were the poets that you thought highly of in that period?

Hayden: Oh, well, in that period, I think that I could certainly name them right off. Countee Cullen, whom I read with almost bated breath. I just thought he was one of the greatest poets that I'd ever heard of. And Carl Sandburg and Edna Millay and—oh, about the time I was ready to go to college, Elinor Wylie and Orrick Johns; some of these poets are completely forgotten now. Orrick Johns and Langston Hughes and the whole—I discovered the poets of the Harlem Renaissance quite by accident. I remember going through the library and getting the

160

volume edited by Alain Locke called *The New Negro*. I discovered those poets and I went to the library and got individual volumes by each of them.

I could say that in that period, oh, when I was about ready to go to college—after high school there was an interim period when I didn't have the money to go to college and I was just hoping and, you know, trying various things, odd jobs now and then, but mostly reading and trying to be a poet—at that time I'd go to the library and get out all the anthologies, and I just knew everybody almost. But the poets I've mentioned I think were my favorites. Of course, I haven't mentioned Lola Ridge—Lola Ridge, who wrote *Firehead* and a book of poems called *Dance of Fire*, and *Ghetto*, and *Sun-Up* and so on. I discovered her about that time. I read *Firehead* and thought it was one of the great poems.

Conversations: From what you've said you seem to have had a taste in nineteenth-century romantic novels and contemporary 1920s poetry.

Hayden: Yes.

Conversations: That seems a strange mixture.

Hayden: It was a strange mixture. I did read some twentieth-century novels in the period we're speaking of. I read the chief popular stuff. I loved Sax Rohmer. I read the Fu Manchu stories.

Conversations: Edgar Wallace?

Hayden: No, not so much Edgar Wallace. I read Sax Rohmer's Fu Manchu, that was my great. . . I obviously, see, have always had this feeling for the exotic, without really being conscious of it. And I used to read all the Fu Manchu I could get my hands on. Then, of course, I read a couple of volumes of the Tom Swift stories, and I read Langston Hughes; of course, I was in college then. I read Langston Hughes's *Not Without Laughter*. I don't think the novel has been reprinted, but it was a novel about a woman who became a well-known blues singer and so on. And I read Carl Van Vechten's *Nigger Heaven*, and things like that. But I tended to read poetry for the most part.

Robert Hayden

Oh, I must tell you this which will surprise you. While I don't seem to have read a great many novels, I became interested in Eugene O'Neill. And I read everything; I read everything. I remember so well O'Neill's *Mourning Becomes Electra* coming to Detroit, and how I longed to go and see that play. And before that time *Strange Interlude* had come to Detroit. I simply didn't have the money to go and see either of those plays, but I had read them. I'd go to the library and just get out all of Eugene O'Neill and read them. I don't know what kind of influence it had on me, but I did go through an O'Neill period.

Conversations: You said you thought of yourself as a poet. Did you have any contact at all with professional poets, published poets?

Hayden: No, not until I met Langston Hughes.

Conversations: When was that?

Hayden: I met him in the thirties. I guess I was still in college. I have a good memory, but today dates are eluding me. But this was in the thirties when I met Langston Hughes. He was the first recognized poet I ever met. He had come to Detroit to see a production of one of his plays that a dramatic group in Detroit was putting on. I was in the play, and I asked the director Elsie Rocksboro, who was a close friend of Langston Hughes, to arrange for me to meet him. And she did. We had lunch together and I did what young poets always do; I showed him some of my poems. He wasn't terribly enthusiastic. He thought that they were too much like other people's poems, which I'm sure they were at that time. And he pointed out that I needed to find my own voice; I needed to find something. I needed to work and find what my own voice was and do something that was more individual, because some of my poems were too like those of other poets. I was a little crestfallen, I guess, but I was very excited to meet this poet, who at that time was, you know, very famous and sort of glamorous. We read about him traveling all over the world, and he was having plays produced, and he had been one of the bright stars of the Harlem Renaissance; so it was really quite exciting to meet him. Then when I went to Harlem— after I was married, my wife and I went to Harlem one summer.

Conversations: About when was that?

Hayden: This was 1940. No, it was 1941; it was the second year of our marriage. She was studying music at Juilliard, and her uncle had been in college with Countee Cullen. So Erma called Mr. Cullen. He remembered her, because he had known her when she was a very young person, and he invited us to come out and visit him. Again I was enthralled, because I had read all of Countee Cullen's poetry, and I was delighted to meet him. I remember that he was very affable, and he was interested in me. There was a poem of mine that he liked—I had had a book published by this time. There's a poem in my early book *Heart-Shape in the Dust* that's called "The Falcon," and he wanted me to read it. He had a copy of the book—maybe I had sent it to him or took him one, I've forgotten now. And I read "The Falcon." I was very flattered to think that he wanted, you know, to hear a poem from me.

We didn't talk very much about writing poetry, about the craft of poetry or anything of the kind. It was really a social evening. The widow and the sister of Rudolph Fisher were also at Countee Cullen's house, and there was some talk about the Harlem Renaissance and the Negro movement. I recall that Cullen wanted my wife to play a Chopin etude. My wife is a pianist, and she did. It was a pleasant evening. Afterwards when I looked back on it I felt that it had been awfully genteel, you know, really very genteel. But it was a chance to meet Countee Cullen, and that was the first and only time that I saw him. I heard from him after that, but I didn't see him anymore before his death.

Conversations: Heart-Shape in the Dust was published in 1940.

Hayden: That's right.

Conversations: How did that come about?

Hayden: Well, that was a local venture.

Conversations: The Falcon Press?

Hayden: The Falcon Press, yes. Louie Martin was the editor of the Negro weekly, *The Michigan Chronicle.* I was working part-time on the newspaper and he became interested. He knew that I wrote poetry and he had a certain amount of faith in me, so he decided that he would bring out a book. He told me to get my work together and he'd publish it, and he did. He organized a little company called The Falcon Press, and he brought out *Heart-Shape in the Dust* in 1940. It was what you would imagine: it was the work of a young poet. Of course, I wasn't all that young when it was published, to be sure; what was I, about twenty-seven or so. But it was the work of a young poet, and there are echoes of other poets in it. It was full of, you know, protest poems, and it was full of poems that were primarily concerned with racial themes. It did quite well. The book seemed to move, and today I understand that people are willing to pay, oh, five or six dollars for a copy of it.

Conversations: Five or six?

Hayden: Well, maybe more, because you see at that time back in 1940, I think it was something like $1.50. Some people have advertised for copies and I think perhaps it's worth more than five or six dollars today. I threatened at one time to round up all the copies that were extant and burn them, but I haven't done that. But *Heart-Shape in the Dust* was a young poet's work, and it did get some serious attention. I remember it got a small review in the old *New York Herald Tribune*. People who knew poetry seemed to know something about it. There are several people now who are writing doctoral dissertations or studies of one kind or another on my poetry. They all go back to that book, and they try to assure me that it's not as bad as I think it is.

Conversations: At that time were you teaching at the University of Michigan?

Hayden: No. At that time I was on the Writers' Project. When I got married in 1940, I had been on the Writers' Project for a couple of years. I was doing various things; I was sort of doing part-time work at the *Michigan Chronicle* office, and by 1940 I was trying very hard to be a writer. I felt myself to be a poet and was trying to write and trying to learn as much as I could about it. I left the Writers' Project and went on to another project, the Historical Record Survey, and I was fired from that because the

W.P.A. projects were winding up and they were getting rid of people; so I found myself without a job. My wife was teaching in the Detroit public school system and she, being rather advanced in her thinking, didn't see why I shouldn't, since I didn't have a job, stay home and write and not worry about it. But oh, I couldn't do that. I was just worried sick because I didn't have a job. But in 1941 we decided that we would leave Detroit and I would go back to the University of Michigan and get my master's degree. And so by 1940 I was married and I had a book published, and then the next year I went to the University of Michigan.

That's when I met my third poet, and that was W. H. Auden. He was teaching at the university; he was teaching a course in the analysis of poetry. He was accepting a few students and I was able to get into his class. That was a marvelous experience. Yes, he was eccentric and odd, but I sort of cherished that. I'm really becoming more and more alarmed by the fact that so many poets now are good academicians in gray flannel suits. But Auden certainly wasn't like that. He was a little awe-inspiring. We all had read his books, you know. We knew that he was brilliant.

When his class began I remember the first day sitting in class really frightened, because I thought, "If he calls on me what will I say?" He was absolutely brilliant. He would quote poems in the original German, and he would quote Latin verses—the range of his learning, the breadth of his knowledge was just extraordinary. He really did inspire us in a sense. His teaching I guess was pretty... oh, he would never have won any prizes for pedagogy. But somehow or other he stimulated us to learn more about poetry and even to search ourselves. He made us aware of other literatures, and he made us aware of poetry in a way that we never would have been had it not been for him.

So it was a marvelous experience and, of course, I had a few pleasant personal experiences with him. He read some of my poems. There were some that he liked very much, and some he didn't like at all. The ones he liked he said were poems that were like algebra, in which you were solving for X. He said that was always the best kind of poetry, whereas there were other poems that were like arithmetic: You add them up and get the sum and that's all there is to it. In the other kind of poetry you have to work; you have to try to find the unknown; you have to work for it and so on. I have remembered that ever since he said it.

He came to see my daughter when she was born. Of course, this was a year or so afterwards—after he had left the campus. But he did drop in to see my daughter. He was eager to see what she looked like, and so he looked down at her in her crib. I've told her, "You must remember always W. H. Auden came to look at you." He helped me to get a job in the library. He was friends with the librarian there, Dr. Rice, who later on was the chairman of the English department, and he spoke to Dr. Rice and he got me a job in the library. He was interested in seeing that I got my poems published. He was a wonderful person. And then years later he and I read together at Columbia University.

Conversations: So you maintained the relationship with him until his death?

Hayden: Not really. We were aware of each other—rather I should put it the other way round, he was sort of aware of me. After I had a New York publisher, the publisher would send him copies of my books. William Meredith has told me, I don't know what the occasion was, that Auden spoke rather warmly of me and said that he hoped that, oh, I don't know, some prize or some fellowship or something would come my way. Of course, later on I guess it did.

I didn't see him for a very, very long time, and then in 1968 or '69, I think it might have been '69, we were asked to read together at the McMillin Theatre at Columbia University. I had heard that he liked the poem of mine in *Selected Poems* published in '67, the poem called "Witch Doctor." So that night at the McMillin Theatre I read "Witch Doctor" for him. I read first, then he read afterwards. And we did have a chance to talk before the program began. We talked about his years at the University of Michigan, and his coming to see my daughter, and so on. But we were by no means close. We didn't keep in touch, but the following year I was invited to his birthday party. I was in New York and I went to, I guess it was, his sixty-fifth birthday party. And that was the last time I saw him alive.

Conversations: You got your master's degree from the University of Michigan and taught at the University of Michigan for two years, before you went to Fisk.

Hayden: Yes. I taught there from—what was it—'44 to '46. I had been a student with advance standing for, oh, two or three years at Michigan, and so I piled up a lot of hours. But it only took me about a year to finish up everything for my master's. And in 1944 I became a teaching fellow in English there.

Conversations: During this time were you publishing in little magazines?

Hayden: Yes. I had a few poems published here and there. In 1942 I won the Hopwood Award for poetry at the University of Michigan. And I had some poems published in magazines. Also in about 1946 I had a poem, "Middle Passage," which now has become a well-known poem, that appeared in Edwin Seaver's *Cross Section*. And then I had a poem in *The Atlantic Monthly* in the forties, "Frederick Douglass," which is the other poem that's become very well known. I didn't have a great many poems appearing in magazines. I didn't have all that much time to write. I was a teaching fellow and I had all sorts of responsibilities and so on, and that cut into my writing time.

But I've always had to struggle to write. I've always found it difficult to keep my teaching going and keep my other responsibilities going and write too. I've really had to struggle to get anything out. I think it's partly due to the kind of temperament that I've had. I guess maybe I had so much struggle in my life that. . . I don't know how to say it. Most of the writers that I admire are able to rise above difficulties of one kind or another. Yet, I always find it very hard to, you know, carry on and keep my work going if other things are on my mind, or if I have other obligations. So that has been a problem for me.

Conversations: You said in an interview in World Order *magazine that was published about a year ago that you're a poet who teaches in order to earn a living so that he can write a poem now and then. Sounds like you resent teaching.*

Robert Hayden

Hayden: Oh, I don't resent teaching, but I don't love it. I never have loved it, and I've always been a good teacher. I'm a very conscientious teacher and also I care about my students. I try to give them a full measure. But I feel always in conflict, partly because until recently I've had to teach rather heavy loads. There was a time in my life when I was teaching fifteen, sixteen hours a semester and trying to write. And, you know, it was almost impossible to live as a poet. So I don't know, maybe I do resent teaching. I know that William James admitted that he had never liked teaching, though he had been an excellent teacher. I would just say that I've always found it difficult, and it has always caused conflicts. I've tried to do an honest job. I've never shortchanged the students in order to do my own work. But there has always been a great conflict between my academic chores and my own creative life.

Conversations: When you went to Fisk was it as far from Detroit to Nashville as it would seem?

Hayden: Indeed, it was. When I went to Fisk, I had never lived in the South. I had had very little experience with the South. And when I went to Fisk in 1946, I knew that a brand new chapter in my life was beginning and that I was in for an experience or experiences which I had never had before. My first couple of years there were extremely difficult for my wife and for me, and I can't say that we adjusted. We never did adjust to it. I think it would have been a mistake to adjust to it, but we came to know how to handle it. We found that it was possible to form relationships with people of goodwill who did not have the traditional prejudices. And we found people interested in the arts, people interested in music, and in dance and poetry and so on. And this made a difference.

But we had many difficulties there, because, first of all, we didn't want our daughter to go to a segregated school. We had never gone to one and we didn't want her beginning her education under those circumstances. What we did, of course, was rather drastic. My wife took her to New York, and we put her in a progressive school. My wife was interested in working with modern dance as an accompanist and so on, and even toured with the dance company. I think that if it was a blessing, it was a very mixed blessing. Eventually we found that being a divided family was no good for any of us. I went to New York for a year—I took leave from Fisk and went to New York for a year. Then at the end of that year, we came back to Nashville, and my daughter went to the regular public school.

Conversations: Was it segregated?

Hayden: Yes, yes. It was segregated. But we felt that—well, two things were influential there. One was that we felt that a great deal of harm was being done by—to her—by the fact that we were a divided family. She didn't quite understand it, you know, at first.

Conversations: How old was she?

Hayden: Oh, she was, what, four, five, something like that. And we also felt when we brought her back that she had some background and we could certainly offset some of the harm that might be done to her in the segregated schools. That was a very, very difficult time for us.

Conversations: Sounds as if you've paid a rather heavy price, emotional and otherwise, to. . .

Hayden: Indeed, we did.

Conversations: To teach at Fisk. Why?

Hayden: Well, for one thing it was very difficult to find a position in another university. Also, I'll go back to this point later, I think I felt that there was a certain amount of good that I could do at Fisk. I found, of course, that Fisk was a pretty sophisticated school and there was certainly nothing. . . well, it wasn't a backwoods institution, let us say. But I think, perhaps, I felt that I could be of some service to the young people there. The other point that I just touched on a moment ago is that in the forties and fifties it was very difficult for an Afro-American to move from one of the schools in the South to a school like Michigan or Harvard or Yale. It's much easier now, but at that time it was very, very difficult. I was at one point in my life considered for a teaching position at the University of Chicago. I was even invited to the university to talk with the various deans—I've forgotten now just what the setup there was. And I was hoping that I was going to get out of the South, you see, and go to teach at the University of Chicago. But it didn't happen. It was very difficult in those days for us to move from the Afro-American schools into the other schools, and that was one reason that we stayed where we were. Jobs were hard to come by.

Conversations: When you were first describing the move from Detroit to Nashville you kept referring to "it," the pressures of the "it." What did you mean by "it"? More than simple prejudice, I assume.

Hayden: Oh, well, yes. It was certainly the racial situation which in Nashville wasn't as bad as it was in some other places in the South, but it was bad enough. The buses were segregated; the schools were segregated; drinking fountains were segregated; and so on. Fisk was kind of an oasis and in the Fisk area, in the Fisk neighborhood, one didn't encounter too much prejudice. As a matter of fact black and white faculty members lived in the same neighborhood and socialized together and so on, and our children played together and all that kind of thing. But the racial situation in the South was of paramount importance to us because it did pretty much limit us: limit the kind of experiences that we could have, limit the kind of things that we could do, limit opportunities in every single way. There was a time, for example, when I never went to movies in the South, because in order to go to the movie you had to enter the theater through an alley and then go up and sit in what we used to call the buzzard's roost, a Jim Crow balcony. So I never went to the movies in Nashville. And even some stores downtown were unpleasant to shop in. The clerks would call Afro-American people by their first names, whether they really knew them or not. And it wasn't out of a gesture of friendliness, it was a way of telling us that we were not on the same level with the other customers.

And then, too, there was a kind of provincialism in the South. People tended to entertain themselves at home to socialize, not to be so much aware of the larger world, not to be so much interested in, oh, the things that we cared about—modern art, and modern dance, and all this kind of thing. There wasn't so much interest in that. Going to live there meant that we had to. . . we experienced something different from what we had had in the North.

Conversations: You stayed at Fisk quite a long time, twenty years.

Hayden: Yeah, more than twenty years, just about twenty-two years.

Conversations: What was your role there? Were you a poet-in-residence or were you. . . .

Hayden: Not at all, no. I guess I started out as assistant professor of English, and then I became an associate, and then about the time I was ready to leave, I became a full professor. And I taught eighteenth-century literatures and I taught creative writings and I taught Afro-American literatures and I taught all sorts of things. I was advisor to the student publication, *The Herald.* I worked rather closely with young people who were writing and who were members of my creative writing class, and who were working on *The Herald.* Later on I worked with the Fisk newspaper, *The Fawn.* I was a regular member of the English department and I did what instructors in English would do.

Conversations: Your second book of poetry, The Lion and the Archer, *was published right after you came to Nashville.*

Hayden: Yes. I had a Rosenwald Fellowship, and while I was on fellowship I worked on that book with Myron O'Higgins and it was kind of a—it was a far cry, I think, from *Heart-Shape in the Dust.* I was trying to write in a way that I had not written before.

Conversations: What way is that?

Hayden: Oh, I can't really describe it. I did go through a period in the forties that I call my Baroque period, a period in which my poems were rather heavily ornamented. But I shouldn't say ornamented, because ornamentation sort of connotes the idea that you don't really need it, you know, that it's something that you can do without. But I'll tell you, the kind of imagery and the kind of texture that I tried to create in my poems was different and was what I call Baroque. It was more involved, for one thing, and more heavily symbolic, I think, too. I lean toward symbolism

171

Robert Hayden

anyway. I guess I was trying to work toward something more or less metaphysical, and I was trying to get away from the straight-forward. . . well, I guess I was trying to get away from protest and from poems that were pretty much restricted in theme to racial matters.

Conversations: This seems a bit odd, too, in light of what you've just said about the shock of moving to Nashville.

Hayden: Well, I wanted to—as a matter of fact, I did write about the South, and I did write my reactions to it. But I guess I wanted to approach those things as an artist and not as a propagandist, because by this time I had really begun to change in the way I approached these racial matters. I'm just repeating myself, but I guess I'll have to so I can get on to the next point. I wanted to deal with the new experiences; I wanted to, and I wanted to exteriorize and objectify for myself my feeling and so on. But, by this time I was trying to do it, as I say, as a poet and not as a propagandist. The technique or the how was as important to me as the what, you know, or the subject matter.

Conversations: The book was published by the Counterpoise Press. How did it come about?

Hayden: Well, Counterpoise was a group endeavor. Some of my students and I got together and decided that we wanted to do something to encourage creative writing at Fisk, and we also wanted to encourage Afro-American writers in general. Again, we wanted to get away from the blatantly propagandistic, and we wanted to get away from the out-and-out protest poem, and we were trying in a sense to make an opportunity for ourselves. Again, this is the forties, and it seemed to me that in the forties there was a great deal going on in the arts, but Afro-Americans, unlike today, were being pretty much ignored. We wanted to do something a little different and encourage one another to do something that was a little off the beaten track. We wanted to encourage people to get away from the obvious poetry that dealt with race and so on. And we wanted to encourage the avant-garde and the experimental—not, of course, that we did it, but we did launch our little movement with the publication of *The Lion and the Archer*. And that's really what the Counterpoise is all about.

We published a little statement; we published a little manifesto. I've forgotten most of the things that we said, but we did get some attention. Sterling Brown wrote a critical article that appeared in one of the Afro-American journals about Counterpoise and *The Lion and the Archer* quite awhile after the series was launched. We wanted to bring out a series of booklets that would be published more or less on a subscription basis. We didn't get too far with it, because it was never all that well worked out.

We published two or three booklets and then we didn't publish anymore. I guess we published four altogether, because as late as '67, or thereabouts, I brought out a group of Margaret Danner's poems, a little collection called *To Flower*, and I called it Counterpoise. I suppose if I were ever to publish another little pamphlet of poems for anybody I'd call it Counterpoise, you know, six or seven or whatever it is. I like the name, and also the idea of encouraging the experimental and the avant-garde still appeals to me. But that's how Counterpoise came about: a group of us got together and sort of drew up a little manifesto. We raised a little money to publish the first booklet and then after that, I guess, I paid for all of them.

Conversations: Your next book of poetry was Figures of Time, *again published in Nashville, this time by Hemphill Press in 1955.*

Hayden: Well, that's still in the Counterpoise series, though.

Conversations: Oh, is it?

Hayden: Yes, that was the third. By that time Counterpoise was not—we had never had a very definite structure and all that, but by this time Counterpoise was the name I was giving to a series of things that I hoped to publish and so on. And the Hemphill Press had done them from the very first. The Hemphill Press was the name—or is, they're still in existence—the name of the printers. They were terribly interested in what we were doing and they used to work with me on designing the booklets and getting the special kinds of paper and all the rest of it, because I've always been crazy about beautifully printed books. And these booklets were rather nicely done. We designed them very carefully with the assistance of the Hemphills.

Robert Hayden

Conversations: By this time it seems that you certainly had a considerable influence on your students. What was your influence on American poetry?

Hayden: Oh, none, almost none. Somebody came to Fisk to give a lecture once and said to me, "You have the best underground reputation of any poet in America." And I said, "I wish it would surface," you know, "I wish it would surface." Yes, by this time I had had poems in anthologies and I had won a Rosenwald Fellowship and I had gotten the Ford Foundation Grant for traveling and writing in Mexico. And I had had poems in anthologies that Langston Hughes and Arna Bontemps brought out. I had bits and pieces scattered here and there, and I had the Counterpoise booklets. But it was a long, long time before I could get a publisher interested in a regulation-sized book of poetry.

And at this time people knew that I was a poet. As I say, I had come to be known, to some extent. I didn't get very many readings. My students didn't care all that much about it. Some of them in my creative writing courses were sort of interested that I was a poet. But, you know, I was first of all their teacher, and they didn't even think that I had the real sensibilities and all of a poet. They really didn't. Maybe one or two did, but for the most part, I was their instructor, and occasionally maybe I wrote poetry. As a matter of fact, years after I had left Fisk some of my students said, "Well, you know, I really was surprised after I left Fisk when I heard about you. I was really surprised to know that you really were a serious poet." You see, your students don't. . . . I was working at this time and writing as much as I could and when I could. And I had received some recognition, but I was still kind of struggling to establish myself as a poet.

Conversations: Your next book was published in London. That seems odd.

Hayden: Well, that was *A Ballad of Remembrance*. My work was known abroad and there was a lovely, lovely person Rosey Pool—who's now dead—a Dutch woman, who had done a great deal of work in American Negro poetry. As a matter of fact, I guess back in the twenties, maybe, when she was a student at a Dutch university, she had been doing research and writing papers, you see, on Afro-American poetry. During the war, she told us this after she came to the United States for a visit, Afro-American poets were quite well known and their works were read a great deal by people who were involved in the underground struggle against Fascism, because they identified with our freedom struggle here and so on.

Paul Breman originated the Heritage series in England. My book, *A Ballad of Remembrance,* was the first in the series. He was a kind of protege—I guess I shouldn't say that because if Paul Breman hears that he will be mad—but he was a young friend of Rosey Pool's and he was interested in Afro-American poets and poetry. She stimulated his interest, and really what is his appetite, by giving him books to read and so on and so forth. So he became interested and wanted to publish the work of Afro-American poets, and he did so by launching the Heritage series in London in 1962. He aimed to bring out rather beautiful limited editions of the work of poets that he admired. And he brought out quite a few of these. Then ten years later in 1972 he brought out my little book, *The Night-Blooming Cereus.* It was kind of a celebration or commemoration of the tenth anniversary of the Heritage series.

Conversations: I'd like to talk a little bit about the Baha'i faith.

Hayden: Yes.

Conversations: You've said that you're not an organization person and that the only organization that you have much cared about is the Baha'i faith.

Hayden: Yes.

Conversations: When did you convert?

Hayden: I was a Baptist and when I went to Ann Arbor to work with Auden and started working toward my master's, my wife and I met Baha'is on the campus and we went to study groups—that's how you become a Baha'i; you're not born a Baha'i. You are required to learn about the faith, to study it, and then to make up your mind whether you want to be a Baha'i or not. And when we went to Ann Arbor in 1941, we met the Baha'is. My wife went to the study groups more often than I did, and she still does,

175

for that matter. She became a Baha'i first. I made some study of it, and I went to study groups and decided that it was the truth, that it answered a lot of questions that I had never had answers for up to that time. And I became a Baha'i.

Conversations: You're now very much involved with World Order *magazine.*

Hayden: Yes, yes. I'm poetry editor of *World Order* magazine. I don't do as much writing for the magazine as I would like to, but I do some. I'll be working on essays and poems, too, for it. And I'm very happy to be able to do it because one of the attractive features of the Baha'i faith to me as a poet, or would-be poet or whatever, is that in the writings of Bahaullah, the prophet of the faith, it's clearly stated that the work of the artist—and by artist I mean anyone engaged in the art of poetry or whatever—the work of the artist is considered a form of service to mankind and it has spiritual significance. If the work is done with great sincerity and devotion and, of course, with knowledge, you know, then it is considered really a form of worship and a form of service to mankind.

I think that today when so often one gets the feeling that everything is going downhill, that we're really on the brink of the abyss and what good is anything, I find myself sustained in my attempts to be a poet and my endeavor to write because I have the assurance of my faith that this is of spiritual value and it is a way of performing some kind of service. Indeed, I feel that very deeply now—I'm not praising my own poetry; I don't mean that I think my poetry is of all that great a consequence to the world— but what I do mean to say is that there is a certain vision of the world that I have. I believe in the essential oneness of all people and I believe in the basic unity of all religions. I don't believe that races are important; I think that people are important. I'm very suspicious of any form of ethnicity or nationalism; I think that these things are very crippling and are very divisive. These are all Baha'i points of view, and my work grows out of this vision. I have the feeling that by holding on to these beliefs and giving them expression in my work, not always directly—most of the time not directly—at least I'm doing something to prepare, maybe, for a new time, for a new world. And so I guess this is what I mean when I say that maybe I'm doing some sort of service, because at least I'm not going along with the crowds, that is trying to divide and exploit.

Conversations: I was going to ask who you wrote to, who your audience was. I suppose in some ways you just answered that.

Hayden: Yes. For a long time, I guess, I wrote for myself and for a few friends. I have a sort of sense of audience today, because it surprised me to know that my work was so well known throughout the country—I'm not being falsely modest, I really have been surprised to know that it has been read in so many courses in Afro-American literature and in just general English courses throughout the country. I have some sense, I guess, of an audience. I think, really, without being dramatic or, you know, being rhetorical, I guess I write for people, really. I guess I have the feeling that people of discernment, people of goodwill will read the stuff. I don't know.

Conversations: I get the impression that particularly since you left Fisk, and particularly in the last maybe fifteen years or so, that you've become much more a public poet in the sense that you have been serving short terms as poet-in-residence at various places and that you have been doing a good many more readings and that sort of thing. To what extent does that ironically hinder you as a poet? Is it part of a poet's responsibility to make himself personally visible?

Hayden: Up to a point, I think, it's the poet's responsibility, but you've hit on something that is very important. A poet—any artist—but a poet, anybody using words, has to be very careful and not become too public, because what happens, or what has happened to me, is that I found myself in demand for readings. Being at the Library of Congress means that I'm really highly visible. Everybody knows that I'm there, because much was made of it when I was appointed. It was in the *Washington Post* and this paper and that paper, because I was the first Afro-American ever to hold that post. And yes, going as writer-in-residence here or a poet-in-residence there. One has to be very careful that he isn't always up before the public and not having any time at all to write poems. It gets to be very difficult, and I

Robert Hayden

don't think that most poets are content to live on what they did two or three years before. I know I'm not.

I'm at the point now where I have decided to cut down on the number of readings I will give in the coming year and to try to make myself less available for conferences and one thing or another and to get some new work out. I intend this summer to go away, to hole myself up and not be available to anyone, and spend two or three months writing—doing nothing but writing. And next fall I will give a reading in September and then maybe another in the fall, and maybe another in the spring. But I'm going to cut down radically on the number of readings that I give, because you do reach the point where the energy that ought to go into the writing is going into public performances and so on. This can be very upsetting, because two or three years go by and you discover that you've not finished the poems that you had started before. And you just have to draw the line and not be quite so public in order to get some more work done. And yet you can't help feeling—I know I so often feel, you know, what a wonderful thing that people care enough that they ask me to come and read and they want to give me honors and so on. How lovely. Though I don't know whether I deserve it, I appreciate it and so on and so forth. But as in all things you've got to try to work out some kind of happy medium.

Conversations: What are you working on now?

Hayden: Well, I'm doing a series of things. I'm trying to write a long poem on Matthew Henson, the Afro-American explorer who went to the Pole with Robert Peary, and I've got four short sections of it done. And I'm working on various poems. Also I'm trying to get a new book ready—a small book. It's going to be published in a special limited edition. I want something to come out while I'm still at the library as consultant.

Conversations: This will be your first volume since Angle of Descent?

Hayden: Yes. I think it's going to be called *American Journal.*

Conversations: Will it be all new poems?

Hayden: All new poems, yes, all new poems. My regular

publisher, Liveright, wanted me to wait until I had, you know, sixty or sixty-five pages. Liveright, of course, has been very good to me and very kind. I've had good luck with publishers; I don't ever fight with publishers. But my editor there felt that a book of less than, oh, fifty or sixty pages would be something that they could not handle. And so this book will be brought out by one of the small presses.

Conversations: Have you done what you want to have done in terms of your work at this point?

Hayden: Well, yes and no to that. I haven't done as much as I would like to do, but I think I have developed in a way that I wanted to. I think my range is fairly wide; certainly my sympathies are broad and human, you know. Nothing human is foreign to me. I do have some vision of life, some vision of the world now that I didn't have years ago. And I have more opportunities to work. I don't have to prove myself anymore. I don't have to struggle for recognition; I've got that. I still struggle to get the poems out, but that's another kind of struggle. But all in all I'd say that I'm happy for what I've done. But I'm aware that there's much more that I want to do, and there's much more that I can do. I'm hoping that I will be able within the next few years to do more work and get out some of the things that I feel are in me, but I haven't been able to get out up to this point.

Peter Buckley

Mary Welsh Hemingway was born in Minnesota in 1908. After attending Northwestern University she worked on Chicago newspapers before going to the London Daily Express. *At the time she met Ernest Hemingway she was a* Time *reporter in London. They were married in 1946. In 1976 Mrs. Hemingway published her autobiography,* How It Was.

Mary Welsh Hemingway

Mary Welsh Hemingway was interviewed by Matthew J. Bruccoli at her apartment in midtown Manhattan on 28 March 1977. The apartment has superb paintings, acquired by Ernest Hemingway, as well as animal skins and mounted animal heads. The phone rings every few minutes. Mrs. Hemingway served a mixture of coffee and chocolate.

Conversations: You're just back from London where you participated in the launching of How It Was, *the English edition of your book of reminiscences.*

Hemingway: Very good-looking book, too.

Conversations: Did you notice any difference in the English reception of the book as opposed to the American?

Hemingway: Not really, because I was there such a short time doing interviews and several programs on BBC that by the time I left very little had come out. Since then the public relations lady of Weidenfeld and Nicolson has been more than energetic in sending me copies of reviews, and I must say a large majority of the reviews are very generous and kind. While I was there I didn't notice any differences in the reception.

Conversations: It's been roughly a year since publication of the American edition, hasn't it?

Hemingway: No, seven months, and since then, of course, I've been crisscrossing the country. One doesn't write books—not these days. One writes them and then has to go out and sell them, making appearances—especially at something which I was unaware had grown so enormously in the United States, book and author luncheons. Every town in the country seems to give at least one or two a year, and I was invited to a great many of those. Very useful when one has handmade, hand-produced audiences of three to four to five hundred people who are willing to listen to authors talk about their work, which I think is very generous of them.

Conversations: And even buy some copies, which is even better.

Hemingway: Yes.

Conversations: The question that I was leading up to was in the months since the first publication of How It Was, *have you had any postmortem reactions yourself about it: "If I were doing it over I would have put in something else; I would have done it differently; I would have made it bigger; I would have made it smaller?"*

Hemingway: Well, of course, one of the great complaints of most of the reviewers is that there's too much, so perhaps if I were to do it again I would do more cutting. I left out so much that I thought was also interesting, with the assistance of that marvelous editor Mr. Robert Gottlieb of Knopf. We cut a great deal which is sooner or later going to appear in print somewhere else, perhaps magazine articles or something. But I think I would have cut, and I also perhaps would have made a short foreword saying explicitly—rather than indicating in the text but not specifically saying—that this is an attempt to be as accurate as possible about everything, but especially about Ernest as I knew him and observed him. Perhaps I should make a little foreword explaining that. I suppose when you do anything, you can't expect everyone to approve.

Conversations: This was your first book?

Hemingway: First whole book; that is, I had made contributions to various other books. One was published during the war from the London Bureau of *Time* and *Life,* the title of which, if I recall correctly, was *Their Finest Hour.* And then another was published by the Overseas Press Club to celebrate its twenty-fifth anniversary, which was in 1964, and was titled *I Can Tell It Now.* That consisted mostly of pieces by various members of the club which had been written during the war and were censorable or for some reason or other couldn't be published at that time. It's still quite a good book, I think. I was assigned the year 1940, which, of course, was the blitz on London. It was a challenging job, and I had a dandy time doing that particular chapter of the Overseas Press Club book. That's what got me started on this thing of mine. I was having such a good time doing it and then realized there was so much more that I would like to have written but our space was limited.

Conversations: How It Was is a big book, and you say it was even bigger before the manuscript was cut. What was the actual writing span on that? How many months from word one to thirty?

Hemingway: Oh, something like ten years, because I didn't have a contract. I didn't have any sort of deadline at all. I began, as I say, with expanding the thing about the blitz on London. Then I had such a good time doing that that I thought why not go back to northern Minnesota and my childhood, primarily, I guess, because at one time I had done a piece similar to that which was published in *Vogue* many years before, in 1953. Then I'd put the thing aside. I went fishing for salmon up in the Aleutian Islands; went down to Antarctica on the first of the Lindblad Explorer journeys down there (the very first one, not the second in which they grounded the ship somewhere); over to Russia; one year chartered the only boat available from the Yugoslav government and then invited a bunch of my friends to go lazily and dreamily down the Dalmatian coast, very pleasant holiday it was; you know, back and forth to Europe. Offhand I can't remember where else I went, but quite a few places around the world. But when I came back there was a manuscript saying, "Hey! How about me?" So I'd get to work again. Therefore it didn't take ten years of writing, by any means; I wrote intermittently. I remember one year going to spend the summer in Idaho and having so many house guests and so much fun that I didn't tap out one single sentence of the book the whole three months of summer and autumn.

Conversations: You didn't write it in straight chronological order? You wrote various sections and then assembled it?

Hemingway: That's right. I started with the blitz, and then went back and led up to it and the thing about getting a job in London because I was convinced that there was going to be a war—even though Lord Beaverbrook, who finally hired me to work on his paper, the *Daily Express,* said in a very stern voice, "There shall be, there will be no war!"

Conversations: I remember from the London section of How It Was *your delight when you got that bucket of peanut butter.*

Hemingway: You can't imagine how valuable twenty-one pounds of peanut butter had become.

Conversations: How long did it last?

Hemingway: It lasted for, oh, I don't know, a couple of years at least. Peanut butter preserves itself very well. Of course we had no refrigeration. My little fridge which I had in my flat in Grosvenor Street broke down, and when I called the company that manufactured it I was informed that they couldn't make any repairs. They were doing something, obviously wartime stuff. So I had to live without refrigeration as a great many other Londoners did, and, of course, refrigeration was new to the Londoners anyway. They had never had it.

Conversations: Do you have another writing project in the works?

Hemingway: Paying bills mostly.

Conversations: You're not planning another book at this moment?

Hemingway: I have a large envelope which is labeled "futures," and it contains all sorts of ideas. There are, I think, parts we cut out of *How It Was* that will make good magazine pieces, but for a whole book—who knows. Also I'd like to do a piece of fiction; I mean a series of short stories perhaps. Would you like to hear about one of them? I think it was published once in *Der Sturm,* the German periodical, but American editors were frightened of it at that time. I think perhaps with some revision it would be acceptable now. It's about a lady who lives in a triplex apartment on Park Avenue, New York, with five concomitant husbands. It's all perfectly reasonable. It's supposed to be a sociological survey, and I find it really very interesting.

Conversations: All the husbands are in residence in this apartment at the same time?

Hemingway: One of the husbands is seldom in residence because he is an archeologist and he spends an awful lot of time down in Peru and Chile digging and in various other parts of the world. It happens that the wife had been particularly interested in archeology when she was in college, so they have that. This particular husband has a family tradition of diabetes, and therefore he feels that he should not father children. On the other hand, he likes being married when he has a chance to be, and so that particular husband isn't home very often. Some of the other husbands are there, and all are very fond of the two or three children this lady has produced during the years with a couple of fathers. They live harmoniously together, one reason being, of course, that they do have ample space. They're not treading upon each other. It can be a good, readable piece, I think, and perfectly reasonable.

Conversations: This story has been published in Germany?

Hemingway: It was published several years ago.

Conversations: Was that your first piece of fiction?

Hemingway: The first published anywhere, yes.

Conversations: You realize that you're duplicating Ernest Hemingway's early experience, when some of his early stories were published only in a Frankfurt, Germany, newspaper.

Hemingway: Yes, I know. The one thing that distinguishes the household in my story from any other household is that there is a total absence of jealousy. I think such a household is fun to envision, if not actually to copy.

Conversations: This story that you have written will be part of a projected volume of short stories?

Hemingway: Yes. I have one that I delayed working on, which is about turn-of-the-century or late nineteenth-century cannibalism in England.

Conversations: Based on fact?

Mary Hemingway

Hemingway: Based on imagination, but I do remember the places and the people to some extent. No, not based on fact.

Conversations: A question I'm sure that you've been asked on every one of your public appearances in connection with How It Was is what plans do you have for releasing in the near future any more of Ernest Hemingway's unpublished work?

Hemingway: As soon as I can get at them. I think that it's time now. There are several short stories, mostly concerned with infantry action during World War II. There is an enormous, long manuscript entitled "Garden of Eden," bits of which I think are quite good and other bits of which I consider to be unpublishable. I think I must have told you the two principles that I decided upon when sometime after I had learned, not having known it, that Ernest had left me total responsibility for all of his unpublished work in his will, which was holograph, signed. He left his property to me, "including my literary property," and made me administrator of it, or executrix. That was an enormous job, and I took a lot of time to think about it. Then evolved what seemed to be the most sensible two principles. The first was that anything that we published under Ernest's name will be his and only his. We may add commas and the absolutely essential "and" or "but," but nothing else. Nobody is going to fuss around and "improve" his work. And the other is that I won't publish anything which seems to me to be of inferior quality to that which was published with his approval during his lifetime.

Conversations: The most important provision of Ernest Hemingway's will for scholars is the one prohibiting publication of letters.

Hemingway: That was not in his will, you know. That was a separate piece of paper, the only piece of any consequence which I found in the little steel file we had in the library of our house in Cuba. It was in one small envelope, interestingly dated on the outside three or four days later than the date on the inside. It was a typewritten thing signed with his official signature, which was with the initial "M" in the middle. That's the way he signed formal checks and contracts and things like that. Whether or not he'd put it aside and maybe forgot about it, why he made this prohibition, who knows? Of course, if you've read my book you might know that I bent a little bit his instructions, or I detoured perhaps a little bit from them to quote a few of his letters to me, which I felt quite certainly he would not possibly have objected to. He must have done it having written something really frightful and sent it off to someone, so he made the blanket thing: no letters. I must have, I assume, both here and at the Kennedy Library I would estimate a minimum of a million words of letters. He was a prolific letter writer. He wrote, I don't remember how many now, but he wrote a great many, for example, to Lillian Ross of *The New Yorker*. There is enough for a whole book, a sizable book, of just their correspondence. I had to point this prohibition out to Lillian because she rightly thought it would be interesting reading and was about to publish it when I had to show her Ernest's instructions.

Conversations: So far you've been able to uphold Ernest Hemingway's wishes and stave off publication of correspondence. What happens after you go?

Hemingway: They could be published then, of course. I won't destroy, I have not destroyed anything. They can be put into the Kennedy Library, where all of his work, his papers, manuscripts, and everything else are going or have already gone. And they can be put there with the blanket prohibition against their publication.

Conversations: In perpetuity.

Hemingway: In perpetuity. Of course, really in perpetuity? If anybody is interested fifty or 100 years from now, who's to prevent publication, except those instructions of mine? And then there is the fascinating possibility that I might wish, of course, in consultation with an editor, to select the very best and most interesting of the letters to various people and make a volume, in contradiction of his instructions. It's an interesting possibility because I think lots of the letters are really highly readable, to say the least.

Conversations: I have read every Hemingway letter that I've been able to see, and they're marvelous letters because he always had something to say. Usually, it seemed to me that the writing of the letter was—and for God's sake correct me—but I get the impression that his letter writing, which must have been a daily stint, was involved somehow with his creative process: that he would write letters to get warmed up or to cool off afterwards. I don't know which, maybe both.

Hemingway: I think a combination. I think it was sometimes warming up and sometimes cooling off.

Conversations: Again and again I'll notice what's supposed to be purely a business letter saying "Yes, you may" is more than that; for example, when he's writing to Charles Poore, who was then editing The Hemingway Reader, *he would not only provide answers to questions that Poore had asked him, but then he would spin off.*

Hemingway: Yes, exactly. Long, elaborate explanations of this or that.

Conversations: "I wrote this story in Madrid at such and such a hotel and the waiter brought up a bottle of . . . ."

Hemingway: Yes, yes.

Conversations: What he called the "rat-trap memory" is very evident in the letters because there's no impression that he was doing research while he was writing these letters. As he wrote them the gates would open.

Hemingway: He just got interested in what he was doing and then indulged himself.

Conversations: All of the details, all of the facts related with an experience would be incorporated.

Hemingway: That's true in that series of letters to Charles Fenton.

Conversations: Which are being sold tomorrow afternoon.

Hemingway: Yes. He wrote to poor Mr. Fenton at such length. I remember at one point one of his letters to Mr. Fenton said, "You don't know what it was like in Oak Park; you don't know anything about how we used to go down the river and swim, and how we used to put goldfish in the reservoir of the town's water supply," something of that sort, "and watch them grow." I don't remember those letters precisely. I'm not sure that I ever saw them all or how I happened to see them. Then, of course, there were the letters, some of which were destroyed, thank goodness. Once in awhile if he wrote a particularly mean, nasty, deriding, hurtful, and denigrating letter to somebody, I was able to intercept it. I remember one time when I was sitting on the front steps at the Finca on a bright warm morning, and he was just about to give this letter, still unsealed, to the chauffeur to take in to mail in Havana. I said somehow or other, "I hope you haven't been too nasty." He was at that moment terribly irritated with something his elder son Bumby, Jack Hemingway, had done. And he wrote this really nasty, vituperative, unkind letter to Jack. I said, "Oh, let's read it over," or something like that. So we sat down on the front steps and phrase by phrase almost I was able to say, "Oh, sweetie, you could tone that down. You know you love this boy; you don't have to be that brittle and that brisk and that nasty to him. Do think about it; do make it a little bit more sympathetic. You can get your point across quite easily without being so inhuman." And in that particular case Ernest went back to his typewriter and produced a letter which indicated quite clearly his feelings about whatever this thing was that Jack had done of which he disapproved. I carefully stood by and watched while he tore up the original. The only things that he threw away, almost, were newspaper wrappings. But in this case I did see the letter destroyed.

Conversations: Speaking of Ernest Hemingway at the typewriter, one of the things that fascinates me about his typescripts, in his letters as well as in his literary work, is the system of spacing.

Hemingway: You can identify his manuscripts always.

Conversations: Yes. But it's also occurred to me that the irregular spacing was not just a nervous thing of somebody hitting the space bar because he couldn't think of a word, but there's some kind of system of emphasis involved.

Hemingway: Could be.

Mary Hemingway

Conversations: He puts extra space around a word the way somebody else might underline it. Or is that just haywire professional thinking?

Hemingway: I couldn't speculate, because he never looked nervous when he was working. I would tend to doubt that he did it as a thing of nervousness. It was just his manner or perhaps he was just searching for a word, but I wouldn't say nervously. What amuses me particularly about his writing in general is that he was an absolute stickler for good spelling. I'm a terrible speller, and I have to use the dictionary constantly, but in spite of his being so forceful and insistent upon good spelling, he himself made amusing mistakes. He never wrote "l-i-v-i-n-g"; he always wrote it "l-i-v-e-i-n-g."

Conversations: And movable with an "e."

Hemingway: And movable with an "e." And many of those words ending in "ing" he preceded with "e," the unneccessary "e." That was his personal preference.

Conversations: Still speaking of typing, you typed two, maybe three of the novels; you typed The Old Man and the Sea.

Hemingway: Yes.

Conversations: Most, if not all, of Islands in the Stream.

Hemingway: Yes, I guess I did.

Conversations: And parts of Across the River.

Hemingway: Yes, I think so. It was all so long ago, I can't remember. There was a young lady named Nita Jensen who worked at the United States Embassy in Havana and came out sometimes moonlighting to type manuscripts and also to take letters. But it was a very haphazard thing.

Conversations: He never employed a full-time secretary the way many of the writers do.

Hemingway: Oh, he wouldn't dream of it. He would feel obliged to provide work for the secretary, and therefore he wouldn't have the freedom to write when and where and how much he wished to do. Of course, his standard habit was working in the mornings and doing other things in the afternoon. Nita Jensen used to come out frequently—oh, this was over a period of a year, a couple of years, no more—and they would have a session in the afternoons. But lots of times we used to go and shoot pigeons or swim or something like that.

Conversations: Is it really true he had a system whereby he wrote dialogue on the typewriter and exposition in longhand?

Hemingway: Pretty much. He used to keep his typewriter on top of a bookshelf in his bedroom and beside it the pad for his handwriting.

Conversations: Unlined, because you can always spot his handwriting by the downward slope.

Hemingway: Yes.

Conversations: He didn't use lined pads at all, then?

Hemingway: No, never did, as far as I know. But then sometimes he would take the typewriter in to the big, big table we had in the library and sit down with the typewriter in front of him and pound away, hunt-and-peck system, because he said he couldn't keep up with the dialogue by hand. He could work faster on the typewriter, even though it was only hunt-and-peck.

Conversations: When you were typing The Old Man and the Sea, *for example, would you get a daily stint, or would he wait until he had a great hunk?*

Hemingway: I'm not sure my memory is accurate about this, but I think he did the whole thing by hand and then I typed it. I remember particularly that in the typing I came across a couple of rather minor oversights—in a phrase something had been left out, or a couple of things, which seemed to me not for poetic purposes, were unnecessarily repetitive—and I would take it in. I remember one time he said, "No, let's leave it like that." Other times he would make adjustments, but there were very, very few. That thing just sort of spun from his head onto either the handwritten page or his typewriter. I can't remember which, really, whether he did it all by hand, or all by typewriter, or a mixture of the two. I don't remember.

191

Mary Hemingway

Conversations: Does the old man die at the end of The Old Man and the Sea, *or is he going to?*

Hemingway: Oh, no, he lives!

Conversations: There are some critics who feel that Santiago is dying at the end of the novel, and your opinion—not just opinion, your knowledge—is that Santiago is going to carry on.

Hemingway: That was my definite, final reaction. I'm sure, you know, that as he was approaching the end of this particular book . . . . He wrote every morning, and I read from the beginning every evening. We happened for once not to have house guests. We didn't have to be fussing around attending to them and having supper served and all that kind of thing, and so I would read peacefully stretched out on the sofa in the sitting room. As we were approaching the end—or as he was—I said something to the effect of, "Darling, I'm afraid you're going to do away with this old man. This is a sleazy, chintzy, shiftless, and careless way to finish a book. Please do consider letting him live." And Ernest, probably sitting cross-legged in his big chair—he had a great huge overstuffed chair with its cretonne-flowered slipcover— probably said something like "Hum"—to that effect. And the following evening I began again—now I was able to read rather quickly through the first whatever it was. It was, as you know, a tiny book anyway. And I made the same point, saying, "It's such a cheap way to cut him off—he's such a nice old man, Santiago. Let him go ahead and fish. He can have several years at least. And perhaps the boy will go back and fish with him and he can have a lovely life, without now being destroyed." In the end, as you know, it finishes up with the boy sitting by the old man, and he has brought him something to eat, and the old man is sleeping peacefully.

Conversations: Dreaming about the lions.

Hemingway: Dreaming about the lions on the beach of Africa. To me that means he is going to survive in order to fish again, which is what his whole life was. As to people who assume that he kicked off, I find that that is very presumptuous on their part.

Conversations: As you probably know, there are several scholars who are convinced that The Old Man and the Sea *was not, in fact, written at the time it was supposed to have been written, but that it was an old manuscript that Ernest Hemingway dug out of a trunk and refurbished.*

Hemingway: Horseradish. Not true. Our habit was from at least the first five, six, or seven years after I went to Cuba and we began fishing. . . . I went there in 1945 and fell in love with *Pilar* and also with the Gulf Stream and its marvelous, myriad inhabitants: birds and fish and men-of-war with those nasty bubbles that trail—I forget what they're called—with long, gelatinous tails that have very poisonous stings on the end—and flying fish, and, of course, a variety of actual fish, as well as dolphin and sometimes those other marvelous mammals, whales. We used to see whales sometimes. Our habit was to anchor *Pilar* in the little bay of Cojimar, which was merely a commercial fishing village. The town's population was almost entirely fishermen who went out as Santiago did in those days with their skiffs and were carried by the Gulf Stream, which flows from west to east across that northern part of Cuba's coast. They would then put their baits down and drift; then our prevailing wind we called the *Brisa*, which blew from east to west, came all the way across the Atlantic and hit the north coast of Cuba. When they had their fish, or when the day was finished, whether or not they had fish, they'd stick up their sails and come sailing back against the Gulf Stream, the wind being stronger than the current of the stream—the current ran an average of about four knots. A definite river, it was cutting through the sea. We could see the boundaries, curling edges of this river, through the rest of the ocean. Now, or even before we left, the fishermen had become prosperous: they were able to add outboard motors to their boats. But what was the original question?

Conversations: Whether The Old Man and the Sea *was an old manuscript dug out of a trunk.*

Hemingway: Oh, yes. Well our habit after our fishing was to go up to the only respectable bar, or the only bar of any pretensions at all, which was called La Terraza. Ernest would invite whomever we'd seen that day. He'd say, "Come and have a drink at La Terraza." People would stand around and chat about their adventures of the day. Ernest had been doing this for a number

193

of years. Indeed, none of our usual drinking friends would ordinarily order themselves a whiskey, but Ernest was buying the drinks and so they had whiskey or rum instead of beer, because even rum, while it was cheap, was more expensive than beer. They would tell a number of stories, which mounted in Ernest's head, in a sense, into this one or two days' fishing by this one man. Anselmo, who was one of the oldest of the old boys, had had an experience quite similar to that of Santiago, the man in the book. By the time I met him he was an elderly old boy, but he still went out by himself every day fishing. But it was not Anselmo's story. Anselmo had never gone through that wild and bitter and strenuous experience. But many of them had had quite similar things, their great catches being eaten up by sharks, that sort of thing, and so it just grew inside of Ernest's head. Anyone who pretends that he dug it out of something else is mistaken—plain and simply mistaken.

Ring Lardner, Jr. is the only survivor of the four writing sons of the great American humorist. He left Princeton to become a newspaperman and then went to Hollywood. Two of his screenplays have won Academy Awards: Woman of the Year *(1942) and* M.A.S.H. *(1970). His screenwriting career was interrupted when he served a prison sentence as one of the Hollywood Ten. That experience resulted in Lardner's satirical novel,* The Ecstasy of Owen Muir *(1954). He reminisced about his famous family in* The Lardners: My Family Remembered *(1976).*

Ring Lardner, Jr.

Ring Lardner, Jr. was interviewed by Matthew J. Bruccoli in May 1977 at the Lardners' apartment overlooking Central Park in Manhattan. They talked in Lardner's utilitarian study, which contains only a few pieces of memorabilia—including a poster for Woman of the Year, *and the cover to the first* Esquire, *to which Lardner contributed at the age of eighteen. The interview was interrupted by a phone call from a movie producer in France.*

Conversations: In a way, the Lardner family is the Bach family of American writing. Offhand I can't think of another family that has produced so many good writers: your father, you and your three brothers, and now a number of the grandchildren of Ring and Ellis Lardner are making their way as writers. Would you care to speculate on why so many of the Lardners are first-rate writers?

Lardner: Well, it does also, perhaps, go back to my grandmother, my father's mother, who had a couple of books published. I can only say that both families were pretty literate—my mother's as well as my father's—so that probably the combination of genes was good for writing, although I really think it's probably more a question of environment. I think we were certainly—my three brothers and I—conditioned by our background, by the kind of things we talked about as children, to be interested in writing, initially as readers, but then as writers.

Conversations: Conditioned by environment, but not encouraged by your parents?

Lardner: Not particularly, no.

Conversations: There was no sense that you were being groomed to be writers?

Lardner: Oh, no, no. Any writing that we did, like the family newspapers we put out, was initiated by us—primarily by my brother John, as the oldest. There was a certain parental encouragement; they read what we wrote and said if they liked it. But they never set us any tasks of writing or initiated such things themselves.

Conversations: But on the other hand, there was not the sense— as there so often is in any professional family—that this is a terrible profession. Go into something else.

Lardner: My wife, who is an actress, has said that to our children, and only one of them is in the profession. There was only that to this extent: my father did say about the time I first started writing things—the Triangle show at Princeton and an article in *Esquire* that I sold a few months before he died—he said, "Isn't somebody in this family going to do something else?" But he didn't seem seriously concerned. He never suggested that it was a terrible thing to be, even though he went through some considerable agonies with writing, especially in the later years. He made us think that newspaper work, at least, was—gave us the sense that it was fun.

Conversations: What was your first writing job?

Lardner: My first job when I left college was on a New York newspaper. I worked for just about a year.

Conversations: Then you went to Hollywood?

Lardner: Yes.

Conversations: How did you feel about Hollywood as a place for a writer to be? So many of us have grown up with the stories about how Hollywood destroyed talent. Did you feel that this was the case?

Lardner: No. I didn't when I went out there, although I do know some examples of talent I think Hollywood did have an adverse effect on. When I went out at the age of twenty I had no particular idea that I was going to stay in filmwriting for a long period of time. I thought it was an interesting place for a young man to be to find out about this business of making movies, and that's the way it turned out. I did find it quite stimulating, but I had in mind that I was quite free to change either the kind of writing I was doing—to change from filmwriting to some other kind—or to do something else entirely. I never said with any sense of commitment that I was definitely going to be a writer the rest of my life.

Conversations: What was your first Hollywood job—what studio?

Lardner: Well, I was hired by David O. Selznick with the idea that he was going to teach me about the film business; but he signed me to a contract which specified that I could do anything he wanted me to, and my first job was in the publicity department. In the course of my first year there he even gave me a screen test. Then after he saw it he said, "You're going to be a writer."

Conversations: What was the first movie that you worked on?

Lardner: Well, I worked on a few movies as the publicity man. As a writer the first movie I worked on—Budd Schulberg and I collaborated on writing some scenes for the original version of *A Star Is Born*, and they used our ending, which was used also in a remake.

Conversations: "This is Mrs. Norman Maine"?

Lardner: Yes, and a couple of other scenes during the course of the picture, so that Dorothy Parker and Alan Campbell, who had credit for the screenplay, said we ought to get some credit—to which we were not entitled according to the general rules of the thing. But they were just being generous, and Selznick vetoed that. Budd had been a reader in the story department there and I was in the publicity department, and we got drafted into this effort to think up an ending. Then after that, even though Selznick didn't think we ought to get credit, he said, "You can be writers now." He gave us a couple of projects to work on.

Conversations: What was the first project that was yours?

Lardner: Well, the first project that was mine, was mine with a collaborator a couple of years after that, because I did do pieces of another thing for Selznick and then a couple of scripts at Warner Brothers that got rewritten. But the first one that really came out as movie was called *The Courageous Doctor Christian*. It was in a series with Jean Hersholt from a radio series, and Ian

Ring Lardner, Jr.

McLellan Hunter and I collaborated on this. As a matter of fact we wrote—no, *The Courageous Doctor Christian* was the second one, that's right. The first one was called *Meet Doctor Christian*.

Conversations: How many Doctor Christians did you do?

Lardner: That was it. We did two.

Conversations: What was the first job you really regarded as a serious work?

Lardner: Well, it was the picture *Woman of the Year,* on which I also collaborated, this time with Michael Kanin. That was the first film that Katharine Hepburn and Spencer Tracy starred in. And that was the film that got the Academy Award for the best original screenplay that year—in 1942. Everything else up to then had either been pieces of important pictures, or the whole of unimportant ones.

Conversations: What effect did winning the Academy Award have on your career?

Lardner: It certainly made a great deal of difference. Really from that time on for the next five years I had no problem getting work in Hollywood.

Conversations: Were you under contract with a studio or did you free-lance?

Lardner: I free-lanced during most of that time. The last of those five years, in 1947, I think, I signed a contract with Twentieth Century-Fox.

Conversations: Was Forever Amber *your last Fox job?*

Lardner: No. I worked on two things at Fox after that before the Un-American Activities Committee hearings in the fall of that year, which interrupted my career for some time.

Conversations: Did it interrupt it or destroy it?

Lardner: Well, it pretty well ended it for the immediate—Well, for a period of fifteen years I wasn't able to work under my own name.

Conversations: You did work under pseudonyms?

Lardner: I worked under pseudonyms, mostly on short films made for television.

Conversations: But it was fifteen years before you had a full-scale assignment again?

Lardner: Yes. One script I had done right after *Forever Amber* was from a book by Margery Sharp called *Britannia Mews*. The movie was called *The Forbidden Street*, which is not important except that they did shoot it the following year and produced it with my name on it as sole author of the screenplay. It came out about a year after I was blacklisted, which was interesting just because it showed that they were not really afraid of those names, and certainly no one made any stink about the fact that my name was on this picture—nobody boycotted it or anything.

Conversations: During your blacklisted period you wrote your only novel, The Ecstasy of Owen Muir.

Lardner: Yes. I started that novel in the Federal Correctional Institution at Danbury, Connecticut. I came out with about, oh, fifty pages of it and finished it during the course of the next two years.

Conversations: Which became something of a cult book. It was originally published in England and then in the United States.

Lardner: Yes. It was first accepted by a British publisher, Jonathan Cape. Then I made a deal here with a rather obscure left-wing firm, Cameron & Kahn, just a month or two later, but I had tried all the major publishers in New York unsuccessfully.

Conversations: Did anyone say okay, but not under your name?

Lardner: Nobody said that, but a couple of editors told me that they thought the real problem, after they had recommended the book and it had been overruled further up, was not so much my name as the fact that it dealt with the Catholic Church in a way that the Church might object to. The publishers were particularly sensitive because of the Church's habit of boycotting a whole firm if they didn't like something. Almost all of the big publishers have textbook departments which are pretty dependent for revenue on Catholic school sales.

Conversations: It's had sort of a second life, The Ecstasy of Owen Muir. *I imagine it sold more copies the second time around than the first.*

Lardner: Yeah. It's been published twice as a paperback—once in 1967 and once in 1972. The first time was kind of an abortive thing, because the company that published it went out of business. I think it was the last book they published—company called Parallax. So that one didn't sell very much. The New American Library edition in '72 has remained in print. It's part of their Plume series, and they do make an attempt to keep those in print. That's had a respectable—not a big sale.

Conversations: The automatic question is how come only one novel? Why didn't you keep writing novels?

Lardner: Well, I guess the main reason was that I had five children I was responsible for, and I think my income from *Owen Muir* in the fifties, for the two years that I spent working on it, was certainly not more than $3000. So when I found that I could do these television films, again collaborating with Ian Hunter, I was able to make a considerably better living.

Conversations: Would you rather write novels?

Lardner: Well, now I have started on another novel after all of these years.

Conversations: What was your favorite movie project? Woman of the Year?

Lardner: Well, I would say that that and *M.A.S.H.* both had some special satisfactions. *Woman of the Year* because it meant a tremendous difference in the way I was regarded in Hollywood and the opportunities to get the kind of picture assignments I wanted. It was really an important change. And *M.A.S.H.* because the only previous picture I had done after the blacklist, a picture called *The Cincinnati Kid*, did get rewritten somewhat and changed from what I had in mind, so that *M.A.S.H.* was my sole screenplay credit; because it was very successful—and again for the second time won me an Academy Award—coming after this long blacklist period it had considerable satisfaction to it, too.

Conversations: Is there such a thing as the art of the screenplay?

Lardner: Oh, yes. Well, at least there is certainly a lot of technique in the screenplay.

Conversations: There's the art of what you write down on paper, but what you write then gets turned over to many other people, so that the thing that finally appears on the screen always represents a collaboration.

Lardner: It certainly does. It represents a collaboration in the main part with the director, the actors, the film editor, the cameramen, the composer of the music.

Conversations: Plus anyone else who was brought in to polish the script.

Lardner: Yes, that can be. And yet I think it is valid to say that writing a screenplay can be a very creative process.

Conversations: Do you feel that the screenplay is your thing and the film on the screen is somebody else's?

Lardner: There is a different degree of that separation in almost every picture. Sometimes a concept that's on paper in the screenplay can be realized on the screen quite directly and truthfully. Sometimes the result on the screen is far removed from the screenplay. You have to realize that the screenplay does include the basic construction of the picture, the breaking up into scenes, and, in a good screenplay, all the important visual elements as well as just the words that people say to each other. I would say that probably of the whole process the construction is the most important part. Now that is also what can be changed the most because it's possible for a director to find whole new ideas for scenes while shooting a picture, depending on the physical location—the kind of background they are shooting in—depending on things that the actors come up with about their roles. So the variation from one picture to another is very great. But ideally the screenplay is the blueprint of the finished picture.

Conversations: If you're lucky. I've heard stories about how on a given script there were ten writers, there were teams of writers. For example, Gone With the Wind apparently had so many writers that nobody knows who wrote that finally.

Lardner: That's true. I think at least eighteen functioned on that, but that was much more the case back in the thirties and forties than it is today.

Conversations: Do you feel that that assembly-line system of screenwriting was justified?

Lardner: I don't feel that it was ever a very good system. The main practitioners of it—Irving Thalberg, David Selznick, Samuel Goldwyn—were in some ways the most fastidious and really the most artistic of the producers in those days—in a day when the producer had the real control of movies. But I think that they all abused the system of having successions of writers on pictures and they probably would have gotten better results if they hadn't done that.

Conversations: In some cases they simply destroyed the ability of some of the writers to work under that system. Every time they gave F. Scott Fitzgerald a collaborator they started a feud. Raymond Chandler, too. Both men were temperamentally and constitutionally incapable of collaborating with anyone.

Lardner: Yes. In that system a man like Selznick was the dominant figure, and part of the way in which he expressed his domination was to tell writers what they should write; and when they didn't please him, to substitute another writer or rewrite himself.

Conversations: Did he really know what he was looking for, or was this a power show?

Lardner: He did know what he was looking for. It wasn't always the best thing, but he was a highly egocentric man with very strong opinions. When he eventually more or less dispensed with writers entirely and wrote pictures himself under pseudonyms—one called *Since You Went Away* and, to a large extent, *Duel in the Sun*—they were not as good as the pictures he had had other people writing. But the whole era of that kind of domination by the producer—which was not only over the writer but also over the director, who was completely a hired hand in those days—that whole system died away in the beginning of the 1950s, I think. I believe pictures have improved.

Conversations: At what point did the director supersede the producer as the honcho?

Lardner: It started really in the fifties. There was some overlapping. There were some very strong directors before that who were able to achieve their purpose. But it was typical before the war; even with a strong director like Alfred Hitchcock, a Selznick would dominate the picture, as in *Rebecca*. It really began, as I say, in the fifties. The cult of the director was strengthened a good deal by the French *auteur* theory, which is about twenty-five years old, I think. It has been applied to American films rather arbitrarily, because it still is not the system by which most American films are made. Even now in Hollywood it is more often the practice than not that the director doesn't come into the scene until there is a first and possibly a second-draft screenplay, and the producer and writer have more or less determined the general shape of the thing. This is not true of certain very prominent directors who are more apt to conceive the project themselves.

Conversations: Who were the most talented writers you worked with in Hollywood?

Lardner: Well, I didn't work with a great many writers, directly that is. I did collaborate with a few, but I was aware of the work of other writers. The ones that I respected particularly included Dalton Trumbo, Michael Wilson, the Hacketts—Albert Hackett and Frances Goodrich, who did the Thin Man pictures and *Father of the Bride* and then the stage play version of *The Diary of Anne Frank*—Sidney Buckman. I'm thinking back more to the older ones. Dudley Nichols. I remember back during my first years in Hollywood, after I left Selznick and went to work at Warner Brothers, I was very impressed with John Huston, who was working at Warner Brothers at the time. This was several years before he got a chance to be a director, and he was an extremely talented screenwriter, I felt.

Conversations: Did you ever have directorial ambitions?

Lardner: It did occur to me a couple of times that there were certain things that I could do as a director. It's possible that if the blacklist hadn't intervened I might have tried it. I do think I lack some of the qualities that are most useful to a director.

Conversations: What qualities are those?

Lardner: Well, certainly a strong self-confidence, the ability to make very quick decisions. The director has to make decisions about a remarkable number of things in different fields, and in some cases to make them very rapidly. And sometimes they are those kind of arbitrary decisions—the sort of thing Fitzgerald had the Monroe Stahr character talking about in *The Last Tycoon*, when Stahr cited the railroad builder's kind of choices where he couldn't possibly know all the factors involved, and the great quality was to be able to make a decision when there was no basis for it. Sometimes it's that kind of thing. A director should be articulate, which I am not always. So I'm not sure how I would have done it, but the opportunity has not come up, and I'm quite sure that it won't. Dalton Trumbo, who did direct a picture, finally—the adaptation of his own book, *Johnny Got His Gun*—I think at the age of sixty-five referred to himself as the oldest new director in Hollywood.

Conversations: You mentioned a moment ago The Last Tycoon. *Did you see the movie?*

Lardner: Yes, I did.

Conversations: Would you care to comment on it?

Lardner: Well, I was certainly disappointed in it.

Conversations: Do you feel that it was a fair or accurate picture of Hollywood when you knew it, as you knew it?

Lardner: Well, it was a picture of some things, some aspects of Hollywood in those days. It showed certain things, in somewhat exaggerated form, that went on that were an aspect of the motion-picture business of the thirties. But I think it was a fairly limited view. It was mostly a few top people. There were a couple of things that were rather nicely done in it. I think the Tony Curtis actor part was good and the Jeanne Moreau was a slight caricature of a type that existed then. But mostly it failed as a piece of entertainment as well as an adaptation of Fitzgerald. I think Fitzgerald is terribly hard to adapt to film. I was approached by David Merrick about *The Great Gatsby*, and I think I finally did say I would discuss further doing it. But I was not really terribly interested in it as an assignment simply because it would either work out well, in which case everybody would practically ignore whoever had adapted it and just say, you know, it was Fitzgerald, or, as was more likely, it would disappoint lovers of the book, in which case the screenwriter would be attacked. I think there are qualities of Fitzgerald's writings which just can't be rendered in that way. I don't think I ever—there was a version of *Tender Is the Night*.

Conversations: Selznick.

Lardner: Yes, Selznick did it. I remember a friend of mine, David Hertz, was working on it for a while. I don't know whose version finally got done. I didn't see it, but I understand it was not successful either.

Conversations: If the subject isn't painful I would like to ask a couple of questions about your H.U.A.C. experiences. Did anybody think that the so-called Hollywood Ten were sneaking propaganda into the movies?

Lardner: Well, that was the big issue that we tried to get brought to the fore back then. My friend Trumbo, for instance, brought a stack of scripts to the hearing and said, "Tell me where the propaganda is." One of the members of the committee, Congressman Rankin of Alabama, had talked about the lying, immoral, anti-Christian filth—as well as un-American propaganda—that was in the films. However, when they called us to the stand they refused to discuss content of pictures at all. They said the only relevant thing was whether or not we or anyone else connected with pictures were or had been Communists.

Ring Lardner, Jr.

The decision in the district court in Washington when we were convicted of contempt of Congress said, in effect, that it was enough to assume that if there were Communists among Hollywood writers that they would try to sneak their propaganda into films.

Conversations: At no point did someone hold up a script and say, "Here: this is the party line"—nobody said that?

Lardner: No. As a matter of fact, in the decision which became the law, really, because the Supreme Court declined to review the appellate court decision, it said not only that it was relevant to the committee's purposes to find out whether some writers were Communists or not, but that to go into the question of what propaganda—what specific propaganda they had put into their films—might be a violation of the First Amendment. It wasn't such a clear question whether Congress had any right to investigate that, so they never faced up to this question of content, and all through the period when hundreds of writers were blacklisted—and some directors and actors—the pictures they had made that had apparently brought them to the attention of the committee were being shown on television. There was scarcely a night on television that you couldn't find some blacklisted person's movie being shown on one channel or another. It came down to the question of either we were right in saying there was no sinister influence in these pictures, or that some new factor, like the smaller screen, had deprived them of the power to subvert.

Conversations: Let's say for the sake of argument you were sneaking in propaganda; but you submitted the script, which then other hands, as we have said, vetted. So that even had you been trying to sneak in something, there was a review process built in.

Lardner: Yes. In those days one man in each studio had pretty effective power over everything—Zanuck at Fox, Harry Cohn at Columbia, Jack Warner at Warner's, and so on. At the time of the hearings, just before they took place, Daryl Zanuck was quoted in a column in *The New York Daily News* as saying, "Yes, there were some reds among the writers." He said, "They even tried to sneak some propaganda into *Forever Amber.*" This intrigued me, so I went back to the notes of our conferences with Zanuck on it. Every time Zanuck would go over a script with the writers and producers and so on, somebody would take notes of everything he said. Not what anybody else said, but just what Zanuck said during the conference. Then we all would get a copy the next day of Zanuck's remarks, so I had them. I found one line that he had cut out that could conceivably have had political implications. The line was spoken by an actor about King Charles II, as characterized by George Sanders. It said of the King, "Charles is every inch a king. He always finds the devious solution." This seemed to be an anti-Royalist line, and Zanuck had cut that out; but that was as subversive as we got.

Conversations: As I understand it, the unspoken assumption was that of course you people were sneaking in subversive propaganda, and nobody bothered to prove it.

Lardner: Absolutely. No one bothered to prove it. They evaded the challenges to prove it. They could not. Well, during the earlier part of the hearings a couple of the witnesses, who were so-called friendly witnesses, did speak somewhat about the content of films. Ayn Rand, the author of *The Fountainhead* and so on, spoke about a movie that MGM had made during the war called *Song of Russia.* She said that it showed Russian children smiling, which was something that hadn't happened in her experience between the revolution in 1917 and her departure from the country in 1926. She didn't remember ever seeing any children smiling. Then Ginger Rogers's mother said that in a picture written by Dalton Trumbo, Ginger had been asked to say the line "Share and share alike—that's democracy," which, as Mrs. Lela Rogers pointed out on the stand, was clearly not democracy at all, but arrant socialism. That's about as much as was said about content of pictures during the whole hearing.

Conversations: You're laughing now. How many years did it take you before you could laugh about it?

Lardner: Oh, we laughed about it right then. It was pretty funny. It was hard to see that the blacklist was funny, and yet the way in which it was ended was really by ridicule. It was absurd, because, as I say, these same pictures that we all had written were being shown on television. It was absurd in the sense that when it was all over with, the same people were hired and went right on writing and exercising the same power to subvert that they had before. It was really because Trumbo, more than anyone else, realized that ridicule was the right weapon to break down this structure that it finally collapsed. It was partly through the Academy, which is a sacred institution in Hollywood because it does have a very close effect on the box office. First, right at the beginning of the blacklist, two pictures won Academy Awards for writers who had already been blacklisted—*A Place in the Sun* by Michael Wilson and then *Roman Holiday* won an original story award. Then when a second picture of Michael Wilson's, *Friendly Persuasion*, looked like it would get nominated for an Academy Award, the Academy passed a rule saying that no blacklisted writer's picture could be a candidate. So there were only four instead of five nominees that year. They thought they had defused the bomb, not knowing there was a booby trap in the separate award for best original story, which went to a man named Robert Rich who turned out to be Dalton Trumbo.

Conversations: The Brave One.

Lardner: Yes. Then the following year a picture two blacklisted writers, Michael Wilson and Carl Foreman, had written won the Academy Award for best picture and best screenplay, and the screenplay was attributed to Pierre Boule, the author of the book. This was the picture *The Bridge on the River Kwai.* Everybody knew that Boule didn't speak English and had never written a movie. Then the year after that—they had had this rule that no blacklisted writer's name could appear as a nominee— there was a picture called *The Defiant Ones*, which had two writers in collaboration, one of whom was blacklisted and one who wasn't. That created an insuperable problem. They had to reverse the rule again so as not to discriminate against the writer who wasn't blacklisted, and it won the best screenplay award. So that helped to make the institution seem ridiculous, and it kind of collapsed of its own accord after that.

Conversations: Did most of you come back, or did some of you just vanish?

Lardner: Well, no, I would say probably less than half came back. Among the blacklisted ones there were some who were older and a number died. Particularly there were quite a few who were not very well established in the movie or television business and didn't have impressive credits. They had to find other kinds of work, and by the time the blacklist was beginning to collapse, they really had nothing to go on. I mean, people would say, "Where are your credits in the last ten years?" There were writers I knew of who became waiters and bartenders, and one became a rather successful operator of parking garages. Lionel Stander, the actor who was blacklisted, became a stockbroker for three or four years. I would say that probably the majority did not return to working in Hollywood again. I don't know what the actual figures are.

Conversations: How many of you went to jail altogether?

Lardner: Just ten.

Conversations: The Hollywood Ten.

Lardner: The Hollywood Ten, yes. There were no other cases after that. We had all challenged the committee on the basis of the First Amendment, but once we had lost our case there wasn't much point in anybody else doing that, so almost all the other witnesses who were called invoked the Fifth Amendment. Whereas if they were blacklisted, they didn't go to jail. A few years later some began to invoke the First Amendment again, and for one reason or another each of these cases—even though some of them went to trial and a few resulted in convictions at that level—each of them ended in some kind of reversal. There was Arthur Miller's case; there were a couple of men on *The New York Times*; there was an actor named Elliott Sullivan; and a few others which all ended in various ways without the person who had so testified going to prison.

Conversations: Impossible question: Would you do it all over again exactly the way you did it?

Lardner: Well, it is impossible. It certainly is relevant that at the time I thought, and I think most of us thought, we had a pretty good chance to win this case. There was some pretty clear language in the Supreme Court decisions that seemed to say that this kind of investigation couldn't go into these areas. So I didn't know that I was going to jail, and I didn't know that I was going to be blacklisted for that long. However, I still think I would have found it very difficult to conform to this committee, and so I might have done the same. But you really can't tell.

Conversations: Whose strategy was it to appeal on the First Amendment rather than the Fifth?

Lardner: Well, it was ours. There were nineteen of us originally, although only ten were called to the stand before they suspended the hearings. Several reasons: one was that in order to plead the Fifth Amendment to this particular question—"Are you now or have you ever been a member of the Communist Party?"—you would have to be saying, in effect, that you or that somebody thought it was a crime to be a Communist. This was at a time when the Smith Act had not yet been invoked against Communists. It's even possible that we couldn't have invoked the Fifth successfully. The courts might have decided that was not a proper use of it, although I think they probably would have. But also it didn't really focus on the issue of did this committee have the right to investigate in an area where it seemed to be constitutionally forbidden to legislate. We thought there was a chance of the courts declaring the committee itself invalid, this kind of investigation invalid, which they wouldn't have done on the basis of invoking the Fifth Amendment.

Conversations: Whose idea was it to look into subversive activity in Hollywood? Was it Parnell Thomas?

Lardner: Well, it had been started some years before by the first chairman of the committee, Martin Dies of Texas, who had had some hearings.

Conversations: About Hollywood?

Lardner: Yes, back in 1941, I think. Thomas had just been made chairman of the committee because the Republicans had won the congressional election in '46, and he wanted to launch his chairmanship with something that would get a lot of publicity. Hollywood has always been good for publicity. It was that terrible John Rankin of Alabama, whom I quoted before, who made the loudest statements about what they were going to do to Hollywood, so it was certainly partly his idea. And he was quite clearly motivated by overt anti-Semitism, among other things.

Conversations: Were most of the Hollywood Ten Jewish?

Lardner: No, they were really attacking—Well, I haven't counted up about that, but I meant attacking the motion-picture business, which generally was thought of in the minds of people like Rankin as being dominated by Jews. No, as far as the Hollywood Ten, I guess the majority were Jewish—Adrian Scott and Dalton Trumbo and I and Edward Dmytryk I think were not.

Conversations: You subsequently had the curious experience of seeing Parnell Thomas at Danbury in the same jail.

Lardner: Right. He was there when Lester Cole and I got there.

Conversations: Did you talk to him in jail?

Lardner: I never talked to him directly. Cole had a few words with him. He was in charge of the chicken yard there. He had been, of course, convicted in the meantime of putting nonexistent people on the government payroll and pocketing the money, to which he pleaded nolo contendere. He was eligible for parole, and I was working in an office called the Office of Classifications and Parole, and I was told that Thomas was very concerned that I would somehow sabotage his parole. But actually a civilian took the job of typing the papers away from me. The only thing I did to Thomas at all was—Ordinarily when I found out that somebody was getting paroled I would be able to let him know about it a day or so ahead. I did know that Thomas was getting it, but I didn't tell him.

Conversations: We haven't touched on your recent book at all— The Lardners: My Family Remembered. Why did you decide to write it?

Lardner: Well, it started with someone else's idea, not mine, to write a magazine article. Harold Hayes of *Esquire* suggested a piece, and I did a piece for *Esquire* in 1972. Then a couple of publishers wrote or called about the possibility of a book, and I thought about it and I was somewhat uncertain. But I did realize there was quite a bit that I remembered that no one else would know, and so I thought of writing just a general kind of reminiscence book of what I remembered. Then when I started reading these letters my parents had written during their courtship, I realized that that was pretty interesting stuff, and that wasn't firsthand knowledge of my own. So in order to tell the story, I would want to go back to that courtship, and that meant doing research not only in those letters but other things. I found myself getting increasingly interested in it and I did it. I quite enjoyed it.

Conversations: How would you summarize your father's place in American literature?

Lardner: I think it's a dual thing—that he is a continuing part of American literature and that some, at least, of his stories will go on being read because of their lasting qualities. But certainly also he has a place as an influence on other writers, and that second one may be the more important of the two.

Conversations: Who are you thinking of?

Lardner: Well, to a certain extent, most of the writers who came after—starting with Hemingway and James T. Farrell and Dashiell Hammett, in his way.

Conversations: William Faulkner told me that he carried a copy of "Sun Cured" around until it fell apart. As you know, the fashionable critical position on Ring Lardner is that he was an unfulfilled writer, who never fulfilled his potential, a writer who died embittered. Do you think that's accurate?

Lardner: There is some truth to it. He was unhappy during the later years. It was largely a matter of health, but it was also a matter of his attitude toward the times. He was a conservative man, a prudish man, who didn't respond well to a lot of the manifestations of the post-war period of the Jazz Age and so on. But I think he largely fulfilled what he wanted to do. Part of my argument in my book is that he became a fiction writer more or less by accident, and I think he realized that he had this facility for the short story. I quoted in my book his statement to me: "If I ever wrote a novel I'd be more bored with it by the time I got through with it even than the reader would." And I think there was some truth to that. There was obviously kidding to it, too. I'm uncertain whether it was just that he never got an idea which seemed to justify a novel, or whether he was temperamentally incapable of doing a longer piece of work. But, in any case, I think the stories and some of the nonfiction and the short plays and so on—what remains is a very impressive body of work. I think he had reason to be satisfied with it, whether he was or not.

Conversations: You've just finished working on the Muhammed Ali movie, The Greatest. *Are you all done with that?*

Lardner: Oh, yes. It's opening next week, as a matter of fact.

Conversations: Are you satisfied with it?

Lardner: Well, I haven't seen the final version of it, but I saw a rough-cut version. I haven't seen it with the musical scores and things that have been done with it. I think the main problem with it is going to be something over which I had no control, which is the fact that Ali at thirty-five is playing himself, starting with the age of twenty-two, and he doesn't quite look right. We have a younger actor playing him at eighteen, but the transition is going to be quite a jolt from the one actor to the other.

Conversations: Do you have another assignment now or are you between assignments?

Lardner: I've started to work on a novel about Hollywood. I expect to interrupt it to do a movie, but I'm not sure what that's going to be.

Wallace Markfield was born in Brooklyn in 1926 and was educated at Brooklyn College and New York University. After working in public relations for Jewish organizations, he published his first novel in 1964. To An Early Grave established him as one of the most promising novelists of his time. It was followed by Teitlebaum's Window (1970) and You Could Live If They Let You (1974). A master of idiom, Markfield writes serious comedy about the Jewish-American experience. A movie addict, he has published a considerable body of film reviews and articles. In 1954-55 he was film critic for the New Leader. He has taught literature and writing at several colleges and is currently on the faculty at Columbia University.

Wallace Markfield

Wallace Markfield was interviewed on 28 March 1977 by Matthew J. Bruccoli in the interviewer's room at the Yale Club of New York. Mr. Markfield had just taught a class at Columbia University and was relaxing with a large cigar. After the taping they walked to Penn Station where Mr. Markfield caught the train home to Port Washington.

Conversations: You recently wrote an afterword for a novel that is going to be republished by Southern Illinois University Press in the fall, The Landsmen *by Peter Martin, and in this afterword you speak rather knowingly, perhaps even sadly, about how the author of a small success feels. Do you think that your own novels come under this category? That is, you get splendid reviews, but your books have not been best sellers.*

Markfield: That's quite true. Well, my first novel received extraordinary, uniformly flattering reviews.

Conversations: To An Early Grave.

Markfield: *To An Early Grave.* And I was never sure at the time that I entirely deserved them. I felt that the book was celebrated by *Time* magazine as a send-off of what Truman Capote called the New York Literary Mafia, that *Time* was only too delighted to stroke me and simultaneously shaft *Partisan Review.* I thought *To An Early Grave,* at least when I started it, was a simple—I can't call it a tragedy—a simple tone poem on aggravation. Tragedy, that is, is beyond us, but aggravation we can aspire to. How could I know the herd of independent minds would *qvell* at each reference to Melorols, F. D. R., and Bogart? All right, I was happy for the success it enjoyed, and I made quite a bit of money—not as much as I might have, with a standard best seller—though movie sales, and this fellowship and that fellowship and lectures amounted to far more than I expected.

Wallace Markfield

I thought *Teitlebaum's Window* was a far better, deeper, richer book, but perhaps one might say they were waiting to get me, though that's rather paranoid. I doubt that. I think *Teitlebaum* came out at the wrong time, too close upon the heels of *Portnoy's Complaint*: too much Jewish mother, carrying too much redolence of milk and matzoh. In the end, the only review that sort of hurt was one in, of all places, the *Baltimore Sun*, I believe, which spoke of all the characters lying around waiting to be remembered and the reviewer's sadness at consigning the broken-down bunch to oblivion. And I felt the sadness of this poor schnook who'd liked *To An Early Grave* merging with my own and the two of us going off together into the stygian darkness.

As for *You Could Live If They Let You*, I received very few reviews, it seems to me. Let's see, only two besides the review in the Chicago paper by my interviewer, which pleased me no end and flattered me, you know, magnificently. There was one, I believe, in another Chicago paper by someone whose name escapes me. He had been a TV critic. He seemed to dig it. If either of those reviews had appeared on the front page of *The Sunday Times*, well, I would have been delighted. Still, it would have made no difference essentially to the sales or anything else. The only thing is that I cannot even claim to be insulted and despised by the establishment, because in strange ways I am, and have been for many years, an establishment writer—if by the establishment one means the avant-garde orthodoxies of *Partisan Review* and *Commentary*, although I'm persona non grata and have been for many years with *Commentary*. The *Times* loves me. And, by and large, you know, I can do no wrong, there. Every department calls me up for a Sunday piece and I turn down, you know, five times as much work as I accept, which, I suppose, is the only definition of the establishment one has in New York these days.

But yes, going back to the original thrust of the question, I know pretty well what Martin must have gone through. One is, in a way, better off in the long run, if you're going to be a fruitful, productive novelist, if your first novel is not singled out for too much attention—if Stanley Edgar Hyman keeps his hands off of it. And this is, you know, a little bit of respect and appreciation for the quite brilliant and feelingful review he did in the *New Leader*, which started the critical ball rolling, I think. But mostly it's a matter of luck. I had a notion, for example, until today when I saw an ad announcing six printings and 106,000 sales for John Cheever's *Falconer*, that it was getting nowhere. Displaced paranoia. But I was on the verge of sending a 'I-know-what-you-are-going-through' note to Cheever.

Conversations: You mentioned the power of The New York Times Book Review *a few minutes ago. Do you consider* The Times *the most powerful review publication in the country?*

Markfield: Yes.

Conversations: Do you feel that they handle that responsibility well?

Markfield: Devastating question. I feel it's impossible to handle that responsibility well under those conditions. I know Leonard slightly—John Leonard, the former editor. Let me go back a bit. In the main, I trusted *The Times*, the book section that is, far more when it was in the hands of an out-and-out Philistine like Francis Brown, who knew exactly what would get the front page, why it should get the front page. One understands the influence of publishers and their ads and the power they enjoy. Yet, I was told by those who worked for him that Brown was of considerable integrity—and considerable stupidity, as well. But sometimes a man of integrity who is stupid is more trustworthy than the bright, bitter boys who run things now.

Conversations: Would it be unfair to say they're by and large a collection of failed writers?

Markfield: Leonard, by his own admission, is a failed novelist. The author of, I believe, three novels, none of which, I confess, I've read. Yet, he did nothing for himself; I know that. You know, he's been consistently ill-reviewed in his own pages. He buries his own books way in the back. The funny thing is I have no grudge against them. They treated me very well with *To An Early Grave*. With *Teitlebaum* I was a victim of too much kindness. Bob Gottlieb at Knopf, you know, let the word get around that this

Wallace Markfield

was his beloved book of the year. He sent it to Leonard and his assistant Richard Locke, a very sweet, Jackie Cooper-faced young man. Locke and Leonard loved it and resolved that they would do their very best by it, give it the very best review they could.

Well, the best reviewer, alas for me, turned out to be Alfred Kazin, whose *Starting Out in the Thirties* I'd reviewed a few years back in *Life*. And I killed it. As to why I killed it, there hangs a tale. He had said, I must confess, some very unkind, unnecessarily unkind things about a very close friend of mine. It was in addition a lousy book on any level, I believe. I stick to what I said. I would not—I know I would not have made a point to review it for *Life* if I hadn't been wounded on my friend's behalf. Well, they sent it to what they felt was the best reviewer, to someone who knew intimately the world of the thirties and would respond to it, the Jewishness of it all, and this was Kazin.

Now, speaking again of integrity, I do believe—although I am not without the taste, the thirst for vengeance myself—I do believe that under the circumstances I would myself have turned the book back saying, "No, I don't think I can be—" I don't know what I would have said, although I think I would have turned it back. On the other hand, I suspect, too, that Kazin in his own way gave me an honest review of the book. He was prepared to hate it, and he saw in it enough to hate even as he had hated *Portnoy's Complaint*. You see there are five or six critics. There's Kazin, there's Irving Howe, there's—when he was writing, at least— Norman Podhoretz, once in a while Lionel Trilling, who had their own peculiar notions of the treatment of the Jew in fiction. I don't know quite what it is. I don't know that I want to know, but *Teitlebaum* would in any case have displeased them—this "establishment" with its orbit of perhaps 20,000 people. I don't know why I'm going off about that. And so, oh, *The Times*, yeah. *The Times* again meant to do very well with *You Could Live*. They sent it, unfortunately—this was an unfortunate choice; I know how they operate. They sent it to a guy named Robert Alter, who is a contributing editor to *Commentary*, who has the word from Norman Podhoretz, who has despised me ever since *To An Early Grave*, where he believed he saw himself caricatured (with, I must also admit, some justice: three lines worth of caricature). So he hated it. I didn't mind that so much as *The Times* head which read "Wallace Markfield Imitates Lenny Bruce." This was most unfortunate and most stupid, in view of the fact that only a year before I'd done a front-page review of Albert Goldman's bio of Lenny Bruce. Just sloppy, dumb. But I tend to believe that what we speak of as *The Times's* power or influence is mostly the work of an underpaid girl from New Jersey, who takes three-hour lunches and tries to do all of her work between four and five. Because whenever I'm called to do a book it's a hasty, breathless British voice begging, teasing, promising, I certainly suspect, all kinds of sexual favors if only I will send in some 1500 words. Nice girl, by the way.

Conversations: Listening to you, it's impossible not to come up with the conclusion that book reviewing in New York—or if that's too cosmic, too sweeping—book reviewing in The New York Times *is largely a game of you-got-me-I'll-get-you; that the reviewers are using the reviews to help friends or tick off enemies.*

Markfield: I think to a large extent you're right. I know that *The Times*, in so far as they possibly can, tries not to give—well, I'm not so sure of that, either. Friends get the books of friends. They do try not to give a book to a known enemy. Out of ignorance they often fail, and I've often argued with myself about the matter of Kazin getting my second book. I tell myself how could they know, and why should they know, and yet it is their business to know these petty matters, to keep up with and to file away all these little silly enmities.

But in all that, I can't blame them, not really. I should insist that the fate of *Teitlebaum* would have been the same even, I think, if it had gotten a front-page review in *The Times*. One must remember that a full two-thirds of the books which get the front-page treatment never make it, not to the best-seller list, not even to a respectable 10,000. I'm not talking merely of non-fiction, you know, the likes of Morris Dickstein's *Gates of Eden*. But, you know, there's no certainty that says *Who Is Teddy Villanova?* will hit the charts, although I should imagine it will do well.

Wallace Markfield

Conversations: Let's back up. Let's go back to beginnings. Brooklyn boy.

Markfield: Indeed.

Conversations: Born what year?

Markfield: 1926. 8-12-26.

Conversations: Went to what high school?

Markfield: Abraham Lincoln High School in the Brighton Beach section of Coney Island.

Conversations: Which produced another fine writer named Daniel Fuchs.

Markfield: I didn't know that he had gone. . .

Conversations: I don't know about the high school, but Brighton Beach was his neighborhood.

Markfield: Yes, yes it was. Well Lincoln, as a matter of fact, if I may boost it, had more writers than you could shake a stick at. Among them, just in the top of my head, Joseph Heller, at least a half-a-dozen *New Yorker* people whose names escape me. Countee Cullen, the black poet. Oh, God, I'm failing my alma mater. But it was a very—it still is a very fine school.

Conversations: You started writing for the high school publications?

Markfield: Yeah, yeah.

Conversations: For the high school newspaper?

Markfield: No, I was never beloved by the faculty advisor.

Conversations: Was there a literary magazine?

Markfield: Yeah, there sure was.

Conversations: And you started publishing there?

Markfield: I was publishing there.

Conversations: And then you went to. . .

Markfield: Brooklyn College. This was during the war; I entered '43 or '44, I forget. I will say '43—'43 sounds logical. Anyway, I love odd numbers.

Conversations: English major?

Markfield: I started as an English major. Then I found out that I had not done well on the entrance test in English, and therefore had been assigned to a required year of composition. My first instructor I found absolutely repugnant, a woman by the name of Dr. Henneberg, whose name will be assigned to a villainous C.I.A. agent in Book Four. We mutually despised each other, and I used to continually carp and nag about the grades she gave me. I'd point it out that I was a high school celebrity. And she'd say, "Oh, you high school celebrities—you're all alike." I dropped English and shortly thereafter found a very good history teacher. And I fell in love with history and I became a history major. Instead of the required thirty credits or whatever, I must have taken eighty. Even now I read history for recreation. I prefer history—I prefer the worst history text to most of the fiction that's around.

Conversations: But in college you were planning to be a writer— you'd picked your life's work?

Markfield: I'm not sure about that.

Conversations: I'll turn the question another way. When did you decide that you were going to be a writer, a full-time professional writer?

Markfield: I was never absurd enough to believe that I'd be a full-time professional writer, because, you know, mine was not a well-to-do family and I knew that I'd have to work for a living. And even then, you know, one knew that writers did not just manage to live by writing alone. But I knew that I had—that I would always write by age nineteen. When I was about eighteen I came across my first copy of *Partisan Review*, and it was a great revelation to me. I was stunned by it. I think the first issue I saw contained a portion of *All The King's Men* by Robert Penn Warren. It was called then "Cass Mastern's Wedding Ring." And

Wallace Markfield

I was deeply impressed by the piece, although I daresay I didn't understand it at all, or I thought I didn't understand it. And I began writing and getting a few stories into the college literary magazine and having lots of trouble with the Stalinists who ran it then, it being the war and somehow, you know, the mood of the popular front. Well, I won't go into that.

Politically it was a very bitter time, and *Partisan Review* suited my anti-Stalinist sensibilities. I sold a story, actually, to *Partisan Review* when I was nineteen, and then another one when I was twenty. And then another one to a magazine called—it was a surrealist magazine published by George Leites, called *Circle*. The magazine went out of business before they could print it, but, at any rate, three stories, three acceptances. You know, my head was turning. And I began writing. At the time I was capable of turning out one bad short story, like John O'Hara, in a few hours.

Then I—well, let's see. We had then started—America, that is, or New York—started to enter the awesome, the awful age of criticism. And I decided that I, too, must become a critic. I couldn't exactly make it as a critic, although in my early twenties I had criticism published here and there. Then I got married at twenty-two or twenty-three, and I fell into someone else's life—very strange. I remember being in the San Remo—I don't know if it's in existence any longer—in the Village. I was haunting the Village at the time and I ran into Anatole Broyard. We became friends. No, nobody becomes friends with Anatole; but we became friendly and he introduced me to someone by the name of Raymond Rosenthal, who, I'm glad to say, just translated the Simone Weil collected works, although he doesn't know French—that's another story.

And Ray and I hit it off immediately. Then he met my now wife—my then girlfriend—and he liked her, she liked him, and Ray and his then wife liked both of us. We became permanent babysitters. Well, they were going off to Italy for a year and they decided, though they had many other friends, to turn over their flat to us. It was the greatest Village pad that has ever been. It was worthy of *I Thought of Daisy*—skylights all over, books from floor to ceiling, enormous living room, charming bunkbeds, etc., etc. We inherited not only the apartment and that library, but—in a manner of speaking, at the age of twenty-three before we were really prepared for it—their lives and their friends including—well, let's see, William Barrett and Harold Rosenburg and Isaac Rosenfeld and a little bit of Leslie Fiedler and David Bazelon and Manny Farber and all kinds of others. Everyone who had ever contributed to *PR* and *Commentary* and *Hudson Review.* We fell to the rear of the avant-garde, I guess.

Conversations: What were you doing for a living at this point?

Markfield: Oh, let me see. For about a year I just couldn't get a job. This was in—I forget when I got married. I think from '48 to '49 Anna, my wife, had intermittent jobs here and there. And I stayed home writing ten- or fifteen-dollar reviews for the *New Leader* and selling the review copies to one or another bookshop, you know, for the usual twenty-five percent of the list. For a while I was an outside reader with a very small publisher called A. A. Wynn.

And then through a wonderful gal at the *New Leader* named—she's dead now—Mary Greene, I landed a publicity job with the Council of Jewish Federations and Welfare Funds. I stayed there for a while, two and a half years, and then I went to another publicity job. Then, oh yeah, then I was fired from the second one, very complicated business. Then I went to Europe for a year and a half, and when I came back we moved to 57th Street. I very quickly and easily found a job doing publicity for the Anti-Defamation League and the American Jewish Committee. That was the bulk of my—how much time did I spend doing that? About twelve years of what I call Jewish publicity.

Conversations: All the time writing?

Markfield: No, not all the time, intermittently. I did, I must confess, very little writing, a short story now and then, not too many. In Europe I tried a novel, although I found the conditions of Europe impossible; never did more than 150 pages. I lost it, regrettably. I'm sure it wasn't very much good. I held off writing a novel. I was fearful of a novel. Then, in 1961, a very, very good friend of mine—he's dead now—the economist Ben B. Seligman came up to the house and said, as was his habit, "Wallace, you're pissing away your time. Do you know that Harvey Swados (a mutual friend) is already finishing his third book, and you haven't even started anything?" And I vowed that no one would ever say that to me again, at least with any justice. So as soon as Ben had left I went into my spare room and I just began something.

Conversations: What year was this?

Markfield: Must have been 1961, and that's when I started *To An Early Grave.*

Conversations: And finished it when?

Markfield: Well, no, this must have been 1960, because it took me about three years. I finished in 1963. It was almost a full year before it was accepted. It was turned down by either seven or eight publishers before Simon & Schuster. Rather heartbreaking, you know, the business of submissions and all. But I had a... well, she seemed to me and I would say she was an excellent agent who believed in the book and never lost hope nor patience. Finally she sent it to Bob Gottlieb, who was at Simon & Schuster then, and he was happy to take it.

Conversations: When did you begin the writer-in-residence routine?

Markfield: Well, I have a friend by the name of Herbert Wilmer, an old, old friend who went to public school and junior high school and Talmud Torah with me, and high school, of course, and college. I lost track of him after college, but I sent him a note after I saw a story of his in *Esquire* in which he had mentioned the name of a girl whom everybody had screwed when we were going to junior high school. I found it very amusing. He looked me up when he came to New York on his way to Europe; he had a Fullbright. And then I sent him *To An Early Grave* when it came out; it delighted him.

Well, for a year after *To An Early Grave* I was doing marvelously, just writing pieces for all kinds of magazines. I was making what seemed to be fantastic money. Quite prolific. As soon as I would finish one article, the phone would ring. Five different magazines wanted this and that, and I had no intention of ever leaving New York. I had started *Teitlebaum* in another form, and I was in no rush to finish it. And then Herb called me from the Coast, as it were: "You want to teach at San Francisco State?" Not exactly writer-in-residence, but something like it. I think they call them "floaters." I said, "Sure." Went out there and we had a grand time for the first year. Then they asked me to stay on for the second year, and then I became a writer-in-residence by accident.

R. V. Cassill had put my name in some bulletin he published only one issue of, I don't remember the name, from Brown University. Trying—and it was a worthwhile objective—trying to link writers who were looking for work with universities that needed writers. I got a call from a chap by the name of—may he grow no older or taller—Adrian Jaffe. Well, he was the head of humanities at a new college in upstate New York called Kirkland. Kirkland was to be the progressive girls' wing of Hamilton College. Would I want to come and see him—expenses paid? I figured why not. So I flew from San Francisco to upstate New York. I found the town of Clinton, New York, near Utica, an absolutely charming picture-postcard town. I had never known such a place, and I was absolutely snowed by the idea, you know, of being a writer-in-residence, good Lord.

So we went to Kirkland, and it was surely the most miserable year I have ever spent—I don't want to go into details, you know, it sounds too much like a bad academic novel. It was a small college. The president, a chap by the name of Sam Babbitt, had a face like Richard Greene—a forgotten Twentieth Century-Fox star—but he had the soul of Machiavelli. And he rather looked like a second-rate printing salesman. At any rate, I had a disgusting time. I wanted to quit after the first year, but I was then in the middle of *Teitlebaum*. I didn't feel like leaving a rather comfortable setup, so we just stayed on for two more years making a total of three in all.

And then *Teitlebaum* was finished in 1971, I think—I'm such an academic vag by now that I lose chronology. By accident I got a job as an assistant or an associate professor, I don't remember, at Queens College, and we moved back to New York, bought a

Wallace Markfield

house in Port Washington. I lasted at Queens College for two years. Markfield, why can't you hold a job? Well, I don't know. A couple of years of unemployment and now at Columbia and who knows what next?

Conversations: Obviously, at least since Kirkland, you haven't believed in the work, and you certainly haven't enjoyed it. Why do you stick with it? The monthly paycheck?

Markfield: Yeah, mostly that. And I'd be telling a lie if I didn't say there's a certain ego gratification. I enjoy the little routines that I've plotted out and recapitulated so often these many years, the jokes I make with the students, or to the students, or of the students. Pretending to misspell my name when I write it on the blackboard, baiting them, teasing them. I dislike writing; I love teaching literature. I love just talking away. I teach a goddamn good *King Lear*, and I teach a good James Agee, so between the two I can manage. Students never treat me as commonplace. Many of them hate my guts, despise me. Many of them love me passionately, madly, fulsomely.

Conversations: Does it interfere with your own work?

Markfield: Not at all. Not at all. Only the rage sometimes interferes, you know. . .

Conversations: The aggravation, you mean.

Markfield: Aggravation, yeah. Not too much, though. I hate to turn into. . . . Nor do I think I ever will; I have too much actual work experience behind me, too many memories of pushing hand trucks through Seventh Avenue traffic, you know, when I was a kid and all that, plus all the years doing publicity work. I mean I know what it is to deal and wheel with switchboard operators and bosses. I know what a real boss is like, as against a chairman, if that makes any sense.

Conversations: A boss is worse than a chairman?

Markfield: A boss is—a real boss is different from a chairman. No, not necessarily worse. I've found many things about academia which astonished me.

Conversations: You wrote an article called "The Graves of Academe," for a publication called Pages, *in which you made two points: point number one was that your colleagues didn't know much about literature and didn't much care for it; and point number two, that the students weren't ready to study literature.*

Markfield: Alas, that's true. I've found many exceptions, needless to say—not as many as all that—amongst my colleagues. I don't want to go into the whole bit of the overspecialization, the Ph.D. syndrome, although it's there. There are so many classes of, genera, I suppose, species of academicians. Some, of course, have given the same lecture for twenty years from yellowing three-by-five cards—all right, we all know those. Others are altogether out of their element, you know, if we go five years beyond or before their periods. Others are careerists. Well, I will not mention his name, but the author of a recent well-reviewed book in *The Times* who looks like Rasputin and seems to believe that he has a feeling for the modern—well, I don't know. At any rate, it astonished me to find how small these people were, how humorless, how, well, I'll stick to small. You see, the article was not drawn from a single university. Well, if it represented anything it represented Kirkland, I suppose, more than Queens.

Queens is a nice, decent place with some very good people; some very bad people, too. The very best of their instructors were young girls, terribly exploited, ranging in age from twenty-five to thirty-five, who worked for half of what the men got and gave five times as much as the best of the big-name, hotshot, full professors. They were summarily fired during what was called an excuse for budget cutting, while the full professors got themselves sabbaticals by putting themselves down for full programs in classes which never met. Remarkable piece of duplicity and they're still doing it. Well, it's not only Queens, they're doing it at every CUNY institution.

Conversations: Let's get back to your work. You don't write every day?

229

Wallace Markfield

Markfield: I've been busy, or pretending that I've been busy, for the last, oh, year, year and a quarter, doing all kinds of articles for this and that. It's worse not writing because I think of writing. Possibly I have for the first time in my life been guilty of consistently missing deadlines—and I hate the unprofessionalism of it—so that I will have an excuse not to do another book. At any rate I haven't—I haven't written, I haven't tried a novel in well over a year. Thinking about one.

Conversations: When you do a novel, do you have what you regard as a good day's work, a target figure—1000 words, 2000 words? Or doesn't it work that way for you?

Markfield: It doesn't. I'm ashamed to admit that a good day's work for me is, oh, a page is. . . 300 words is a very full day's work for me.

Conversations: In how many hours?

Markfield: Well, a working day for me begins—I'll put in seven or eight hours. It's crazy. I suppose I'm what Alden Whitman called Joseph Heller—a "bleeder." I don't know why I'm that way and how it came to pass, but I no longer have the will or the energy to do otherwise.

Conversations: How many drafts do you do? How many drafts did Teitlebaum *take?*

Markfield: Well, basically I do only one draft, so by and large I will cut, you know, at the end, but very little else. In other words, when the book is finished, it's pretty well finished, you know, that is, a final draft.

Conversations: And you write on the typewriter?

Markfield: At least half on the typewriter. I have to have—I'll have scratch pads and I will rewrite a sentence. Sometimes I cover ten, twenty pages—this is madness—with the same sentence or certainly the same paragraph. Dialogue, I should say, comes very easily to me. Dialogue I can write instantly and easily on the typewriter. Physical descriptions, you know, are really murderous to me. I'm never satisfied with what I do. I'm always. . . . Well, every writer has his problems, I guess. But I've often, well, I'll often quit and consider a good day's work two lines. I think it's a James Agee syndrome.

Conversations: You've mentioned Agee's name twice in this interview. I take it that Agee is a presence in your life.

Markfield: Yeah, he's a figure, a presence to be sure, although I never met him. I had one opportunity and I screwed that all up. I was just telling my class today about it. I was then reviewing movies in the *New Leader,* and after work I went to see *Moulin Rouge.* I hadn't had dinner and I was very headachy. I didn't much care for *Moulin Rouge,* and after it was over I was hastening for the exit when a fellow by the name of Manny Herbsman who worked for *The Hollywood Reporter*—I used to call him Manny Schmuck; a sweet little guy, I was very cruel—he came over with a tall, pale, extremely dark-haired fellow in tow. And he said, "Wally, I want you to meet. . . ." I never even gave him a chance to finish his sentence. I waved and was gone, and, of course, that was James Agee. And I've often fantasized what the meeting and the ensuing several hours—and I'm sure that it would have been several hours—might have been like.

In fact, I had Agee as a real character in an aborted novel, which *Multiple Orgasms* is a part of, when Laura Pauline Goodfriend and her soon-to-be-husband go to the Museum of Modern Art and by accident James Agee is there looking at a—I think a Braque exhibition—and I have three or four pages of that episode; then he walks outside with them and he takes a taxi. It's a section. I have a feeling I would like to use Agee as a real character, and I have no idea how.

Conversations: What has influenced you most about Agee? His writing, or do you see Agee as a symbolic figure, or both, or something else?

Markfield: Well, I think, along with everybody else, that he was one of the most gorgeous writers America has ever produced. I go back continually to his movie stuff, his criticism. Whenever I write about the movies I'm always conscious of it, as I'm conscious of Warshow and Manny Farber. These are the three

231

whom I have the highest regard for. And I know that possibly without even meaning to I've swiped phrases from Agee, you know, I look at my work sometimes a year later and I say, "Oh, God, this is awfully Agee-ish." True, only I notice it, but it bothers me all the same. But it's like a recurring tick. I'm deeply envious of this fantastic talent, this employment of language of Agee's. I'm not sure that *A Death in the Family* is an altogether successful novel. I've found it, you know, the most beautiful experience. And what the devil is a successful novel?

Conversations: You've worked as a movie reviewer. Your own novels are full of the movies. You've written a lot of articles about the movies. You're obviously a certified movie nut.

Markfield: Absolutely.

Conversations: Obvious question is how come you've never gone out and gotten a job as a screenwriter?

Markfield: I think times were against that. In the mid-thirties you could publish one decent, well-liked novel and you almost automatically got a call from the Coast. The studio system needed writers, devoured writers, but by the middle and late sixties, Hollywood—well, the studio system was dead and it never occurred to me to, you know, simply go out and try my luck. I'm not sure I wanted it that way. You know, had somebody given me a novel and said write a screenplay, I would have done it.

Conversations: What's the best movie you ever saw? What's your favorite movie?

Markfield: I guess, from the top of my head it would have to be *King Kong.* No movie has affected me more, you know, the more I see it. . . .

Conversations: The original King Kong.

Markfield: The original *King Kong,* yes.

Conversations: In what way did it affect you?

Markfield: Well, I spent like 6000 words trying to and probably not coming even close to it. What way? I guess in every way. Fay

Wray in that scanty dress was my first sense of the erotic, I think. And *King Kong* was my first knowledge of what tragic destiny might have been. Although, oddly enough, I didn't see it until I was—let's see '26 and it came out in '33, that's seven—I don't think I saw it until I was about thirteen, so it seems to have coincided with my Bar Mitzvah, my introduction to manhood. I don't know, every time I see it I see something else in it. I think the last five minutes are beyond belief, you know, for pure powerful tragedy. I would like to say that Cooper didn't know what he was doing, but it turns out, I think, that he knew all too well.

Conversations: There's a literary anecdote I've heard about a young writer who arranged a meeting with an older writer he greatly admired. He went to call on this grand old man of literature, and the old man said to him, "I didn't like my father. Why did you become a writer?" Why did you become a writer?

Markfield: Indeed, indeed. Well, it beat working, I thought. How? I really don't know. Certainly not because I believed I had something to say. No, it was, I think the customary reasons. I don't remember who said it, but I was like everybody else, just like all of my students are now. I was able to see myself as a writer, but I could never quite see myself writing. I could never, you know. . . the stains and pains of writing were quite beyond me.

Why did I become a writer? Well, let's see, my mother would have far preferred, and I think I too at the time, that I become, not a lawyer, a doctor. I had no bent for math or sciences. I was always—I guess it was the only talent that I had. There was ego fulfillment and satisfaction in it. And oh, yes, yes—no small thing—one could get girls by dint of being known, you know, to be a bit of a campus hero. At the time the culture hero had, well, was no longer the psychoanalyst but the writer, and so, you know, what do you do? This young, dark creature with a light fuzz up over her upper lip—I'm describing the archetypal Brooklyn College girl. "What do you want to do?" "Well, in a small way"—pause—ellipsis—"a writer." That must have entered into it, I don't know. One did impress girls that way. I used to even write bad poetry. Not much of an answer, I know, it's. . . .

Wallace Markfield

Conversations: It's a pretty good answer. Freud remarked that writers become writers for three reasons: fame, money, and the love of beautiful women.

Markfield: Fame. The money never. You see, it's only now that money is—at my ripe age—is a consideration. You know, the market place is immensely important now. It's changed the complexion of everything. But certainly fame and the love of beautiful women. And when I was in college they didn't have to be that beautiful.

Conversations: Let me ask you a nuts-and-bolts question. Have you ever figured out what you've averaged per year over the years from your writing alone? Not from teaching, not from public relations. What have you averaged as a writer in, what, twenty-five years of professional writing?

Markfield: Not really.

Conversations: Twenty?

Markfield: No, I would say professional—my professional writing begins with novel one, so let's say from '64 to '74 to now '77.

Conversations: Thirteen years.

Markfield: Thirteen years. God, no, I never did figure it out. It could average a hell of a lot more if I wrote faster, I know. Not simply novels, but articles. *The New York Times* now pays—I pick that as an example—$850 per piece. Now one should not, if one is truly professional, spend more than two weeks at it, and I would have no trouble. I could write continually for *The Times* or for *Harper's* or for *Playboy* or this one. I don't and I can't because I know that—let's say if *Playboy* were to offer me some movie piece or nostalgia for, what, 2500 bucks, I'd spend four, five, and six months, you know, before I would finish it. So you know, at those rates. . . . But, let's see. What have I made out of my books? I really never figured it out.

Conversations: It's a nosey question.

Markfield: No, no, no, no. It's a good question. I would say about ten grand a year would average, maybe eight grand a year. It's really hard to—I guess between eight and ten, you know.

Conversations: The point I was sneaking up on is that being a writer is a lot like being in show business. There are a couple of stars who get the Las Vegas salaries, and a lot of other people just make a living.

Markfield: Yeah, and there's the third category: those that don't even make a living. You know, I truly can't—on a certain level, I can't complain. I shouldn't. Well, I can, and I do. But I really shouldn't. I feel that, you know, the bitterness I am subsumed by now is totally unjustified.

Conversations: But you are bitter.

Markfield: Yeah. Right now I'm bitter. I don't know exactly why, but nonetheless I'm bitter. Bitterness is a terribly self-defeating thing and doesn't get any work done, yet the knowledge of that doesn't help too much. I'm basically—well, it comes to this: whether I'm tired of the Jewish thing, whether I'm genuinely tired of it, whether I've said all that I have to say on that subject and with those characters, I don't know. I want to do a novel which may or may not have Jewish characters, but which offers, well, a good read, a page turner.

I've been doing some research and I've read in the past year or so, I don't know how many hundreds of, well, bad books: thrillers, doomsday books, melodramas, espionage, and I find myself surprised to thoroughly enjoy stuff like Lawrence Saunders's *The First Deadly Sin*, or Judith Rossiter's *Looking for Mr. Goodbar*, which is an atrociously written book, and yet I found it immensely moving. And I find so many brilliant ideas—I would include in that a really stupid book called *Audrey Rose, Whose Little Girl Are You?* A dreadful book, but a brilliant idea, and I'd give my molars and eyeteeth to have come up with that idea.

I find, too, that by a kind of cruel contrast, the finest writers of our time—I mean, of course, Bellow, or, let's say, on another level, Cheever—can't plot to save their lives. Well, Cheever is perhaps a bit better, but *Falconer*, for example, is a beautifully written—that is line-by-line, sentence-for-sentence—piece of work. But there is no reality to the setting or certainly not to the character Farragut. He's one dimensional. But Cheever, you know. . . . I read it with great pleasure. What I'd like to do and what's giving me God-awful trouble is come up with. . . . Oh, Lord, this sounds like Jacqueline Susann, but I'd like to come up with a very solidly plotted novel with a traditional beginning, middle, and end. Perhaps even a thriller, or my own definition of a thriller, with the obligatory sex and violence, murder and mayhem, which also has every bit of the art that I believe can be brought to this genre. I'm not thinking really of Graham Greene. I'm not thinking of anybody. I have moments and beginnings and thoughts, but thus far I cannot put it all together.

You see, a few years ago I was able to just begin. At present I'm obsessed by the line "At this moment in America." I know that four, five, and ten years ago I'd have a sheet of paper in my typewriter and I'd begin "At this moment in America" and the first paragraph would get itself written. And without any sense of a plot or a character I would eventually three years later finish the book, a book. Now I have no such confidence. I'm waiting for another kind of character to whisper in my ear and till such a time, till such a time, we will continue in a state of bitterness, I suppose. But nothing is altogether lost.

Donald Ogden Stewart was born in Columbus, Ohio, in 1894. After graduating from Yale he started a business career but became a humorist by chance. His first book was A Parody Outline of History *in 1921, which was followed by* Perfect Behavior *(1922),* Aunt Polly's Story of Mankind *(1923),* Mr. and Mrs. Haddock Abroad *(1924),* The Crazy Fool *(1925),* Mr. and Mrs. Haddock in Paris, France *(1926),* Father William *(1929), and* Rebound *(1931). His autobiography* By a Stroke of Luck! *appeared in 1975. Stewart became one of the highest paid writers in Hollywood, winning an Academy Award for* The Philadelphia Story. *He has lived in London since 1952.*

Donald Ogden Stewart

*Donald Ogden Stewart was interviewed by Matthew J. Bruccoli on 8
May 1976 at the Stewart home in the Hampstead section of London.
The living room walls were covered with the modern art collected
by Stewart's wife, Ella Winton Stewart. During the interview she
tended the plants that filled the room. Stewart dispensed a drink he
had just invented called "wine."*

*Conversations: In the twenties we had a golden age of humor:
there was Stewart; there was Benchley; there was Lardner; there
was Dorothy Parker; there was George S. Kaufman. America was
full of wits. Now there is no one around who could be considered
a major American humorist. What happened to American
humor?*

Stewart: Well, it isn't as easy as that because at the end of the
twenties there came a thing called the "Crash" and everybody
was worried about money. Before that my father went broke. My
family went broke. I, who had thought that I might become vice-
president of the Second National Bank of Columbus, Ohio, found
that I couldn't get a job, and if it hadn't been for a man named F.
Scott Fitzgerald I would have been on my can, because I had my
mother to support. I had to make a living for myself, and I went to
New York in desperation—without a job, without anything—and
ran into Scott Fitzgerald, and he suggested I go down and see a
man named Edmund Wilson who was an editor at *Vanity Fair*.
Edmund Wilson asked me if I'd ever written anything, and I
hadn't—I really hadn't.

Conversations: Not even at Yale as an undergraduate?

Stewart: No. I was on the *Yale Daily News* as what was called the
assignment editor, and the assignment editor ran the competition
for the next. . . . I heeled successfully and made the *News*, but it
didn't mean anything in terms of writing. I ran competitions for
the next assignment editor. In the course of that, it suddenly

239

Donald Ogden Stewart

occurred to Edmund Wilson or myself, "Why not do a parody of Scott Fitzgerald?" That had never occurred to me at all. I hadn't done any parodies. I wrote a parody of a little bit of *This Side of Paradise*, which was Scott's first book, and took it down to Bunny Wilson and started to read it to him. It was awful, because Bunny just sat there. Somehow this sort of thing has always happened to me—three rooms away a man began to play the flute, and if you're going to read a parody of anything, the flute is not the thing to accompany it. And I got madder and madder, because Bunny wasn't laughing and there wasn't any sign of recognition. But I went on reading this attempt at humor, and suddenly Bunny began to laugh. I've never felt so in love with anybody as I became with Edmund Wilson during that. He began to laugh even louder, and then the flute stopped playing, and I felt, "Well, what can you lose?" So I went on. After I had finished a certain amount of it, Bunny said, "Well, Don, that's not bad. Could you do some more, and perhaps do another parody of another writer?" So I, who had devoted my life to making good at Yale and getting ready to become vice-president of the Second National in Columbus, Ohio, suddenly became a writer. It scared the bejesus out of me, because how did I know it was going to go on.

I sent for my mother, whom I was supporting. She came down to New York, and my life became that of a writer. I got a job writing monthly pieces for *Vanity Fair*, and then Mother and I thought we might like to go over and see what Europe was like. I had enough money by that time to do that, so she and I went to Paris. In Paris, I happened to meet a man named Ernest Hemingway and a marvelous couple of people named Gerald and Sara Murphy. Little by little editors began to accept articles that I wrote about Hemingway and about Fitzgerald and the Murphys and so forth. And a man who had not the slightest idea of becoming a writer found himself cashing checks which turned out to be good. They were from publishers.

From there, I went on to writing my first parody book which was called *A Parody Outline of History*, and that happened to catch on. So this young man who had meant only to be a modest vice-president of a bank found himself a writer with people reading his books. From then I found out that—I didn't find out that I could act, but a friend of mine at Yale named Philip Barry had written a play, and he asked me to take a part in it. I found that when I walked out on the stage, people began to laugh at what I said.

Conversations: You hadn't acted at Yale? Or at prep school?

Stewart: No, oh, no. I hadn't ever thought of acting. The play was *Holiday*. Katharine Hepburn and Hope Williams were in it, and it was a hit. The next thing I knew—oh, they had discovered something in Hollywood called dialogue. Up to then, they had had silent pictures, and they began to find out that you could use words and get laughs and suspense and so forth. This would have been about 1930 or so.

Conversations: What was your first movie?

Stewart: My first movie was—I'm not quite sure—but I think it was something called *Laughter*, which I did for Paramount in New York.

Conversations: How about Brown of Harvard? *I thought that was your first?*

Stewart: No, *Brown of Harvard* was a silent.

Conversations: You worked for the silents before you did talkies?

Stewart: Well, I did that, yeah, but that was just a mistake. They didn't have anybody else to do *Brown of Harvard*, and as I had gone to Yale, it seemed naturally the thing for me to do.

Conversations: But Laughter *may have been your first talkie?*

Stewart: I'm not quite sure it wasn't, yeah, but that was for Paramount across the river from New York. And that worked out all right. Then there was an actress named Tallulah Bankhead. Paramount brought her over and I wrote a picture for her and from then on it was a continuous life in motion pictures. Then I also did a couple of plays, acted in a couple of plays, and wrote three or four plays myself.

Conversations: Now in Hollywood. . .

Stewart: It was just luck.

Conversations: In Hollywood you became most closely associated with MGM, didn't you?

Donald Ogden Stewart

Stewart: Yeah, well, at first I did, yeah. And then I worked for different companies.

Conversations: You worked closely with Irving Thalberg for a while?

Stewart: Yes, very closely.

Conversations: How do you recall Thalberg?

Stewart: Well, Irving—if you don't mind my calling him Irving— was marvelous, because he knew what he set out to do when he became a movie producer. He knew movies. And if you didn't know movies, Irving would set you right, and you would be sure of yourself. I learned a great deal from Irving Thalberg about dialogue, about drama, about moving pictures. And I owe a tremendous amount to him.

Conversations: Did Fitzgerald get him right in The Last Tycoon? *Do you recognize Fitzgerald's Monroe Stahr as Irving Thalberg?*

Stewart: I wouldn't be able to say, toots, because I—if Irving was Monroe Stahr I can't remember the picture well enough to criticize it—Irving was something you felt sure of. He was younger than I. He had gone through a certain political life that I was just beginning to discover. Irving, when he was in a Brooklyn high school, used to go on the corner and make speeches for Socialism to people. I didn't know anything about Socialism until I began to feel terribly guilty about the money I was getting, and this was about 1929 or '30.

Conversations: What was your salary?

Stewart: Well, it started out around $500 a week. It wasn't long before I was getting $3500 a week and that wasn't due to any—I mean, I had nothing to do with that. I could write dialogue suddenly, and I could write pictures, and it began to work. When I finally ended up in pictures, it was because I had discovered something called Socialism. I felt so guilty about the money I was making and the people who were having to stand in breadlines and jump out of windows and things like that—this would have been after 1929. I happened to be in London and I discovered— well, I accidentally went out to talk to the doorman who had gotten me a taxi cab. I asked him if he knew anything about

242

Communism and he said, "Well, sir, I'm afraid I don't, but I think if possibly you went to a book shop, you might find out something." So I got into the taxi cab and drove to Boots' Book Shop, I think it was. They had a book by a man named John Strachey called *The Coming Struggle for Power.* I bought *The Coming Struggle for Power*, and it opened up a whole world for me, the world of Communism and Socialism and the working class.

When I went back to Hollywood after that I helped organize various institutions. There was one which was against a man named Hitler. We had begun to read about him. And there were other fights that we participated in. They weren't fights—we would hold meetings and have various speakers come out, senators and so forth and so on, and it all began to work out. We found that we could fill the auditorium; we could get crowds. Then a curious thing happened. Something called the Un-American Activities Committee arose in Washington in Congress, and they began to attack us for being—for God's sake, for being Communists. And we didn't know anything, or we didn't know very much about what Communism was about. We wanted to help the poor.

Conversations: You never became a member of the Communist Party?

Stewart: No. I came awfully close. I don't want that "no" to be a sort of a purification of myself. It wouldn't have taken much for me to have joined the Communist Party. When it got to be a showdown, when they began really to investigate, I found out that I was on the edge of being kicked out. By that time I was making $4000 a week and at the same time I had married the widow of Lincoln Steffens. She and I decided—she also was what might be called a left-winger—that it might be a good idea to get the hell out of Hollywood and New York and see what was going on over in Europe. So in '51 or '52, we got on a boat and landed in England, and we've been here ever since.

Conversations: You were not subpoenaed by Congress?

Stewart: No, I was never called up. The only danger I was in was that the legal department of my Hollywood studio . . . .

Conversations: MGM?

Donald Ogden Stewart

Stewart: Yes—suggested that it would be a good idea if I came down to the legal department and gave a few names of Communists. That was the end. I mean, there's something about giving names of other people that didn't sort of come together with my idea of what I was trying to do for the poor people. So Mrs. Stewart and I found ourselves on this boat, and we've never been back.

Conversations: Would you like to go home?

Stewart: No, it's been . . . .

Conversations: For a visit?

Stewart: Well, I might, but I don't know whether anybody would remember me anymore. That was twenty-five years ago. It's been a marvelous life. London, England, is marvelous to live in, and I've been very happy here ever since.

Conversations: Did you have trouble working after you left America?

Stewart: I didn't try to work anymore. I had three or four plays I'd written. I put those on—one in Sweden, one in Germany, and one in Italy, I think. The plays worked out all right. My writing life went on. I did three or four films here in England.

Conversations: Under your own name?

Stewart: I think—I can't remember that—but I think under my own name. There was one picture for which I had to take my father's name, Gilbert Holland. He was Gilbert Holland Stewart, and I very cleverly said that this picture was by Gilbert Holland.

Conversations: To make it distributable in the United States?

Stewart: Yes. I don't think that by that time—I think that I couldn't have gotten any pictures accepted or bought by film companies.

Conversations: What movie was it that Gilbert Holland did?

Stewart: I can't possibly remember. I only did three or four over here, and I got my plays on, and it's been wonderful. It's really been a marvelous, fulfilled life.

Donald Ogden Stewart

Conversations: When you left America you were prepared to pay for your convictions, because you must have been leaving a very nice contract.

Stewart: Oh, sweetie, I wasn't prepared for anything. I didn't intend to live in England for twenty-five more years. I only knew what I believed in, which was left-wing politics. I was very much a left-winger. I would not have given the names of any of the left-wingers that were with me. I think I was fairly honest about my life from the moment—I tell you—from the moment that the "Crash" came in America and I was getting $3500 a week. I began to feel that I ought to do something about that besides contribute to charity and things like that. And the thing I did about it was to become politically involved up to my neck in helping the poor people. In other words, I stepped out of my . . . . My father had been a Republican judge in Columbus, Ohio, and I had been a Republican judge's son. I had done all the right things at Exeter Academy and Yale. I had been a boy on his way to belonging to the best clubs and so forth, and when the "Crash" came it just seemed that you joined a different group. You stepped down from the Racquet Club.

Conversations: Irving Thalberg, after his high school Socialism, who was making at least ten times what you were making in Hollywood, became a conservative. He fought Upton Sinclair, and helped fight the Writer's Guild.

Stewart: Well, I don't really see how you can compare Irving and me, because Irving was a Socialist in high school . . . .

Conversations: And outgrew it.

Stewart: And outgrew it. You might say I was an upper-class member of the Racquet Club, and outgrew it. I discovered something else.

Conversations: Did you ever talk politics with Thalberg?

Stewart: No, I don't . . . at least if I did, he wasn't on my side.

Conversations: He was a strong Republican.

Stewart: Yes. He was a very strong Republican, and he knew exactly what it was he was after. He was going up and I was going down. But not in moral terms. I found myself in finding the lower classes and trying to help them. That sounds a little noble and I don't mean it to be that. I think I joined my father and my brother when I discovered the poor, because we never were very rich or anything like that. I just felt so comfortable to be with the people who were having a bad time. Now I don't mean that to be a noble statement or any praise of myself: it just happened naturally. I became a member of the working class, and actually the working class would have laughed their heads off at my idea of being a member of the working class at $3500 a week. But it was my way out of—oh, climbing, snobbery, all of those things that you'd rather not be connected with.

Conversations: Can you give me some idea of Thalberg's working habits?

Stewart: No. He worked his ass off. He was a very intelligent man. I don't know whether he went to college or not. I only knew that I trusted him and believed in him, and he taught me an awful lot about screenwriting, and we got along together. But aside from that, I wasn't close to him at all. You didn't get close to people at Metro-Goldwyn-Mayer or any of the studios. At least if you did, you were in danger of ass-kissing, and as you know a Yale man doesn't do that. That's a joke.

Conversations: There is a wire from Fitzgerald to Maxwell Perkins telling him to send the opening chapter of The Last Tycoon *to Joseph Bryan at* The Saturday Evening Post. *Bryan had never dealt with Fitzgerald and thinks that you might have directed Fitzgerald to him.*

Stewart: It would never occur to me to try and sell Scott. It would be impossible to think of, of selling Scott to Joe Bryan. I mean I liked Joe and I liked Scott and think they . . . . You see, my first wife and I lived on the Payne Whitney estate. To live on the Whitney estate and to go . . . . Our friends were all rich and good dancers and things like that, and Joe and his lovely wife were all part of it. There was no connection as far as . . . . Until I discovered *The Coming Struggle for Power,* I lived the life of the rich, and it was great. It was very nice. I've no objections at all to the Whitneys or anybody on the north shore of Long Island. I've had a hell of a lucky life. I mean I've had the best of both worlds. I have enjoyed the Whitneys—Jock is a very nice guy and I loved his sister Joanie. My first wife was wonderful. I mean I've really had a hell of a lucky life. And then with all the kind of lucky success with books and plays and films and acting and everything—what the hell, I've had it, toots. I ought to die.

Conversations: You've had a hell of a life; I'll agree with you there.

Stewart: Yes, and it hasn't been a climbing life.

Conversations: It came to you?

Stewart: No, after I discovered John Strachey and Karl Marx . . . . You're talking to a guy who's been lucky as hell. I made all the best clubs and then I made all the best poor people. I don't think it turned me into a horse's ass. I mean it could have, but I never got out of that sort of feeling—"Well, you lucky son of a bitch!" But the main thing is I've enjoyed it. I really have had a hell of a wonderful time. I don't know what's going to happen tomorrow or the day after tomorrow, but up till now it's been wonderful and I'm so appreciative of it. I'm appreciative of Ella and I was appreciative of my first wife, and it just seems to me that life has been marvelous.

Conversations: You've done it all.

Stewart: I haven't done anything, sweetie. How can you write successful books, plays, scripts? How can you make $3500 a week? How can you have two marvelous wives? How can you be sitting on your ass in this room without . . . . Somebody's paying for this. I mean, everybody isn't that lucky.

Conversations: In your next life you're going to be something terrible.

Stewart: Yes. I'll write to you. I'll let you know—"Don't come; it isn't worth it."

Conversations: How about the word "talent"?

Stewart: All right, but isn't that luck? Well, toots the only bad time in my life was when Father got into trouble and Mother got to drinking, and I got out of that. Mother stopped drinking and she and I had a lovely time together. You don't think that something awful is waiting for me?

Conversations: Surely what you did with your talent wasn't luck.

Stewart: But that's the only thing I deserve credit for, I think. I've enjoyed the whole damned thing, really. And I'm still enjoying it.

Conversations: Who are the two or three most exciting people you knew along the way in terms of genius or personality?

Stewart: Oh, I couldn't—

Conversations: You knew Benchley; you knew Ring Lardner; you knew Hemingway; you knew Fitzgerald.

Stewart: I would think Benchley was the most satisfactory person. He was humor. He was the enjoyment of life.

Conversations: Who were the most talented people you knew in Hollywood? What I'm leading up to is the claim that Hollywood destroyed writers. Do you feel that Hollywood destroyed writers by giving them too much money?

Stewart: I think, toots, that the money you got in Hollywood was bad for you.

Conversations: How?

Stewart: In making you too safe. I don't think that you ought to be too safe. My father was a respectable judge in Columbus, Ohio, and yet he died with a suit against him for having taken money for some cause—I forget what it was now. You never know when it's going to hit you. Ella could turn on me tomorrow and I wouldn't know what the hell to do. I haven't lost friends, perhaps . . . . The minute you get safe or get to feeling safe or get to feeling that you've done it yourself, I think you ought to look over your left shoulder because . . . . I don't know, I'm eighty-one years old, and it's a little late to worry about that now, I think. I hope it is. But if Ella would die that would be awful because she's been so good for me and to me. But Mother and Father. Well, Mother died—thanks to my luck and everything, I think Mother died happy. Father was in trouble when he died. You can't possibly tell—you can't possibly tell what's going to happen tomorrow.

Donald Ogden Stewart

Conversations: A man you didn't like named John O'Hara said, "One of the secrets of a happy life is don't live too long."

Stewart: Well, that's a typical O'Hara remark, if I may say so, because it isn't true. Live as long as you can, but don't be afraid to accept happiness—don't be afraid of your happiness.

Conversations: But you've just told me how guilty you felt about your unearned happiness.

Stewart: Yeah, yeah. Well, I should have felt guilty. It's getting a little late that's the only thing.

Conversations: Let's get off this funeral subject. I'd still like to know about the writers you worked with in Hollywood. Did you work with Hecht or MacArthur?

Stewart: No. I knew them very well, but I never did a picture with them.

Conversations: Did you work with Anita Loos?

Stewart: No. I knew her well.

Conversations: I know you knew Dorothy Parker. Did you ever work on a script with Dorothy Parker?

Stewart: No.

Conversations: How about Dashiell Hammett?

Stewart: No. I didn't work with any of those people. Knew them well, yeah.

Conversations: Would you say that in the case of Dashiell Hammett Hollywood money made serious work seem unnecessary?

Stewart: Sweetie, how could I say that?

Conversations: Because he quit. The Thin Man was 1934—

Stewart: I wouldn't be able to have any opinion about Dash. I never was a friend of his in the same way I was a friend of Benchley's or Dottie's. I don't think I could tell you if I sat down for a week or two weeks or a month. When I say to you I've been lucky as hell and happy as hell, I couldn't prove that. It just seems to me now that I've had a hell of a marvelous life.

Conversations: One of the things you escaped is the bottle. You were a drinker but you were never a drunk. Some of your close friends became alcoholics. Fitzgerald, certainly.

Stewart: Yeah, I never—I would never think of Scott or Hem as drunkards. They were fun to be with; we had fun. I don't know, I didn't see much of Ernie after he had a couple of years in Spain and so forth. So I don't know. I would hear stories about him drinking in Florida, but it never.... You see what also happened to me was that I changed from Fitzgerald and Hemingway to John Hay Whitney and Bobby Benchley. It's not possible to sum up my life.

Conversations: Do you think these people were just natural-born alcoholics, the way other people are natural-born diabetics? Or did the writing life in the twenties contribute to this alcoholism?

Stewart: No, no. For instance, Ernie. I would never think of Ernie as an alcoholic. Scott might have been a bit on the alcoholic side along with Zelda, but....

Conversations: What are your memories of Zelda Fitzgerald? What did she look like?

Stewart: Impossibility of getting close to. I never felt any closeness to her. Scott I knew out in Minnesota before *This Side of Paradise*. I don't think I know any drunks. There have been people in my life that you couldn't count on. And at "21" or other places they might go overboard the way I would. But if you ask me, "Did you ever know any drunks?" I didn't. Maybe it was just that we'd get drunk one night and be all right the next day. I wouldn't be able to categorize anybody, I don't think. They had good nights and bad nights and so forth; but Dottie, for instance, or Bobby.... No, I am beyond judging anybody now, I think. I think that at eighty-one I cannot. I can't hate anybody. I can't let out cheers for anybody. But goddamn it, I loved an awful lot of people. I would have bad days maybe with them, but I can't remember those. I'm too old for you, toots. I'm too near the grave to give you any opinions about anybody. I liked so many people and I've such a good life that I don't think I ought to fart around with it. Let's just say—"the lucky son of a bitch." Would you put that on my tomb?

Thomas Tryon was born 14 January 1926 in Hartford, Connecticut. He attended Yale University, where he received a B.A. in 1949. After Yale, Tryon embarked on a career as a professional actor. He worked on the stage in New York and in television soap operas before going to Hollywood, where he appeared in The Longest Day *(1962) and* The Cardinal *(1964). His first novel,* The Other *(1971), was written while he was working as an actor. The tremendous success of the book encouraged Tryon to quit acting and become a full-time writer. His other works include* Harvest Home *(1973),* Lady *(1974), and* Crowned Heads *(1976).*

Thomas Tryon

On 31 March 1977 Robert Dahlin interviewed Thomas Tryon at the author's fashionable apartment on Central Park West in Manhattan. The interview was conducted in a grand room decorated in an African motif with predominantly white furniture and overlooking the Park. The interview was interrupted at one point so that the principals could make use of the well-stocked bar in the room.

Conversations: You have been quoted as saying you got into acting by accident and you had always wanted desperately to be a writer. How did you get into acting?

Tryon: This comes under the heading of oft-told tales. I had come down to New York from Yale. I was doing postgraduate work and studying at the Arts Students League, and at that point I wanted to be an artist. I had had to register while I was at Yale as a kind of cartoonist. I had a Sunday page about six times through the year where I would do a series of panels reflecting campus life or New Haven life, that kind of thing. I have often said that it was then my ambition to become a *New Yorker* cartoonist, and I think that's fairly accurate. But it happened through friends who were rather well connected at the Cape Playhouse, which was then run by Richard Aldrich.

Conversations: Gertrude Lawrence's husband.

Tryon: Yes. It was, in fact, Gertrude who more or less set me on my path. I was hired to work at the Playhouse mainly, to begin with, as a sign painter. I had become very adept at painting signs, because I had worked for the Reunion Bureau at Yale for three successive Spring Furors, and I was always painting signs. So that really was why I was hired, ostensibly, at a very small, nominal salary.

Conversations: So you were working in art rather than words at that point?

Thomas Tryon

Tryon: Yes, I was. And it just happened that that season—which was 1949, I think, or '50, something like that—Dick Aldrich had booked his own production of *Caesar and Cleopatra*, which had closed on Broadway with Lilli Palmer. He replaced her with Paulette Goddard—really, of all people in that part—and he'd booked her big summer tour in that production. So we really had no sooner gotten to the Playhouse and kind of shook down when it was announced that we, the entire contingent of backstage people including apprentice staff, of which I was a member, were going to have to be in the show. A lot of people didn't want to, but I thought, "Oh, this will be fun."

I had always been interested in the theatre. I had been in our class play as a senior, and I had put on lots of plays when I was a kid. I was very into the whole thing, so I thought it was terrific. They came around parceling out the armor, and I was at that point, I think, an assistant stage manager. I was unique in that I wore a helmet, so you could see virtually nothing of me except a little bit of face sticking out from underneath this helmet. And yet after the opening night performance of the production these two guys arrived backstage and they wanted to put me in the movies.

Conversations: You must have cut a mean figure.

Tryon: Well, I can show you pictures. It's a hoot, with all the body makeup and the greaves and the cape and the helmet. I didn't even carry a spear. Actually, I carried a buccina, which is that Roman trumpet. In any case, they were, in fact, accredited talent scouts for Howard Hughes, who then owned RKO. They really wanted to put me in the movies. Well, everybody thought that was a hoot, including Gertrude, who instantly became my mentor, and said, "No, no, no!" She sent them packing. She said, "He doesn't want to go to Hollywood." She said that if I wanted to become an actor I must get parts, and I must go back to New York, and I must study, and I must get stage experience, etc., etc. As a matter of fact, the guys did come back again later that summer and take photographs of me. Then they went off and I never did hear from them again. But I was very cool toward the whole idea of jumping on a train or plane to run off to Hollywood.

But through that summer I did play some other parts. I played my first part of any substance in a stock production of *Happy Birthday* with Imogene Coca. And got my first professional review; it was a rather decent review from Elliot Norton. Little by little I started getting these parts. As a matter of fact I just bumped into somebody at the gym yesterday who came up and reintroduced himself and said we were in a play at Dennis with Betty Field. I had forgotten all about that one. She was married to Elmer Rice; it was something Elmer Rice had written. I had a small part. Anyway, I got these small parts and then when I came back to New York I decided, based on these talks I had had with Gertrude, that I would become an actor.

Conversations: So you were ready to give up art for acting at that point?

Tryon: Uh-hm. That's really just about what happened.

Conversations: Then you hadn't yet turned your thoughts to writing, per se?

Tryon: Not at all. That didn't come for another fifteen years, really.

Conversations: Had you written at all when you were younger?

Tryon: No. I realized I could write when I was in college and I had to do term papers and things of that nature. I wrote a brilliant thesis.

Conversations: On what?

Tryon: On Henry James. I got straight A's in English. There were some rather bad courses we had. They don't teach much at Yale; they really don't. I don't know if they teach much anywhere, but at Yale they certainly don't. We had a course on the English novel. And the novels we had to read were *Marius the Epicurean*—Walter Pater "burning with his gemlike flame." I think we got *Tess of the D'Urbervilles*, and bad Dickens—I mean second-rate Dickens. *Nicholas Nickelby* is not the best Dickens that there is, and I don't understand why they would go on the assumption that everybody had read all there was of the good Dickens, and what was the other one?—*Nicholas Nickelby* and...

Thomas Tryon

Conversations: Martin Chuzzlewit?

Tryon: Yes, exactly. *Martin Chuzzlewit.* Well, *Martin Chuzzlewit* has Hexnef, and Mrs. Gamp, and characters like that, and they're marvelous, but I don't consider that really prime Dickens in the face of *Great Expectations,* say. They presupposed that you had even read *David Copperfield,* which I, in fact, hadn't. But it was my love for Dickens that later stood me in good stead, because, although I kind of fell into it through a different area, I know that someday I'm going to get into that kind of Dickensian full-out thing when I finally decide that that's where I'm going to go.

Conversations: Fully-textured?

Tryon: Yes, exactly. I don't remember what that thing was I wrote about Henry James, but it had to do with his pictorial sense, which seems strange at this remove, because he doesn't have much of a pictorial sense. Perhaps I just thought he did.

Conversations: That's interesting, though, because your books are quite filled with sensory perceptions.

Tryon: Enormously. Well, that's a combination of my painter's eye and my movie eye—all those years in pictures. I see things very graphically, and I see them, generally, very cinematically. I direct my scenes and I move my actors around in my head. I know exactly, where Gottlieb, my editor at Knopf, says, "I don't really care what the room looks like." I know where they're sitting and everything. I want to know everything; I want to know the smell and the weather and the time and the clothes. If they wrestle, I want to hear that. If they're eating, I want to hear the clank of spoons in the dining room. I want to know if she's messy and drops her crumbs or the egg falls on the napkin, and what the napkin looks like. It's that kind of detailing that I find important. I don't find it in too many other writers. I mourn it, really. I get so tired of these kind of flat-out things that are telling a story but there are no characters there.

Conversations: And it's all very sparse and cold.

Tryon: Yes. And I just finished a book that they gave me from the office to read because they thought it was up my alley and they wanted a quote. Well, needless to say, they are not getting the quote. The two protagonists didn't even come together for 150 pages.

Conversations: How did you get to Hollywood and into writing?

Tryon: Well, that's very simple. I listened to Gertrude's admonitions about waltzing off to Hollywood. She had just waltzed back from Hollywood after having done a disastrous job in the Laurette Taylor role in *The Glass Menagerie*. She was so bad and disappointing. I mean, this is a woman—I loved her and respected her and I thought she was tremendous, but she was just awful in that movie. Gertrude was awfully, awfully miscast. I guess they thought because Vivien Leigh had done a southern accent so successfully that she could do it, but she didn't. It was another five years before I ventured. I started playing extras on television. That's how I broke into the business, mainly through a friend of mine, who now lives down in the Caribbean with his wife. Bill was casting director for many of the important TV kitchen shows at that time—by that I mean the Paddy Chayefsky—what they used to call kitchen dramas. There was Goodyear Playhouse and the U.S. Steel Hour. . . .

Conversations: Studio One?

Tryon: Well, Studio One was something else, but I did do Studio One. I played most of the dramatic shows as an extra. No lines, just as an extra. But that brought me money and enabled me to study. I was fortunate in studying Sandy Meisner at the Neighborhood Playhouse. I got a good solid training from him. Then things started moving. I started playing bits, and what have you. By the time I left for Hollywood I was playing leads on television. In the interim I had done my first Broadway show. After studying singing and dancing for about six months, I went and auditioned, and I got in the show.

Conversations: What show was that?

Tryon: It was called *Wish You Were Here*, the Josh Logan musical with the swimming pool on stage. And how I got in that show in itself is a long story—I won't bore you with that. But I stayed with that show for, I think, about eighteen months, and then left to do a season of repertory with Jose Ferrer, and played in my first classics.

Thomas Tryon

It was at that point I was seen by another talent scout. Although now my position was considerably altered from that opening night at Dennis when I was playing a centurion, I don't think the parts I was doing then were much bigger. This woman was some cohort of Hal Wallis's. She had me round to talk, and she thought I should meet him, which I did. He wanted me to fly down to Key West to play the part—of all things—of a priest, a very small part of a priest in *The Rose Tattoo*, with Magnani and Burt Lancaster. I didn't much like the part and I didn't want to do that, particularly if it were to be my screen test. So I said no. And he said, "Well, all right." Then they flew me to the Coast. He had just signed Shirley MacLaine; she had done that one picture for Hitchcock called *The Trouble With Harry* and she was going to become a big star, so I tested with Shirley. We did two scenes: one from *Summer and Smoke* and one from *The Rainmaker*—both parts that she was right for, and both parts that I was right for. Neither of us ever played them. But on the basis of those tests I was signed to a contract, which was then split between Hal Wallis and Paramount. They each had a chunk of me, and so I moved to California and started my movie career. And that went on from 1955 until—for about ten years.

Conversations: Why did you leave acting to go into writing? Did you find acting not fulfilling?

Tryon: Absolutely. That's exactly what happened. As time went by I had been under contract to three or four major studios. I had been with Disney, and actually I liked working at Disney at that time. It was a rather—well, I won't say exalted position, because you're never exalted if you're working for Walt Disney: there's no one except Walt Disney. But it was a happy period in my life; I did enjoy it. But things got to a point where it just was not satisfying, and I wanted to get into directing.

For your purposes, I have to be very particular about that. I did not have any idea that I was going to have the career I have now as a writer, as a novelist. The desire to direct gave some birth to the idea for *The Other*, in a little book called "The Apple Cellar"—Bob Gottlieb got it under a wholly different title. The first night we met he said, "The first thing that has to go is that awful title." I said, "Oh, okay. I've got a lot of other titles." He

258

said, "Like what?" I said, "Well, it was originally called 'The Apple Cellar.'" And he looked at me with this perplexed expression and said, "What on earth does your book have to do with a man who sells apples?" He may have been pulling my leg. I'm sure he doesn't even remember that, but it was called "The Apple Cellar." It was a considerably different book, but behind the notion of writing it, you see. . . . The big mystery here concerning Tryon is why I elected to do it as a novel at all.

Conversations: What I would think you would do is a screenplay.

Tryon: Exactly. That was my forte—that was where I felt familiar. God knows, I had written and rewritten a lot of my own lousy dialogue and I understood the form; I understood the meaning of the film. At least, I think I did. Why I didn't go directly to a screenplay I don't know. I just felt I wanted to write a book.

Conversations: So is this your first really big writing project? Had you tried to write a screenplay before?

Tryon: No, no, no. I hadn't tried to write anything except another book, which was a satire on Hollywood. It was a very long book; it was like my learner's permit. It really taught me how to write. I don't know at this point how much I knew about writing. I know that I locked myself up for two years and did that book, and I thought it was terrific. I sent it off and it came back so fast it made my head spin.

Conversations: Were you discouraged that soon?

Tryon: Well, it's very painful. When people write me and ask me all these questions, I can't answer them. But I empathize because I know how sad it was when a publisher sent a manuscript back to me, an editor sent it back, and then an agent: a very important agent here in town—Lord.

Conversations: Sterling Lord.

Tryon: Sterling Lord. He said, "Dear Mr. Tryon, we have no plans for publishing a book of this nature," or something like that. "Yours sincerely, Sterling Lord." The editor is a friend; now is a friend—I mean he's more than an acquaintance. He took me to lunch, and he said, "Tom, I know you've got a good book in you.

The satire—this won't do, but a good strong, heavy book on Hollywood would be terrific."

Conversations: This isn't Gottlieb you're talking about?

Tryon: No, no, no. So it was at that point that *The Other* was born as "The Apple Cellar." After all of its vicissitudes of eighteen months, I then sent the book back to this editor, and he turned it down. He sent it back to me with a list of criticisms, all of which I followed to the nth degree.

Conversations: Because you believed in them or because you felt that you should?

Tryon: Because he was an editor and I hadn't had any help really from much of anybody. I thought he obviously knows what he is talking about, and I'll just do these things. I just did those things and sent if off again. Well, it went to Random House and Random House grabbed it like that.

Conversations: So then the first novel sort of disappeared into the closet somewhere and stayed?

Tryon: They just had it in their hands not five minutes before you rang the bell. My secretary said to my manager, "What is this thing—he's got this enormous manuscript." And Arthur said, "Oh, that's so and so and so." He wants me to publish that book. It's a very funny book; it really is. I don't dare show it to Gottlieb, however, because my then-agent told somebody else that if she had read that book before she read *The Other* she never would have read *The Other*. It's rather turgid, but the situations are very funny.

Conversations: So the efforts you took in writing the first book, which didn't turn out all that successfully, nevertheless taught you something as you were going along?

Tryon: Oh, indubitably.

Conversations: And these self-taught hints or tips led you to The Other.

Tryon: Well, I went out and I got a whole flock of how-to books. Among them was that brilliant little book *The Elements of Style*.

Whenever anybody says, "How did you learn to write?" I say, "You go out and buy *The Elements of Style.*" I really think that that book contains everything you need know about writing. It doesn't tell you how to write, but it tells you, I think, how to write well. Was it Coleridge who said, "The difference between prose and poetry is that prose is words in their best order and poetry is the best words in their best order"? That's how Coleridge made the distinction between the two. But I think that Strunk and dear, beloved E.B. White—you don't really need to go much farther than that, although I have all sorts of books in there. Paul Horgan has a marvelous book called *Approaches to Writing*, which is very succinct on the subject. But none of those books will teach you how to write. I had a secret that only I and I alone knew, which was that I could write, and I had known that all my life.

Conversations: At least since your thesis on James.

Tryon: Well, that was just a stop along the way. The time came in Hollywood when I said, "Let's knock off the crap." I said it to Arthur, who is my manager, and we were in an entirely different business then. I said, "We've really got to stop this. We want to do a movie; let's do it." So he said, "Well, how will we do it?" I said, "I'm going to write it." But there is the interesting thing, the mystery—why didn't I say, "Scene 1," you know, blah-blah-blah? I rewrote that novel nine times. I rewrote it completely while, unbeknownst to me, Gottlieb was setting it in galleys. I'm out there and I'm rewriting—adding new characters and scenes, the whole thing. He had to yank it when he found out what I had done. But I was obsessed with that book.

Conversations: Had you plotted it out when you began?

Tryon: No. It was so funny, because it started out to be that awful book that everybody writes—about a little boy growing up in a small Connecticut town. Everybody's written that book—there was only one child and a much more important relationship with his mother. It was not terribly autobiographical, but I suppose it was close enough. It wasn't until I invented the other brother that it started to happen. My belief in it was so strong that it carried me through some very heavy periods. And I lugged that manuscript with me all around the world, literally.

Thomas Tryon

Conversations: It must have been pretty dog-eared by the time you finished?

Tryon: Well, it was. But I remember doing a picture in Australia. My co-star was Carolyn Jones, and from my trailer on the set I'd hear clack, clack, clack from hers. When I asked her, "Well, Carol, what are you doing in there?" She said, "I'm writing a book." I said, "Oh," and I had them get me a typewriter. So now I was going clack, clack, clack. She said, "What are you doing?" I said, "I'm writing a book." Well, we both did, you see. I took it with me to Italy and to Spain, everywhere, and I got to the point where I didn't want to do movie work anymore.

Conversations: So you were acting at this time then?

Tryon: That was acting, yes. I did not stop acting until the book sold in May of '70. Has it been that long? It was published in May of '71, but it sold in May of '70. I did the final editing of it in the last two weeks of May and June. I went back around the fourth of July and I fulfilled my last acting commitment. When I finished that I said, "That's it." And I'll never go back to it again. I never will.

Conversations: Did you have a sense of the kind of book it would be, of the haunting quality at the beginning?

Tryon: Uh-hm. I had no idea that it was going to be the success it became. Gottlieb predicted it. It was a little heady for me to encompass and, as a matter of fact, the day it sold I began my second book. That has not seen the light of day either.

Conversations: I had assumed that Harvest Home *was. . . .*

Tryon: Oh, no. There were four books between *The Other* and *Harvest Home*—parts of four books. And we did the movie of *The Other*. I wrote and produced the film.

Conversations: You have said that you weren't in love with the movie.

Tryon: Oh, no. That broke my heart. Jesus. That was very sad.

Conversations: Even though you had written the screenplay?

Tryon: Yeah. Yeah. That picture was ruined in the cutting and the casting. The boys were good; Uta was good; the other parts, I think, were carelessly cast in some instances—not all, but in some instances. And, God knows, it was badly cut and faultily directed. Perhaps the whole trouble was the rotten screenplay, I don't know. But I think it was a good screenplay. It was not that difficult a film to do if you just decided what the film was going to be. A lot of the horror scenes were cut and the music was taken out. I was a party to all of this dismemberment and desperation. But there were scenes that were shot that could not be cut, because they were just shot in one master shot with nothing to cut to, so you couldn't take a part of it out. So Uta's whole introductory scene, which was a lovely scene between her and the child in the kitchen which established their relationship, her belief in the boy's relationship with Holland, giving Holland a reality that he—that whole scene went because the audience was just fidgeting, but there again I never looked back. I learned an enormous amount and I have never looked back. Arthur says, "Oh, there'll never be another *Other*." And I suppose there'll never be another *Other*. But there have fortunately been. . . I'm having the same problem now. On my fifth book, Bob has had, I think, six projects in his hand since last September, probably.

Conversations: You mean six from you?

Tryon: Yes. We cannot agree what is to be the next book. It doesn't matter what it is. It's the kind of thing it is, and he will only settle for that. I have three books he wants me to do, and I won't do any of them until this fifth book is out of the way. It is driving me crazy. At this point I'm pulling up stakes and I'm going to Europe, because I just have to clear my head out. It's too heavy.

Conversations: I guess there is no answer to that mystery of why Thomas Tryon sat down and wrote a novel instead of a screenplay. It just came out that way for The Other.

Tryon: I wish I could say, "Well, it's like so-and-so," because I'm sure other people have done a similar kind of thing. It was the right thing to do; it was what I wanted to do. There was an impulse there that I perhaps didn't even recognize. But I said, "Oh, yes, of course, now is the time for me to write a book."

Thomas Tryon

Conversations: So then what did this do to your thoughts of becoming a director?

Tryon: Well, it was all step-by-step up to the point of whether I was going to become a director or not. The picture got done mainly because the director who did it wanted to do that property, and he was a known director; he was a known commodity.

Conversations: You had thought about directing it yourself then?

Tryon: No, it was too complicated. When I saw what the thing was going to be, I then continued as a writer from the novelistic aspect of it. But I didn't have any pretension about directing this project. When one of the boys isn't there, and I'm loaded with children, and dogs, and cows—all the things that can make your life really miserable. . . . God knows, when they were down in that apple cellar it was miserable and cold, and trying to coax performances out of those two kids. . . . Sixty people in a room a quarter of the size of this one. It was very heavy.

Conversations: Maybe it was just too demanding an idea.

Tryon: Well, the interesting thing is that now it's almost ten years from the beginning of that dream. I've been offered my shot to write, direct, and produce, and I don't want it. How the world turns. I said no.

Conversations: So it would seem that you are finding writing more satisfying.

Tryon: Oh, yeah.

Conversations: Was it the success of The Other *and that sort of eeriness that led you into horror again in* Harvest Home?

Tryon: Bob was very sure that my second book, while not "The Son of The Other," or "The Other Strikes Again," should be something in that genre. He kept saying "No, no, no!" until I gave him *Harvest Home*. It was about a young couple who leave New York and move to the countryside and get involved with a farinaceous deity, and he said, "That's it. Go. That's your second book."

Conversations: Had you been happy with the first three proposals that you had sent to him? Would you have happily gone ahead and written those books?

Tryon: Yes. I would have, happily.

Conversations: You don't regret that you went into Harvest Home?

Tryon: No. As a matter of fact, probably now number five really should be a horror book. I'm meeting with him tomorrow to try to finally thrash this thing out, because, God knows, he's had everything else thrown at him. He says, "No! no! no! no!" I said to Arthur the other day, because it was a marvelous project I had, "What the hell happened—why did that go up in smoke?" It went up in smoke in an hour's worth of time with Gottlieb, and I can't even remember now why. Bee and Willie from *Crowned Heads* are both in that second book. They're from that second book. Little did I know seven years ago that he was going to have such a demise. I expect to do that book. It's another Hollywood book.

Conversations: One of the criticisms of Harvest Home *was its violence.*

Tryon: Misgauged. Same with *Crowned Heads.* I was just reading in the paper that they were hissing and booing *Black Sunday* at the preview because of its violence. When they were finished they attacked the producers, the makers of the film. I remember at the sneak preview of *The Other* this woman attacked me with her pocketbook; she was hitting me with her pocketbook. It's strange, because you think, "Well, people can take anything today," and they can't. You can't violate sensibilities to that degree. I really didn't think that there was that much violence in *Harvest Home.* Some grisly things go on, but they don't happen on stage. That scene does not happen on stage, and it's not described. It's after the fact when Jack Stump is discovered. And then I think maybe the scene of the killing of the Harvest Lord was heavy, but the whole book builds to that scene. I thought that I handled it, what can I say, tastefully. But I am goddamned if I know what people want. I just don't know.

Thomas Tryon

Very few people really recognize what *Harvest Home* was—my object in writing that book. It's a rather contrived plot, but what I wanted to do was take that classic gothic heroine who goes to the mansion and somebody says, "Don't go up in the attic." She goes up in the attic, the poor bitch, and she discovers whatever it is there. There's always a light in the window, and the Saturnian hero, and she's imperiled, and all that. But she ends up okay, and he usually turns out to be terrific—I suppose the progenitor of that is Rochester. I wanted to take that and make her a him, take the heroine and make her a hero. And so that was Ned Constantine, and, of course, that's exactly what happens. He goes and he gets mixed up in something. He doesn't want to see it, and he doesn't want to face it, but there it is and he ends up screwed. It was not in the tradition of the lady gothic, but it was my own kind of gothic novel. I'll never write another one like that, but that was what I was trying to do.

Conversations: Was it fun to work in that tradition?

Tryon: Yes. For me it was enormous fun, because I pulled out all the stops. And the book was the least successful of all of my books. Now *Lady*, which was a simple labor of love, and I had no expectations about that book whatever, is my biggest seller. It is gentle, quiet, nostalgic, reminiscent. The textures in that book are totally different. I just don't want to be typecast. I never wanted to be typecast as an actor, and I don't want to be typecast as a writer. So I keep looking around for different kind of things to do.

As far as violence for the sake of violence or for the sake of shock, no. People say to me, "Where do you get all these sick ideas of yours?" And I say, "Well, all you have to do is read your morning newspaper." It's true. Read *Time* magazine, read any continually edifying account of the news, and you will see these awful things coming. Is it Michigan, about the child murderer? Five or six kids have been murdered in this one town and they're looking for somebody. They don't know who he is. There's a plot; there's a plot. You know it. It doesn't interest me. It might if that were all I could do, but I want to do other things. The book I really want to do now, Bob won't let me do until I have done another book in between. As I say, I feel that he would like to have a creeply crawly, suspense or something, but it has to have a wellspring, as he calls it.

Conversations: Touch something within you.

Tryon: But it has to come from something in the story that is not dragged in, that is not extraneous. *Crowned Heads* he felt did have that. But I don't know, as I say, I am not interested in painting violence for the sake of violence. I would much rather paint a field of daisies or something.

Conversations: I assume Lady *was, in fact, the most autobiographical of your novels.*

Tryon: It was, and evidently people felt that. It has not been made into a movie, and I think it just hasn't been made into a movie because women stars are not the thing just now. There really isn't anybody around to play that part, with maybe the possible exception of somebody like Audrey Hepburn, who I think would make a good Lady. Bette Davis called me and she said, "Oh, if I was twenty years younger how I would love to play that part." I said, "Bette, yes, if you were twenty years younger, you could play that part." Of course now she wants to play the Widow Fortune in *Harvest Home.*

Conversations: She'd be marvelous in that.

Tryon: Yes, she would.

Conversations: Is Harvest Home *going to be made?*

Tryon: Yes. They're doing a mini-movie for television for the fall. They're doing a screenplay on it now, I think. But see, there again I just didn't want to get involved. I said, "Take it. Go. Take it and do it. I don't want. . . ."

Conversations: Because of your experience on The Other *as well as your Hollywood experience before?*

Tryon: Well, it's just that I know how difficult that thing is going to be to do. I mean it has more than just children and dogs and cows. It's got all those women; and the costumes have to be just right; and the locale has to be just right; and it's got to all be done on location with lots of night shooting, and plenty of crowd scenes, and all that.

Thomas Tryon

Conversations: So you aren't even interested in doing a screenplay at this point?

Tryon: No. They will find out that the minute you start adjusting any of that screenplay the whole thing's going to fall in on them. And I mean it. It's built that way: the minute you take a brick out it's going to cave. It's very delicately balanced.

Conversations: You said there were several projects that you had suggested between The Other *and* Harvest Home. *Were there several you suggested between* Harvest Home *and* Lady?

Tryon: No. It was very strange. I started writing *Lady* while I was on location for the film of *The Other*. I also got the idea for *Harvest Home* up there on location. It was a very strange community. I did *Harvest Home*, and at that time *Lady* was a short story. It was about forty pages, and I told Bob that I wanted to do it as a book. He objected violently to that. But I went ahead and did 100 pages in outline form—just to show how wrong he could be. He said, "Oh, Tom"; he said, "You're absolutely right. You have to do it." So that was the easiest book; certainly the realest book. The only problem with *Lady* was in the cutting of it. There was so much; it was so long. I got the message from Gottlieb not to worry; "We" would cut it when I finished it. I was working on it in Paris at that point, and when I came back and laid this thing on, he gave it back to me and said, "All right, now go cut it." So where was this "we" crap. I was the one who had to cut it, and I had to take out some sections that I loved very, very much. As a matter of fact, they were the violent sections.

Conversations: Oh, really?

Tryon: Yes. And I have often wondered if some of that sharp, grating thing would not have been good in that book as a balance against all that kind of. . . the gentle kind of thing.

Conversations: It's very interesting that the violence was the part that was taken out.

Tryon: Yeah. Well, it seemed to be the one section that I could take out and, well, it abraded, but in a good way, I felt.

Conversations: Do you cut when you write?

Tryon: Oh, God, yes. I always overwrite. I can't help myself. Yeah, and I have to cut and cut and cut and cut.

Conversations: *Is it in plot development or the writing itself?*

Tryon: It's usually in plot development—extraneous things, extraneous characters. That's what I'm involved in now— mentally trying to take this book and cut it back to its essentials, because I'm still trying to find out what the hell this book is all about.

Conversations: *The new project?*

Tryon: Yes.

Conversations: *You said* Lady *started out as a short story. Had you any intention of publishing it as a short story?*

Tryon: That's how I wrote it, to be published as a short story.

Conversations: *It just never saw light that way because it turned into a novel instead?*

Tryon: No, because when I read it I thought, "Oh, my God, it's a book. I can use all of my childhood around that character." It's a very carefully structured book. It doesn't seem, I don't think, apparent. It seems to kind of meander, but it's very, very carefully structured. You know what it was like as a short story? It was rather like "A Rose for Emily." It was about the same length, and there were quite a few similarities. And I'm not a Faulkner fan. That story happens to be relatively straight prose, but, Jesus, I can't handle him.

Conversations: *So then after* Lady *were there several projects that came up before* Crowned Heads?

Tryon: Well, no, there was only one and it's this book, the book that shall be nameless. I worked on it for six months, heart and soul. I was just pounding myself to death. I got about 200 pages and Bob loved it. And I gave him another 200 pages and he hated it. He said, "What happened?" I said, "Well, I don't know." He said, "Well, can you fix it?" I said, "I don't know. I'm bored with it." And I was. He said, "Well, why don't you abort it?" Well, that word just got my back up. He said, "Well, you wouldn't be the first writer to abort a book." Well, I didn't want to abort this, but

I did chuck it under the bed and was very depressed for about a week. Then I thought, "Well, I'll do something." So I took him in six, eight different projects and we discussed them all. This one he liked because blah-blah-blah; this one he didn't like because blah-blah-blah. We finally resolved that there was going to be this book. I said that I would go home and take out of the typewriter the book that's in there, the first draft of "Fedora." I was just really noodling with it because I was afraid that maybe I was going to get writer's block or something. At that point I didn't know what writer's block was because I'd never had it, but I'd heard about it. I'd had this idea for a book called *Crowned Heads* that came out pretty much the way I had originally conceived it.

Conversations: In the separate parts?

Tryon: Yes, in three parts. Bob said, "Well, tell me about it." I said, "No, I don't want to." And I really didn't. I said, "You won't want it. It's not a novel." And he forced it out of me. "Oh," he said, "it sounds terrific. Do it." So I went home and I finished "Fedora" and I brought him that. Of course, he guessed the twist right off because there was one sentence in it that I subsequently deleted. He's awfully canny; he knows me, and this thing was kind of glaring, you know. But I did "Fedora," "Lorna," and "Willie." I really was writing under the gun because he wanted me to be done by Labor Day and this was June. Then he said he liked it so much he wanted a fourth story, and that's where "Bobbitt" was born. "Bobbitt" drove me absolutely crazy, that story.

Conversations: Why?

Tryon: I don't know why. To this day, I don't know why. I couldn't get it. I wanted it to be light; it was very easy to do heavy, but that was not the purpose of its being in the book. It was supposed to be kind of a leavening between Lorna's snake and Willie's death, and I don't know, it just was so difficult. I think it was probably the least effective story of the group, although some people think it's the best.

Conversations: The other three then came relatively easily to you?

Tryon: Oh, yes. "Fedora" was so much fun. I really enjoyed the writing of that. And "Lorna," I had made all those notes for that story while I was down in that place and they were all in the file. I just pulled it out and I wrote it in about a week.

Conversations: Where were you when you wrote it?

Tryon: A place down in Mexico called Jalapa, in that place where she is. That's where I was and I imagined a woman coming there and this whole thing, because of the snake and the temple. So that was fine. The Willie thing—as I say, I had that character in another book. I liked him, and I liked the fact that he had that relationship with somebody you'd think is his wife and it turns out to be his mother. I didn't plan—that grew; I mean it really just grew.

Conversations: You mean the ending?

Tryon: Yes.

Conversations: You read too many newspapers.

Tryon: I don't want to do it. But I have to. I said, "I'll try it and see what happens with Gottlieb," and that's where it went.

Conversations: You're talking about the violent ending?

Tryon: Yes, yes. And I'm sorry if it offended anyone, but I wrote it and I'll take the responsibility for it. It just seemed inevitable that that's where he should go and that's what should happen. I didn't like it, and it was very painful for me to write. It's the most painful thing I've ever done. But that's where it went, and that's where it ended up, and that's what happened.

Conversations: Was it a conscious decision of yours not to write a Hollywood novel until something just came out?

Tryon: No, that was Bob's. You see my second book was a Hollywood novel, 700 pages worth. And he said no. That was a killer; that really was a killer when he said no to that.

Conversations: I'd give up after 700 pages were turned down.

Tryon: Well, you either do or you don't. It's that simple. I'm ready to give up now. I've been walking around for weeks saying, "Why don't you just quit." I don't have to write any more.

But I want to. I've got to go through this agony and this is only the beginning agony. Then the agony of all those months of being alone—locked up with that thing. Go on and that's agony. Then it's agony when it comes out and the reviews aren't what you want—they sting you and they hate you and. . . .

Conversations: You do read your reviews, I take it.

Tryon: Well, less and less. Paul Horgan once told me to put the reviews away and not read them for two years. I think it's generally good advice, more so for writing than for any of the other things, except maybe a concert musician or a singer or something like that. The good reviews aren't helpful, and the bad reviews are less.

Conversations: Isn't that, perhaps, as specific in the criticism?

Tryon: No, no. They're not creatively critical. I don't think there's really any point in reading them. You don't learn anything from them. Hepburn says she doesn't read her reviews, and I would judge that she probably doesn't. I think most people do. You know if somebody calls you up and says you got a brilliant review in *Time* magazine, that's terrific. The guy at *Time* magazine loved *Harvest Home*. And Walter Clemmons in *Newsweek* hated *Harvest Home*. So what can you do? Then there was a guy who reviewed it for *The New York Times Book Review*—he's now on the *Miami Herald* or something. He didn't review the book; he reviewed the money I was paid for the book. It enraged him that I got that amount of money, which at that time seemed like a lot.

Conversations: What was it? Do you remember?

Tryon: Oh, I don't know. It was $250,000 or something ridiculous. Everything has changed so much. When he finds out what I'm getting for my next book he will really clobber me. We should get into this, I suppose. I think my biggest problem as a writer is overcoming the image of the movie star, the actor turned writer.

Conversations: Do you have trouble being taken seriously because you were the glamorous star?

Tryon: Yes. It's very, very difficult. It persists from book to book, but I live in the hope that one day all will be forgiven and forgotten and I will be accepted just as a writer.

Conversations: You want to be thought of as a storyteller?

Tryon: Well, I think that's what I am. I don't know really what makes a great novelist. Suddenly John Cheever, whom I have admired enormously ever since the Wapshot books, is our new Tolstoy. Well, I'm in the process of reading *Falconer,* and it's a mighty fine book; there's no doubt about it. But it's like they just discovered him or something. I don't see any point in writing a book unless you are going to tell a story, and I just happen to have a lot of stories. There is something going on today; there's something wrong with people who tell stories.

Conversations: Do you find plotting comes easily for you?

Tryon: Yes. Plotting comes easily. Character comes easy. Background comes easy. It all comes so easy, why is it so difficult? Why is it so hard? You see, I don't think I write crappy books. There are people who think I write crappy books. I saw Kevin Kelly from the *Boston Globe* last night at the theatre, and he told the story about how much he had loved *Crowned Heads* and wanted to do a piece on it. The literary editor said, "Oh, no, that's all right. I'm taking care of that." And she took care of that, you see. But they hide those reviews from me at Knopf and I don't get to see those reviews unless I go in two years later and read them.

But you see, it doesn't really matter, and Maugham said it. He said it's not all these concomitant things that come with it. You get the fun, the pleasure, the agony, the horror of writing the goddamned thing. That should be all that you get. If you get money besides, terrific. If you get the other things of the success syndrome, the fame and all of those things, that's terrific too. But I've had the fame so I know how ephemeral and how silly all that is and it really doesn't matter. What matters to me is getting up at six o'clock and hitting the keys.

Conversations: Six o'clock?

Tryon: Yes. That's when my working day starts.

Thomas Tryon

Conversations: Do you have a regimen that you follow?

Tryon: Well, I work from six o'clock in the morning to six o'clock at night or eight o'clock or ten o'clock at night—sometimes I work through to midnight, depending on how things are going. Now I read somewhere, possibly in the *Voice,* that the woman who wrote *The Thorn Birds,* writes 30,000 words in a day, at a whack. How can she do that? I was trying to figure: if there were 200 words to a page, that's something like.... I have been known to do thirty pages and they all went into the book, but that's a lot. And I bet those thirty pages had a lot of dialogue, which uses up space.

But I have a discipline that has seen me through a lot in ten years. It's not that easy. There's something that makes it possible for me to get up at that hour: the day is quiet; the doorbell hasn't started ringing; the telephone hasn't started; the maid isn't in; all the people who troop through here.... I can start my work. If I were a sane person, I'd generally have a good day's work done by nine o'clock in the morning. Then I could quit and do whatever I want, because I figure if I do ten good pages a day that's plenty. But I don't. I do twenty, sometimes thirty.

Conversations: Do you write straight through a book, or do you rewrite as you go along?

Tryon: No, I rewrite as I go along. I very often will take to bed with me the pages that I wrote that day and rewrite them before I go on to the next day's work. It depends on how involved I am at a given moment. See, now I have been working on another book.

Conversations: Besides the nameless one?

Tryon: Yes, besides the nameless one, and that's really the book that Bob bought, but its status is rather precarious at the moment, only because it's a book I want to do. It's very light and very different from anything I've ever done before, and he wants a heavy thriller blockbuster. Well, this is a thriller in a way. It's a very bizarre thing, and again it's a labor of love. But I go on the premise that if it's a labor of love, its chances of survival are higher. You see, none of these is the book I want to do.

Conversations: There's yet another.

Tryon: Yeah. There are two major books. One of them I want to save for another five, six years. But there is this book that I want to do called "Final Cut." It's about Hollywood, and Bob doesn't want two Hollywood books in a row. Ergo, my pain. And, you know, I think anything would do—*McGuffey's Reader* by Thomas Tryon—just anything, just to get the book out of the way. Then I can go on and do this other thing, which is pretty big, but it's good. So I don't know.

Conversations: But with all these discussions that you have had with Bob Gottlieb, you have said that Bob Gottlieb really changed your life.

Tryon: It wasn't so much that he per se changed my life, but I was suddenly given the opportunity to be a writer. I'm sorry, if I'm going to make a choice between acting and writing, writing is going to win. If I'm going to make a choice between movies and writing, books are going to win out—for me. I just think a writer is a much better thing to be. I wasn't very happy in Hollywood.

Conversations: Does he guide you along in the creation of the book? Do you work closely together?

Tryon: I guess. I don't just say, "Okay, I'm now going to go away and write *the* book." We have a marvelous working relationship, really very, very good. He has told me that he enjoys working with me. He only has four or five people every year whom he works with. But it's a marvelous relationship, and I am very trusting of it. At this juncture, I just pray that it continues to be that.

Conversations: Getting back again to the cross-fertilization of Hollywood and books, is Billy Wilder going to do "Fedora"?

Tryon: As far as I know he's doing it. He wanted me to do the screenplay with him and I begged off. There is not a line of dialogue in the screenplay that I wrote, and there is not a single scene in the entire movie that I wrote. Now that's something of a feat. He is very angry at me because I didn't like his screenplay. But they paid half a million dollars for that one thing. Five hundred thousand dollars they paid for "Fedora," exclusive of the other things. The protagonist who tells the story is now David O. Selznick! He's a movie producer, being played by Bill Holden. Fedora is a German girl played by Marthe Keller.

Conversations: Does this make you angry or disturb you?

Tryon: Of course it makes you angry. My God, what do you think. I mean it's foolish beyond foolishness. Now there are some very good things in there, but Fedora dying by throwing herself under a train because she wants to play Anna Karenina? I mean it was close enough to Garbo to begin with. She throws herself under a train, because she wanted to play Anna. It's lacking in that marvelous Billy Wilder humor, mordant wit. It is a project that the studio just said, "We pass." He's taking it elsewhere. I said I would be happy to help him in any way that I could, but there really wasn't much I could do. I never heard back from him again. But there is no mystery; there is no suspense. She suddenly says in the scene, "Well, I'm Fedora." I mean there's nothing of his trying to find out or sensing any mystery. What's the point? I ask you, what is the point? Take the money and go to the bank. That's all you can do, and that's why when they asked me to do the script for *Harvest Home*, I didn't want to be a part of it. I just don't want to be a part of it.

Jill Krementz

*Robert Penn Warren, poet, novelist, critic, and teacher, was born in
Guthrie, Kentucky, 24 April 1905. He was educated at Vanderbilt
University, and thereafter did graduate work at the University of
California, Yale, and Oxford, before returning to teach in
Tennessee. He early became associated with the Fugitive group of
poets, and during the 1930s began to compile his own body of
poetry, which now runs to some dozen volumes. His teaching of
literature, in association with Cleanth Brooks, is enshrined in a
number of texts, such as* Understanding Poetry *(1938), and*
Understanding Fiction *(1943). In the late 1930s he also turned to
fiction and began a series of novels including* Night Rider *(1939),* At
Heaven's Gate *(1943),* All the King's Men *(1946),* World Enough and
Time *(1950),* Band of Angels *(1955),* The Cave *(1959),* Wilderness
(1961), Flood *(1964),* Meet Me in the Green Glen *(1971), and, in
1977,* A Place To Come To. *Warren has won most of the literary
honors his country can bestow, including Pulitzers for Fiction and
Poetry, the Bollingen Prize, the National Book Award, and the
National Medal for Literature.*

Robert Penn Warren

John Baker interviewed Robert Penn Warren one morning in spring 1977 at the author's home, a converted barn in Fairfield, Connecticut. They talked in a spacious room with a lofty ceiling, sparsely furnished with a few chairs and a piano. An alcove off the room was filled with books. During the interview Eleanor Clark, Mrs. Warren, interrupted briefly. She, too, is an accomplished novelist, having written Rome and a Villa *and* Baldur's Gate.

Conversations: I'd like to start, as one should, at the beginning—about when you were growing up as a boy in Kentucky. Were you always a big reader?

Warren: Yes, both at my father's house and my grandfather's house—I spent my summers with my maternal grandfather—and both houses were full of books. My grandfather was a great reader and had a tremendous range of knowledge about poetry. He quoted it if he found somebody to quote it to. And he had been a captain in the Forrest Cavalry in the Civil War. He was interested in military history and American history; he talked American history a great deal. He knew a great deal about it, particularly Civil War history—he knew that very well. He had fought in many battles, and he would draw the ground plan for the battles of Austerlitz and the Bridge of Lodi, and would explain the tactics of battles that he had been in, various battles of the Civil War.

He was a very entertaining old grandfather to have, you know. He was very bookish, in that sense. He loved to read Egyptian history, for some reason—a history of civilization was his favorite reading. So I spent one summer building a pyramid and putting everything in it—then made a discovery of it all the next summer. It was a lovely life. I'd see a white boy once every month, maybe. It was a very remote farm, had a lot of woods on it, and this prowling the woods or reading or talking to my grandfather—that was about all there was.

Conversations: Where did you get the books? Obviously it was too remote for libraries. Did he have many, many books in his house?

Warren: There were books in the house. He was, I think, rather a failure at this stage. He had been a farmer—a tobacco farmer—but he also ran a tobacco dealership at one time. His daughters always said that their father was a visionary—didn't put his mind on practical matters. He was always wrapped up with books or something. At one time he had some barns full of tobacco on consignment, you see, which he forgot to insure, and they burned. So rather than go bankrupt, which was the easy way out, he stuck by his debt and paid it off—but that took a long time and set him back deeply. But that's why they called him a visionary. They also called him an inveterate reader, the daughters did. I thought they meant Confederate reader.

Conversations: I can see the confusion.

Warren: I had it quite mixed up at that age, six or seven. Confederate reader was a special kind of reader. I didn't know what kind it was.

Conversations: Now Kentucky was a border state; which side would he have been on?

Warren: Oh, our people were all Confederates. And, in fact, he wasn't a Kentuckian; he settled there after the war. He couldn't go back to Tennessee, because he had had a son once who was chasing down and hanging guerillas under the Brownlow government, the Federal Government of Tennessee. So the relatives of these guerillas, these outlaws—both sides were hanging without much trial. My grandfather said they gave them a fair trial, it just didn't take very long! He had murder charges against him from all these guerilla families. Also all of his property was confiscated by the Brownlow government. So he was on the run. He couldn't go in the state of Tennessee for years, until things had settled down. So he just took refuge outside.

But my father's people were native Kentuckians, and they had come over early, in the pioneer section of the state. My father was a very bookish man, and much more so, in one sense, than my grandfather, because he had set out to be a lawyer and actually published some poetry in his youth. I only knew this because I stumbled on a big book once in the house when I was about ten or twelve called *The Poets of America*. It was some big anthology from about 1895, something like that. And I was looking into it, and there I saw a picture of my father.

Conversations: And he had never mentioned it to you?

Warren: Never, because he felt that was a part of his life that he had put away. He never mentioned it; he never mentioned it again. I showed him four or five poems there and the picture and a little note—a little bibliographical note—and I showed it to him. He took it away from me and it disappeared, so he must have destroyed it. But when he was an old, old man, way up in his eighties, he sent me a poem or two he had found in his papers—on old yellow paper falling apart, and the old purple type ribbon that he had used back in the nineties—without comment; he just sent those to me in an envelope.

Conversations: How old were you when he sent them to you?

Warren: Oh, I was then fifty years old. But his had been a well-lost literary career, and I didn't know him well until long after. I left home early; I was fifteen when I left home. I didn't get to know him well until after I came back from graduate school and then taught at Vanderbilt. After my mother died, then he and I traveled a great deal together and got very intimate in that last phase of his life—about 1931 until his death in '56, when he was eighty-six years old.

Conversations: So he lived to become aware that you had become a major writer?

Warren: Oh, yes.

Conversations: And at the last, I guess he was responding to the notion that you had carried on what he had wanted to do.

Warren: Well, this is rather intimate and I think not that relevant, but it created a strange kind of. . . . His own life, his youth, was spent taking care of a whole brood of stepbrothers—half brothers and sisters. His father died when he was quite young; his mother remarried, then died when he was very young, and he had four or five little brothers and sisters then. And then the farmer married the first girl down the road, as it was common to do in those days. So he had a house full of children. He was a veteran, too, of the Civil War. And there was no connection between the two families. They lived in the same community but they had no connection. They never visited; they never saw each other. His stepmother and her children had no connection with my mother's family at all. They met on the street and they said, "How do you do?" That was it.

As was so often the case in farming in those days, a man didn't know where he stood financially, and my grandfather was a man of property, had a good place. But he had debts as well, so that when he was dead, he left very little. My father was then about fifteen or sixteen. He dug in, but his older brother ran away to Mexico and made a good life for himself as a mining engineer. My father took over. He was the next son and educated himself in various ways, simply by ferocious reading, for one thing.

A few years ago I was writing an essay, a long essay on Cooper and I was using my father's books. I noticed at the end of every novel there was the date when he had finished it—1891 or whatever it was. He was very methodical. And until he died he spent hours a day reading all sorts of things. He was reading Freud, Marx, and things like that. He kept on. He was totally alone in the last part of his life, and I've never understood this isolation that he imposed on himself. One thing about it, I think nobody around was interested in the things he was interested in. Nobody around with the same interests. So he would just rather read than talk about things that didn't interest him.

Conversations: But you were interested, anyway, as a boy.

Warren: I was interested. I'd listen by the hour, and that was all to my benefit. But my father said he'd be a lawyer or a poet, and he wound up as the village banker. The bank failed in '27 and '28, and then he banked a few years after, and then made a comeback. After a few years of misery and struggle, I was just getting my first job during the first years of the Depression. It wasn't a very happy period.

Conversations: What did you think you would become as a child? Did you expect to become something like a writer?

Warren: Well, I didn't expect to become a writer. My ambition was to be a naval officer and I got an appointment to Annapolis. Well, it was political; a friend of my father's was a Congressman and he got me the appointment. Then I had an accident. I couldn't go—an accident to my eyes—and then I went to the university instead, and I started out in life there as a chemical engineer. That didn't last but three weeks or so, because I found the English courses so much more interesting. History courses were also interesting, but the chemistry was taught without imagination, taught purely by rote, you know. It was not done well—nothing there to catch your imagination.

Anyway, John Crowe Ransom was my freshman English teacher, and that made a difference. A real, live poet, in pants and vest, who had published a book and also fought in the war— he was just back. As a man, he made no effort to charm his students, but everything he said was interesting. In the first term he took me out of his freshman English and said, "This is not the place for you. Come into another class of mine"; and I did. At that time at Vanderbilt there was an enormous student interest in poetry. Boys would literally line up to buy the next issue of *The New Republic* or *The Dial* magazine. There was a great distinction to seeing the first new poem by Hart Crane or the first new poem by Yeats. This wasn't just a small group; it was rather widespread. Even an All-Southern center on the football team wrote poems.

Conversations: An extraordinary place to have been. Was there anywhere else like it in America at that time?

Warren: At that time, as far as I know, none. There were four or five small groups of writers' societies among the students, and that continued for years, up until right now. But then I was invited to join the Fugitive group, all grown men, and several of them quite well recognized as writers already.

Conversations: Why did they call themselves Fugitives?

Robert Penn Warren

Warren: It's explained in the first little editorial in this little magazine, the pilot issue: "We fly from nothing so much as the South and the magnolia." They were rebels, in other words, and supported modernity as opposed to the apologetic Southern literature. They were quite unconcerned with the official Southern literature, quite contemptuous on the whole. One young man who later became a professor in France and head of a department in Wisconsin—who had the biggest private collection of Baudelaire—well, he would keep you up all night reading aloud to you from Baudelaire and explicating poems. He had a little private university on Baudelaire. It was a strange kind of ferment going on there for fifteen years or more. But the university had no part in this; the university had no interest in it.

Conversations: So you published your paper, The Fugitive?

Warren: It was published by a businessman in town who financed it and put up the prize money—the Maxwell House Coffee Company gave money for prizes, believe it or not. But it started as a philosophy club which was composed of young businessmen in town and several young instructors at the university, and they met in town in people's houses—they had no connection with the university. Some began to write poetry, and then poetry became the main interest.

Conversations: Were they critics as well?

Warren: There was a great deal of argument about critical theory, and Tate and Ransom, of course, became well-known professional critics as well as poets. And Davidson and several others in the group became professional writers. But it was really a university outside of the university. It had no connection with the university. They were the people who were moderns. The strange thing was that at Vanderbilt I thought that Marx was a member of a firm that made clothes, and I thought that Freud was a man who took and cured Jews of syphilis or something like that. I was very retarded in some ways, and very modern in terms of poetry and literary theory. But I went to Berkeley then, and out there they knew all about Marx and Freud. But they hadn't heard the news about poetry. Even at Yale graduate school they hadn't heard the news.

Conversations: How about Oxford? You went to Oxford for a while, I believe?

Warren: That's right, I wound up there. I was following scholarships; I was just simply doing that. Wherever I got the scholarship, the biggest scholarship, that's where I went. Oxford was a much more worldly place, of course, much more dispersed. At least to me it was. Most of my friends there were, with two or three exceptions, people who were aviators or people like that. I didn't even know Spender, though he and I were there at the same time.

Conversations: You didn't join the Poetry Society or anything like that?

Warren: No, I didn't join it. I visited once or twice, but I saw I wasn't very attracted by it. I wrote a big part of my first prose work, my first novelette, there—my first fiction.

Conversations: And then when you came back to America you began teaching, I believe.

Warren: I went to Tennessee, because that's where I wanted to live. I wanted to live in the middle of Tennessee, and I had the idea held out to me that there was going to be a place at Vanderbilt opening up the next year—and there was. But I was finally fired in '34—let go. So I went to Louisiana State University and found a new life there with an old friend, Cleanth Brooks, who was already there.

Conversations: And you collaborated with him on a number of books, I know.

Warren: Yes. We did those textbooks and books of that sort. They always came out of our class notes and just ordinary conversations; they weren't jobs. They just grew out of our normal life, and only by accident a publisher passing through asked us to parlay a kind of textbook to be used in teaching a course in the sophomore year, which was photocopied. And then it was printed as a book on the press. LSU was a big, big place, with thousands of students a year taking that course. A publisher passing by saw it lying there—Crofts, old Mr. Crofts of Crofts Publishing Company—and said: "This book shouldn't waste in here." He said, "Just let me—where's the Press?" And he walked across the hall to the Press and came back and said, "I bought it from them."

Conversations: An instant deal.

Warren: And then another publisher passed through and saw some more notes, some of the poetry notes, and seemed to feel we had an understanding of poetry. So, by a real collaboration, we put our notes together and argued the poems, which was fun. So we put that book together, and we loved that. So this was a natural development; we had no intention of setting ourselves up as a textbook factory, which, in fact, we did do.

Conversations: But what were the essential principles behind your teaching? Were you trying to teach your classes in a way that hadn't been taught before?

Warren: Well, I guess one thing not to be forgotten is the kind of reading we had done and found to be profitable. This was the age when Coleridge was a great revelation—Coleridge's analyses of poetry—and the time Ivor Richards was just beginning to write. And then both of us read fairly widely—widely being a relative term—in the history of criticism. Now what we used to be given out in some of our own classes was a piece of biography, and the poem was always neglected. You got the biography, and the social history, and everything else, but you didn't get the poem.

Conversations: Exactly. Then a few lines of quotation and that was it.

Warren: A beautiful line, that was it. And the intent was to answer that question—*why* is it a beautiful passage? *Why* is it an effective passage? Turn the cart around and the horse around a little bit.

Conversations: So you were zeroing in on the text very closely?

Warren: Not on the text very closely, but the text as a starting point, not the ending point. But now this brings up a whole question that is often distorted—the question of historical scholarship. Until a few years ago, when Brooks's old tutor at Oxford died, he and the Oxford man were joint editors on a whole series of eighteenth-century texts on Percy, the Bishop

Percy letters. Now on the one hand, Brooks is an eighteenth-century scholar; on the other hand, he is interested in theology and is very deeply involved in the affairs of the Church. And he is, you might say, a theologian and moralist, so he's concerned with anything but the little cut of lines of poetry, you see. It wasn't a question of one thing denying another. It's a question of what is the strategy of teaching poetry. And the relation of poetry to the other topics, to the other things in life, is there, too. But you can't discuss the poetry as poetry unless you know what poetry is, and how it relates to other activities. The main starting point wasn't trying to develop a system for teaching poetry.

As far as the other side was concerned, there was never any assumption which denied the history of it, or denied social or moral reference, you see. I used Brooks as an example because he's a perfect example of it: he's a professional scholar of the eighteenth century and known for that. Now I am not a professional scholar of the eighteenth century, because I find the eighteenth century rather dull on the whole.

Conversations: Yes, I wouldn't have thought it was sympathetic to you, really. But I have read you on "The Rime of the Ancient Mariner" and also on Melville's poems.

Warren: He's a wonderful poet.

Conversations: He's a wonderful poet. They very much neglect him.

Warren: He's very neglected. Only Melville has now been rediscovered. It took so long; he was lost in general, of course. My wife's grandfather was a friend of Melville's. He was a young lawyer with literary tastes who knew Melville and was one of the few friends Melville had. In the next room we have several of his last books which the widow sent to my wife's grandfather with her mourning card and with a note at the death of Melville. But for a long period there, Melville was simply not known. I didn't read a Melville novel until the movie came out, *Moby Dick.*

Conversations: Really?

Warren: And I read it in the movie edition—that was in 1923, or something like that. John Barrymore played Ahab, and they changed the whole story around. But they published the thing,

287

the right text. I read that edition, and that's what got me really started on Melville. But the English had an edition as early as 1907, and there was none available in this country.

Conversations: I didn't realize that he had fallen as far out of fashion as that.

Warren: He fell very far out of fashion. And the poems weren't published until right before 1940, '38 or '40. A Princeton scholar, English, published a few notes on them in an anthology in the late thirties. Then there was a small selection in '46, which I reviewed. I wrote my first piece about Melville on that book. That book hooked me; I got so interested in Melville I began working on a book then in '46.

Conversations: And during the thirties you also began to write on some of your contemporaries. I remember you did a piece on Thomas Wolfe, and you also wrote on some of Hemingway's work.

Warren: I did the Wolfe as a review. I did the Hemingway because Scribners asked me to do a preface to a new edition of Hemingway. I did a good bit of reviewing during that period. Every five dollars meant something for several years there, and reviewing was the way to get the five dollars. Now sonnets could get you as much as ten dollars, but it took a long time to write a sonnet. More often it got you fired!

Conversations: So for most of the thirties you were writing reviews and poetry, side by side?

Warren: Side by side, yes. And you could get liquor cheap at that time. For instance, a sonnet would buy about a gallon of corn, or maybe two gallons of corn, according to the sonnet. This was before Prohibition.

Conversations: I'm amazed you didn't become a writer of epic verse at that rate.

Warren: Well, I wasn't ambitious.

Conversations: Did you see your role as a critic essentially as a didactic one? Did you see yourself instructing the reader about the work in question rather than simply delivering your opinion on it?

Warren: Well, put it this way. In a classroom you are stuck with the idea of a point you are trying to put across to persuade your listeners. When you're trying to write a review, it's usually to make sense of the thing for yourself. The emphasis is different— at least it was for me. Writing about a poem for a review or for an essay, like on "The Rime of the Ancient Mariner" or the Melville thing, I'm trying to make sense to myself; and as a textbook operation, the classroom is different. You have a fixed audience for a special purpose. That makes it different.

Writing poems or novels I'm trying basically to make the thing right, put it that way—to create the thing as it should be, as I want it to be, as I hope it will be, rather than trying to think of how many copies it'll sell, or whom I'm writing for. You're bound to have a few people in mind that you respect, whom you know well, whose opinions mean something to you, who are there somehow as a possible audience. But that small, little bitty audience is all that you have to think about—that's my experience anyway. You want to make a thing that works, put it that way. How do you know whether it works? You don't know until you see it work on people. But you have to go with the nature of the thing in the process of writing the thing, it seems to me. It carries its own logic.

Conversations: Like a sculptor finding the actual form in wood or stone?

Warren: Something like that, yes.

Conversations: And bringing out the inherent quality in it?

Warren: That's right, that's right. Now you want that to communicate, but I think communication is not your first thought—not my first thought. It's to make the thing right, that's my first thought. If it's made right, it will communicate, put it that way.

Conversations: Sometimes, perhaps, even to only a small group of people?

Warren: Maybe a small group.

Robert Penn Warren

Conversations: But you've never consciously written anything with a view to scoring a popular success? You've never deliberately aimed at a large audience?

Warren: No, I never have. I like a large audience, but it hasn't been aimed at.

Conversations: Has it surprised you on the occasions when it has come?—All the King's Men, for instance, your first great success?

Warren: It surprised me, quite a surprise.

Conversations: What first made you interested in writing fiction? Obviously this was a long way from your thoughts when you started out writing criticism and poetry. What was the catalyst that made you want to become a novelist?

Warren: It was an accident, although I think I can trace it now. I began to know people who were novelists, like Ford Madox Ford and Katherine Anne Porter—writers of fiction, rather; she wasn't a novelist then; she was doing novelettes and short stories—and Caroline Gordon and a few other people who were actual writers of fiction. I saw a good deal of them. I didn't know Ford well, though he was a great talker. And hearing these people talk about the inside of fiction, how fiction is built, its subtleties, what it's really like, was like hearing Ransom or Tate talk about the inside of poetry, back in the Fugitive group. I began to see that they weren't so different. They had the same kind of art, with the same complications inside them and different purposes, of course. So as I heard people like that talk, I began to shift unconsciously, I think, in my own attitude toward fiction. And that's the general background.

Then when I was at Oxford, my last season there, my last term there, Paul Rosenfeld was one of the three editors of the old *American Caravan*, which was an annual, a big annual, publishing more or less advanced American things by more or less younger people—a book with 1000 pages or more. Paul Rosenfeld, let's see, the other editors were Lewis Mumford and Van Wyck Brooks, but Rosenfeld I knew the best and I saw a lot of him in and around New York. Rosenfeld either wrote or cabled me at Oxford: "Won't you write us a novelette for our next issue about those tales I've heard you tell? About Kentucky in your boyhood?"

Conversations: These are things that your grandfather had told you?

Warren: The night-rider wars, the tobacco wars, yeah. And so I said why not?

Conversations: Was the story of Billy Potts in your famous poem one of the things that you heard from him, too, or did you hear that from somebody else?

Warren: No, I heard that from an aunt, an old aunt, a great-aunt, who was the sister of his dead wife. But I said why not? I was staying in all day long writing my dissertation and I was sick of writing it by night as well. And so I wrote this novel at night after I had finished my day's work with the dissertation and sent it in. It had some pleasant notices in the press, and then I was asked by publishers to do novels; and I wrote two novels which were not published, I'm glad to say. When they did find a publisher, when times got a little bit better, I went through them finally. A publisher said, "I'll take them, but I'll publish them after I publish novel number three"—which actually became novel number four later on. But meanwhile I had gotten started on a third novel, gotten this prize from Houghton Mifflin.

Conversations: Oh, yes, the literary fellowship.

Warren: And I started a novel with them, so I withdrew these other projects, you see, all this tangle, and just buried them.

Conversations: Have you ever looked at them since?

Warren: Not once.

Conversations: No sense of regret or anything at what might have been?

Warren: No, I'm just happy that they weren't published, that's all.

Conversations: In terms of writing, do you find the writing of a novel easier than poetry, for instance?

Robert Penn Warren

Warren: Well, you can write more poetry lying down. You can't write novels lying down, that's one difference. You have to sit at a typewriter and type it out—that makes a big difference. No, a poem for me and a novel are not so different. They start much the same way, on the same kind of emotional journey, and can go either way. *All the King's Men* was a verse play first, before it was a novel—a complete verse play.

Conversations: I didn't realize that. I thought somehow the play was composed out of the novel.

Warren: No. Two plays: the first play, which is quite different, was written in 1937 and I finished it Christmas '39, in Rome. I spent the years '39 and '40 in Rome. I wrote that and laid it aside.

Then I wrote another novel and some other things, and then brought it out to look at the play again, and I saw this would not do because it was not getting at my main point—my main point being that the man, who is a strong man and takes over, actually is a fellow moving into a vacuum, which means the weakness of others. It's their needs he fulfills. A little play doesn't give enough of the context around a situation that makes such a man possible. My idea was—it's simply stated this way—you have his gunman and chauffeur, who's a stutterer. The man gets killed. The stutterer, thinking of his boss being dead, says, "He could talk so good." And he feels that his boss is an orator, a speaker for this man—he fulfills some vacancy or some weakness on this man's part. Now with each of the other characters, he is fulfilling some need that each person has—and it is a rather large cast—chiefly the need of the narrator, who somehow can't find the way in life. He was bright enough. . .

Conversations: But ruthless and cynical and shallow.

Warren: Ruthless, cynical, and shallow, and can't find the meaning in his life, a thing to do that will be significant. So the strong man, the man who doesn't hesitate about what he is going to do, is the man who is his other half. So each character then has a relationship of this kind to the main character. You couldn't do it in the play. You haven't got time to do it in the play, and your cast is too small to make it significant. Even the girl has a relationship to him in some way, and I saw that only a novel

292

could accommodate this fact about them, my dreamed-up fact about them.

So I started again, taking a character who has no name in the play—he speaks only one line—a nameless newspaperman whom I just picked out of the play. He's there in the play as an English newspaperman and I make him this other character, the narrator, just because he's the first thing that I see that is lying there, this newspaperman in the manuscript. So I pull him into the novel and make him start it. But actually it started differently from the way it is printed. A very good editor, very fine editor—Lambert Davis at Harcourt—in looking over my manuscript told me: "You can't start here. Your novel starts over here." Now it starts where he said it should start, not where I had it. It starts on this trip on the road, further along in the action. I had much more exposition beforehand and sort of lost control of my narrative before I even started it, and he saw that right away.

Conversations: It's a hell of a good beginning.

Warren: Well, without him it wouldn't have been that way. But that was the basic reason for the shift in the programs. It wasn't anything beyond just hiding what I wanted it to mean. And then I did a version which was done in New York a couple of times; and then it was done in Germany; and it has been done in Moscow for 2½ years, so I'm told. I've heard only from the actors—one of the actors has written me about it. I don't hear it officially, you see; and it was done twice, two companies simultaneously, in Warsaw and Krakow—the state theatre in Poland.

Conversations: That's extraordinary, that they should be so fascinated by it in Eastern Europe and Russia. Partly because they see in it a sort of critique of the American system, do you suppose?

Warren: Well now, it's hard to know. They also did a movie of it, their own movie. Now I know this because one of the actors, again, wrote me a letter and got it sent out, and he sent me stills from the movie. He was playing Jack, the narrator. He said they started out to have a very fine movie, because they had an actor playing the politician who understood the complexities of the role. But he died in the middle of the movie, and they had to get another one; so they got a Party hack, who took a naive view of it.

293

Robert Penn Warren

He said they did not get the movie they hoped to get out of it. But this was also done in Bulgaria, which follows Russia very closely.

Conversations: It seems to me that a lot of your most successful novels have been based in some way or another on a historical incident, which you've then imagined yourself into and, in a sense, reconstructed. Is this something that you like to do? All the King's Men is a good example of that, but it's not, by any means, the only one.

Warren: No. I'm sometimes said to be a historical novelist. The first one was *Night Rider*, about the tobacco wars when I was a child, and I saw it, so I guess that's not historic.

Conversations: It's history now, but it wasn't then.

Warren: It wasn't then, you see. And also the novel about Nashville in the thirties, *At Heaven's Gate*—it wasn't history then. I was living there when I was twenty-five years old, and I was seeing those same things happen. Then *All the King's Men* was not history. I never did a day's research in my life on these novels. They were coming out of the world I lived in, but not a historical one.

Conversations: World Enough and Time, for instance?

Warren: Well, *World Enough and Time* was a straight historical novel.

Conversations: You even called it a romance, as I recall, a historical romance—or was that the publisher?

Warren: No, I put the word "romance" on. *World Enough and Time*, that's about a case in Kentucky in 1825, which Poe had written a play about and many novels were written about it before. It's a story about the young idealist who can't find an object for his idealism, you see. He creates a dream world in which he can play the hero. It's a story about the romantic temperament, that's what it is. I was really thinking, I suppose, somewhere in the back of my mind about Hawthorne and some of his materials. It is a historical romance, but it's a philoso-phizing one—that's the difference. I have a modern man telling it and commenting on it as a modern man, you see. The modern man claims to have the documents—as I had some documents—and sees them in the modern way.

Conversations: Yes, you've got the dual sensibility working.

Warren: That's the idea of that one. Now the other one, *Band of Angels,* is a Civil War story which is a true story, or partly true, about two girls—they must have been octoroons—whose father was a rich planter near Lexington. His wife died quite young— she's not the mother of these children. He then takes into his house a yellow concubine—she may have been, say, a quadroon, but he can't be sure. The story is a very well known one in middle Kentucky, or was at one time. By this yellow girl he then has two daughters. He raises them as his own daughters. He drops all of his friends, so the daughters never see anybody except the father and their mother and the household. The father takes them on trips and travels with them as his daughters, of course, and is delighted with them, fond of them. He then puts them in Oberlin College when they get big enough, which is the only coeducational school in the country—also an abolitionist school, but that doesn't matter, because he's never admitted their color, you see.

Then when they are big girls, grown girls, college age, he dies suddenly, and dies in debt. The two girls are seized at his grave by the creditors, the sheriff and all of the creditors. This causes a great scandal in the state. They are sold off to a downriver trader, and that's all we know about them. But that much is in the record. Of course, you can't have two, so I got rid of one of them right quick—I never had but one. And then the question is: Why couldn't the father admit that? You see, he couldn't bring himself to face the fact that they weren't white; but to make a manumission legal, he'd have to denominate them as slaves, and he couldn't face that motive, you see. He just kept postponing, thinking it would work out or maybe that they'd get married and live up North or something. But in my book she goes to the Civil War as a slave.

The whole story is about an investigation of the nature of freedom. I mean she's never free—you can't set her free from the fact of the relationship to her father. Until she can forgive her father, she's not free. You see, that's the nature of freedom as she

295

experiences it. It's not just a piece of paper in the story, or the Battle of Gettysburg. The story is inside her. She marries a white man and is passing as white. That's a philosophized historical novel.

The last two books are, again, different. *The Cave*—once again, that's a modern story, set in my lifetime, based on the Floyd Collins case in 1925, which I couldn't care less about then, because I was interested in John Donne and the Greeks by that time. I couldn't even be bothered to go see the place. But later on I crawled every cave in that whole region. I've done a lot of caving, just to see what caves were like—but only when I was writing the book. I'm afraid of caves.

Conversations: Yes, that comes through in the book, very powerfully.

Warren: I'm afraid of caves, sure. But that happened a long time ago, in my lifetime. Usually it takes about ten or twenty years for me to write a novel. I carry it around with me and I try to talk about it to friends, and gradually tell the story to myself by telling it to somebody else, trying it on other people. I quit that now because I have nobody to talk to. You can't do it to your wife, poor woman; she's got her own troubles. You can't do it to your children; they're too busy, you see. And your friends all have their jobs.

Conversations: I can see your problem.

Warren: Everybody could write 100 stories, you know, 1000 stories—the question is: Why does this story pick on you? Why this story and not that story? My guess is now this: The story or the poem you find to write is the story or poem that has some meaning that you haven't solved in it, that you haven't quite laid hands on. So your writing it is a way of understanding it, what its meaning, the potential meaning, is. And the story that you understand perfectly, you don't write. You know what the meaning is; there's nothing there to nag your mind about it. A story that's one for you is the one that you have to work to understand.

Conversations: So for you writing is always an act of exploration, essentially?

296

Warren: Exploration and interpretation. It's not just steno-graphic work.

Conversations: Which means that the people that you look for as protagonists, whether in a story that really happened or something you simply conceived yourself, have to be people who don't understand themselves?

Warren: In most cases, yes. Who don't understand their own role anyway, their own meaning. Or, perhaps, get misled by their own motives.

Conversations: Somebody once said he thought all your novels were essentially about idealists betrayed by their own ideals. Is that fair enough?

Warren: That's pretty fair; that's pretty fair. That would certainly apply to the young murderer in *World Enough and Time*.

Conversations: It would. And in a sense it would apply to the man in Band of Angels, *too, because his ideal was to create this world in which these girls could live.*

Warren: That's right, and it would apply to the hero, Mr. Munn, of my first published novel, *Night Rider,* and it would apply certainly to the last two novels I've written. Now *Flood,* I'm not sure of that one.

Conversations: You deny, with perfect justice, that you're a historical novelist in the usual sense of the word. Do you consider yourself a Southern novelist? Nearly all of your novels are set in the South.

Warren: All of them are, without exception. There are scenes outside the South. My current novel has scenes in Chicago and one other novel, *Wilderness,* has scenes in New York City—the draft riots in New York City in 1863. But you can't write with inner authority about a world you don't understand and you understand your world usually by the time you're ten or eleven years old. Short stories are a little different. Now I'm in awe of a writer like Katherine Anne Porter, who can write in various countries, with a wonderful sense of national differences.

Robert Penn Warren

Conversations: Yes—who can write about, say, a Mexican bandit leader. You presumably would find that very difficult to conceptualize.

Warren: I find that difficult and I would simply take the world I understand best. And I've had to do that.

Conversations: Here you are living up in New England, and yet the landscape that haunts your mind throughout your novels and poems remains that of the South.

Warren: Well, poetry's different. I have many poems about Vermont and a few about Greece and a lot about France. But poems are more personal transactions between you and yourself. There's no reportage, you understand. For a novel you have to be able to tell what food to eat, what hour of the day—a thousand things, you know, that depend on information, and I just don't know that much about anywhere else. I lived in Minnesota, for instance, but I can't imagine myself writing a novel about Minnesota life, except if it was to get into the world of straight business or the academic world, where the occupation carries its own mores and habits.

Conversations: And where the setting doesn't count?

Warren: The university could be Berkeley, or it could be the University of Minnesota, or it could be Yale. If I had to write a university novel, I wouldn't give a damn which one it was. They're all alike. Also I guess, I have an abiding concern with American history, but especially with Southern history. And I read a lot of history—for a nonprofessional I read a lot, anyway.

Conversations: You've never written a formal book of history of any kind? You've never been tempted to do so?

Warren: I wrote a little essay for *Life* magazine and I published a book called *The Legacy of the Civil War*, but that was just an assignment—a request from *Life* magazine. It turned out longer than *Life* wanted, and so I published it as a book. It's just a long essay. I wouldn't think of sitting down and writing a piece of history as just another piece of history.

Conversations: So the actual writing of history—simply reconstructing events and trying to make it colorful narrative— wouldn't have any interest for you?

Warren: No, no. I wouldn't have any interest in doing that. Really, I'm terribly interested in history, but writing it is not for me. It's a very demanding profession. If you're going to be a good historian, it's a very demanding profession.

Conversations: Do you think the many-sidedness of your work as critic, novelist, and poet has meant, to a certain extent, that your reputation has become diffused? There are a number of people who regard you as a great poet, and another number of people who regard you as a great novelist, and yet your achievement itself is so varied. Americans love specialization, as you know, and you're difficult to categorize for that reason.

Warren: Well, I have only two roles, essentially: poetry and fiction—and only a certain kind of fiction. But I don't regard myself as a professional critic. It's like teaching; it's part of my social life. I had to teach for a living in the early forties. I couldn't have managed without it. I enjoy teaching a little bit. But I've quit teaching, except for one term a year, around two days a week. And I haven't taught more than one term a year and only two days a week at most for—since the 1940s. But I like to keep in touch with the young.

Conversations: So you'd never give it up?

Warren: If I weren't paid to teach, I would pay for the privilege. But it's also a way of talking about ideas. When I have an idea, I want to talk about it, and the only way you can do that is to teach. Also, you can find certain people that you can't find outside. There are not too many of them in the teaching profession, but there are some—the real humans—brave men who love their learning and who love ideas. Now if you hang around the university, you can get some of that rubbed off on you, or at least you can talk to people like that, and you can profit from it. When I'm not teaching, I miss that very much. You can't do it by social life at a party. You can't do it by, say, having six people to dinner. Occasionally you can, but not very often. That sort of association involves teaching at a good university, and I've been very fortunate in always being in places where there were some people. . . .

A real critic, like Cleanth Brooks or I. A. Richards, has a system—they use a system. And it's his main interest, and he's concerned with that, primarily. I'm not. I'm interested in trying to understand this poem or that poem, but I'm not interested in trying to create a system. I'm interested in a different kind of understanding, you might say, a more limited kind of understanding. I'm interested in my enjoyment, put it that way, more than anything else. I've certainly written some criticism, but I usually take it from my class notes. I'm just not a professional critic. That business is just something that happens, like my garden. I like to garden in the same spirit. But writing fiction, poetry, that's serious—that's for keeps.

Conversations: But even that, I think, may have, shall we say, diluted the way in which you are regarded. There was a recent review on the front page of The New York Times Book Review *of your latest collected verse in which the critic with an air of astonishment wrote, that behind our backs Penn Warren has turned into our greatest poet. That was the gist of his review, it seems to me. He'd clearly been thinking of you mostly as a novelist, and perhaps a novelist to whom he wasn't particularly drawn; yet as a poet, he found you extraordinary. Now other people are more interested in your novels. What I'm trying to say is: Do you feel that it dissipates your impact to be so active in both fields?*

Warren: I think it does, but it's something I don't worry about. It'll shake down, but it's nothing to worry about. And, after all, novelists and poets are both fictionalizers, of course, and not such rare birds. I don't find an absolute difference, as I said before. At a certain level an idea takes hold. Now it doesn't necessarily come with a form; it comes as an idea or an impulse. It may be one verse of a verse play. It isn't labeled when it comes to you. I've started many things in one form and shifted to another—quite often, in fact. Now I've quit short stories entirely. Short stories interfere with poems. I have written stories mostly because I needed the money, mostly in the thirties.

Conversations: These were primarily written for magazines and such, for immediate publication?

Warren: I wrote them the best I could, but I wrote them for money. I found that the short stories were eating up poems, or they could have become poems. I got some very good prices for some of them. But I quit it quite deliberately, because I found the main thing was to follow a narrative in verse.

Conversations: Yes. Sometimes even in sets of poems you'll follow one thought through. . .

Warren: Yes, that's right.

Conversations: A series of five or six poems.

Warren: That's right. And it could at one stage turn into a short story. So I just don't write them as stories. Just quit, deliberately.

Conversations: Well, that's one habit you kicked anyway.

Warren: I kicked that one.

Conversations: If you had your choice and somebody said you could only be remembered for either your poetry or your fiction, which would you prefer to be remembered for? Which has been the more important to you? Is that a ridiculous question?

Warren: Well, I think it's a question that has to be treated within certain limitations. Of course, one would like to be remembered, period. So I do work that is worthy of me—honest. But I feel poetry is much more personal than fiction. It's more personal for me—and I suppose that answers your question.

Conversations: Yes.

Warren: You're closer to trying to investigate your own values and the meaning of your own life in poems than you are in a novel. At least I am. In any case, I think I'd make that choice if I were given a choice. But that doesn't mean that I don't feel that I could start a new novel now, with complete commitment to it. I'd do it because I felt I had to do it. I'm not just in search of a money deal, or so one might say: "He writes novels for the Book-of-the-Month Club and the Literary Guild." I try to write the best

Robert Penn Warren

novel I can, period. But the interesting topics, the basic ideas in the poems and the basic ideas in the novels are the same. They concern the same basic things.